ROMAN SATIRE

ULRICH KNOCHE

ROMAN SATIRE

Translated by Edwin S. Ramage

INDIANA UNIVERSITY PRESS

Bloomington & London

Published in Canada by Fitzhenry & Whiteside Limited,
Don Mills, Ontario

Manufactured in the United States of America

Library of Congress Cataloging in Publication Data

Knoche, Ulrich, 1902–1968.
    Roman satire.

    Translation of Die römische Satire.
    Bibliography
    Includes indexes.
    1.   Satire, Latin—History and criticism.
I.   Title.
PA6056.K613   877′.01′09   74–25014
ISBN 0-253-35020-4   1 2 3 4 5 79 78 77 76 75

Contents

Translator's Preface

Ulrich Knoche's *Römische Satire* needs no introduction to scholars and students of classical studies. Since the first edition appeared in 1949, it has remained the most valuable general study of Roman satire that we have. This is not only because of the great amount of information that is contained in these pages, but also because of Knoche's insights into the nature and history of the genre. The reason for offering an English translation, then, is obvious: it is an attempt to make this important study available to a wider circle of readers, experts and non-experts alike.

The importance of *Römische Satire* is shown by the fact that by 1971 it had appeared in three editions. It was first published in 1949 under the auspices of the Wissenschaftliche Editionsgesellschaft. A second edition containing a supplement updating each chapter appeared in 1957 and was published by Vandenhoeck and Ruprecht. The third edition, upon which the present translation is based, appeared posthumously in 1971 under the same publisher's imprint. This contained revisions of Chapters I, II, and III carried out by Knoche before his death and a bibliographical supplement by Wolfgang Ehlers covering the years 1956–1968/9.

What follows contains a minimum of changes and additions. Although what Knoche says from time to time begs for qualification or even rebuttal where modern scholarship or the translator feels differently, no attempt has been made to offer commentary. Such instances are not very frequent, in fact; the great majority of the author's judgments and conclusions are as valid today as they were when he first put them forward some twenty-five years ago. Besides, this kind of commentary would be distracting and would contradict the general purpose of the translation, which is to present Knoche's study in a way that is as faithful as possible to the original.

In keeping with this purpose, an attempt has been made to produce a translation as close to the German as relatively readable English will allow. The odd expansion, addition, or adaptation that is necessary for sense will perhaps be excused.

There are, however, a few changes and additions of a mechanical nature that need explanation here. The major difference between the original and the translation lies in the removal of many references to ancient and secondary source material from the text to a series of notes (pp. 159–73). This has been done only after lengthy deliberation, as a means of reducing distractions and interruptions in the narrative. The notes have also made minor expansions possible; article titles, for example, have been added where Knoche chose to omit them. In a very few instances it has been natural to include a sentence or two of the text in a note.

It should also be pointed out that a series of selected readings in English has been added to the appropriate note in each chapter. These are easily recognized because they appear in brackets [. . .] to set them off from the original. There are a few other incidental additions indicated in the same way.

Titles, words, phrases, and sentences from languages other than German that Knoche uses have been kept, with a translation following each in parentheses. Quotation marks are used here to indicate words and passages taken directly from other writers.

A few minor changes have been made in Professor Ehlers' bibliography by way of Anglicizing it, but nothing has been omitted. A number of errors in the German text, many of them typographical, have been caught and corrected. No doubt new errors have crept in and for these I apologize in advance.

The translator's bibliography has two purposes—to bring things up to date as far as recent publication is concerned and to include a few pieces of the earlier scholarship on satire not mentioned elsewhere in the book. Brief articles dealing with textual details have as a rule been omitted.

Some thirty journals in the field of Classical Studies were asked for titles of articles on Roman satire that were forthcoming or accepted for publication at the time this book went to press. I would like to thank the editors of the following publications for their gracious replies: *The American Journal of Philology, Antichthon, L'Antiquité classique, Arethusa, The Classical Bulletin, Classical Philology, Classical Quarterly, The Classical World, Greece and Rome, Gymnasium, Latomus, Maia, Mnemosyne, Phoenix, Rivista di Studi Classici, Transactions of the American Philological Association.*

I am grateful to my colleagues at Indiana University, Professor Hans Tischler of the School of Music and Professor Wolf Rudolph of the Department of Fine Arts, for being so willing to help with many points of translation. They, of course, are not responsible for any misinterpretations that may appear in what follows.

The two publishers, Vandenhoeck and Ruprecht and Indiana University Press, came to a quick agreement about publishing an English translation. As the person between, I appreciate this very much.

Ms. Carol Boner, who edited the manuscript for the Press, has been most efficient and extremely tolerant. Her patient attention to detail has brought any number of important improvements to the text.

I must also thank Harrison Shull, Vice-Chancellor for Research and Development and Dean for Research and Advanced Studies at Indiana University, for providing funds for the typing of the manuscript.

Finally, there is the matter of a dedication. The author's original dedication has been kept—and with good reason. Hopefully, it will not be inappropriate to provide one for the translation as well:

To The Memory
of
Ulrich Knoche

EDWIN S. RAMAGE

Bloomington, Indiana
December, 1974

To

Hellfried Dahlmann

Foreword to
the Third German Edition

IT WAS the intention of the author that this third edition of *Römische Satire* be completely revised in the light of the scholarly literature that has appeared since 1948. More specifically, Ulrich Knoche's ambition was to expand and elaborate the central chapters on classical Roman satire. The supplementary sections added to the second edition in 1957 represent preliminary studies toward that end. Unfortunately, Professor Knoche was not permitted to carry out his plan. When he died in the summer of 1968, only the first three chapters were in a revised form. And so if the book was to become available in print again, the editors' only alternative was to replace chapters I–III with the revision which was found in Knoche's estate, and to reprint the text of the rest of the book from the second edition. We hope that the reader will excuse us for letting the study appear in this uneven form. Hopefully, the high quality of Knoche's work and respect for the author will justify our following this course.

To meet the needs of the person using this book, Professor W. Wolfgang Ehlers (Hamburg) has gathered together the more important secondary literature at the end of the text.

THE EDITORS

ROMAN SATIRE

« I »

Satire:
A Roman Literary Genre

ANYONE attempting a historical treatment of Roman satire has to free himself right at the start from the contemporary concept of satire and the satiric. Nowadays we understand "the satiric" as a specific attitude which can be expressed in a number of different ways. As Schiller says, it is to be contrasted with the elegiac mood. So conceived, satire feeds on the tension between what is ideal and what is real, and its purpose is to portray reality as a situation causing aversion or even disgust. The satirist wants to present reality, or at any rate a certain part of it, in a mirror, as it were, whether it be parody, caricature, a utopian theme, or something else. And so today we can speak of a satiric novel, a satiric epic or drama, a satiric piece of music, and even a satiric person. This has been brought out again only very recently with a surprising array of examples in the capricious and ingenious study of Gilbert Highet.[1]

To the Roman way of thinking this kind of thing would be inconceivable. The Latin word *satiricus* is not attested until relatively late times, actually only from the third century after Christ on. The ancients used it almost without exception to designate the poet who writes satires. Isidorus, for example, speaks of *satirici a quibus generaliter vitia carpuntur, ut Flaccus, Persius, Juvenalis vel alii* ("writers of satire who generally criticize vices, like Horace, Persius, Juvenal, or others").[2] Even in antiquity the word *satura/satira*, from which the adjective is derived, did not simply denote a specific attitude of mind involving the contemporary scene, but was the term used for an independent literary genre of a particular kind with well-defined limits and a unique profile. This is the way Quintilian puts it,[3] and long before him Horace had defended this view and had spoken explicitly about the "law" of this literary genre.[4] The fact that Horace did this completely as a matter of

3

course shows that such a concept of satire had been current well before his time. Lucilius is the earliest ancient witness to the fact that this notion was well established and generally accepted in antiquity. For in a programmatic poem in Book 26, the earliest part of his collection, he contrasted his satires with other literary forms and other likely intellectual activity and expression.[5]

Actually, the ancients differentiated two kinds of Roman satire, as Quintilian shows.[6] The one kind made use of a metrical form only; this, then, was verse satire. Quintilian names Lucilius, Horace, and Persius as its representatives, though he makes a point of referring to other writers of verse satire belonging to his own times without naming names. From our perspective today we would add Juvenal to the list; he had not yet become prominent in Quintilian's time.

The other kind of satire, the so-called Menippean, is marked by a mixture of prose and verse and was established among the Romans, as Quintilian once again tells us, by Marcus Terentius Varro, the polymath. Perhaps he went back to an older form, quite naturally following a Greek model.

Quintilian with complete confidence claims verse satire as a unique creation of the Romans, and he specifically excludes the Greeks: *satura* ... *tota nostra est* ("Satire ... is wholly ours.") are the words he uses,[7] with just the same comprehension of genre which Horace had so clearly expressed much earlier.[8] And in the sixth century after Christ a Greek author still felt this way when he described Lucilius and his successors as writers οὓς καλοῦσι ῾Ρωμαῖοι σατυρικούς ("whom the Romans call satirists").[9] If all of this is correct, then it appears that we are in the position of tracing a purely Roman literary genre from its beginnings right down to the end of Roman times.

But contrary to Quintilian's testimony, certain scholars have undertaken to search for Greek prototypes for Roman satire, and in doing so they have marshalled those Greek works in particular in which the writer could be giving expression to a satiric spirit—a spirit, of course, not as the ancients understood it, but as we understand it today. And here they find ample evidence based on the well-known ridicule of the Greeks. Some have pointed to satiric epics like the *Battle of Frogs and Mice* whose subject matter probably points even toward Egypt. Others have put forward comedy, mime, the phlyax plays of Rhinthon, the old iambic poetry, Hellenistic biography, epigram and the Hellenistic lampoon, silloi, the poetic moralizing of a Phoenix of Colophon, Callimachus with his iambics and invectives, the curse poem, and many others as the Greek source or model for Roman satire. Some even want to understand *satura* as a Latin variety of the Cynic diatribe, so to speak (Terzaghi).

There can be no doubt that a great cross-section of Greek writing, especially works of the Hellenistic period, exerted an influence on the individual writers of Roman verse satire. Indeed, they influenced each and every one of the satirists to different degrees in theme and subject matter. And it is a well-known fact that the Roman poet was quite ready to adopt and assimilate influences passing from one literary form to the other.

In spite of their efforts, however, scholars have had little success in deriving Latin verse satire as a whole from the Greek, and they will probably never be successful. For it is a unique phenomenon, as the ancient writers themselves knew and insisted, a unique form of expression, which, in spite of its receptivity to stimuli from the Greek-speaking world, did not lose any of its individuality and originality. Quite to the contrary, it was just because of this that it could and did evolve with its special energy, meaning, and versatility.

On the other hand, we should not for this reason lose sight of the real issue and overlook the fact that Roman verse satire influenced other literary forms. Not only thematic borrowings, but even verbal reminiscences of the satirists are to be found in the fables of Phaedrus or the epigrams of Martial and still later in Ausonius. They are present in great profusion in the invective of Claudian or in the polemic excursions of Rutilius Namatianus as well as in Sidonius and other writers. In the same way, the Menippeans of Varro had their influence on Seneca and probably on the Emperor Julian, an influence that extended right down to the time of Martianus Capella and even later. All of this, however, is proof of the effectiveness of satire only; it is not evidence that can be used directly for an understanding of the historical development of the peculiarly Roman *satura*.

The concept of Roman verse satire as a clearly defined genre, a notion passed on to us by the ancients, has also been disputed from another point of view. No one would take exception to the well-known fact that the personality of the individual poet to a very high degree determines the special character—perhaps it could be called the special profile—of his satire. This is the reason that Wilamowitz, for example, went so far as to state quite directly that there really is no Latin satire, but only Lucilius, Horace, Persius, and Juvenal.[10] Now anyone who

knew the great man was also aware of the supreme enjoyment he found
in paradoxes, at least insofar as they served as a challenge to thought
and reflection. And so I think that a double problem faces us here. On
the one hand, there is the task of describing the historical development
of Roman verse satire as a homogeneous Roman literary genre, while on
the other, the individuality of the poets who regarded satire as their
particular field of literary endeavor and the significance of their separate
personalities will have to be brought out clearly in broad outline.

« II »

Origin and Name of the *Satura*

OUR first task is to search out the origins of Roman satire and then to see what meaning should be attached to its name.[1] In the passage mentioned earlier, Quintilian says only that Lucilius was the first to become famous as a writer of Roman satire, but he does not call Lucilius its creator or originator.[2] A comment of the grammarian Diomedes, who was writing toward the end of the fourth century after Christ, but who was naturally following an older scholarly tradition, takes us a step further: "At one time," he says, "a composition consisting of a number of different individual poems was called *satira*. This is the kind of thing that Pacuvius and Ennius wrote."[3] As in the passage from Quintilian, the singular *satura* is used in its primary meaning here; it is a collective noun standing for the genre and does not designate an individual poem.

Should Ennius, then, be considered the originator of the Roman *satura*? The much-studied chapter of the historian Livy seems to militate against this idea.[4] The passage is an insertion and is to be derived not from a historiographical source but from one that is antiquarian and literary-historical and, in its essential parts, apparently pre-Varronian.[5] Livy, then, provides the following account:

1. In 364 B.C. during a great plague, because none of the usual means of appeasing the gods had helped, the Romans introduced scenic performances into Rome for this purpose. Before this the only "performances" were those of the Circus Maximus. And so they called in performers from Etruria who in simple Etruscan fashion danced to the music of the flute without any text or any synchronized movement.

This account sounds authentic and warrants our belief. In the last analysis, its source could easily have been the records of the priests. But the literary-historical conjecture follows immediately and is simply

not plausible. It would be believable only if it were free from contra-
diction and reinforced by other reliable, independent documentation.
But this is not the case.

2. Livy, then, goes on: The young people in Rome imitated this in
the period that followed and the word *satura* was now applied to the
religious dance that still had no verbal aspect. The young people also
exchanged insults in rough verse and brought their movements into
harmony with the words to some extent.

In this passage, then, Livy has combined a reference to the old Italian
verses of burlesque, raillery, and lampoon which certainly existed at an
early time and among which surely were the *versus Fescennini* (Fes-
cennine verses) with his account of the first appearance of Etruscan
ritual dancers in Rome who had been introduced from outside for pla-
cating the gods. The relationship he sees is a causal one, and it is not
a likely interpretation of the facts.

3. Further development of these bantering exchanges makes up the
next stage in Livy's narrative. These presentations, he says, were produced in the next period by *histriones* (actors). The word is derived
from *ludio* (actor), the Etruscan designation for the performer. But
ludio (*Lydus* = Lydian = Etruscan) itself in all probability originally
referred to what is Etruscan and only secondarily and through popular
etymology was connected with *ludere*.

At this point, Livy goes on, the exchange of song was no longer
improvised, but the text was recorded so that from now on the presentations took the form of miscellanies (*saturae*) filled with music. Now
the song and action already described had to fall together with the flute
music in the proper way.

For our inquiry here it seems significant that in this passage the
saturae are equated to "miscellanies" and are apparently an early form
of dramatic performance of the Romans developed from the *versus
Fescennini*.

4. Livy now goes on to the invention of the literary drama by Livius
Andronicus. According to the tradition, this writer was the first to
bring a coherent plot to the performance already described: *ab saturis
ausus est primus argumento fabulam serere* ("After the *saturae* he was
the first to put together a play using a plot."). This is assigned to 240
B.C., the year determined by Varro as marking the beginning of Latin
literature. Later Andronicus also established the role of the *cantor*
(singer) who sang to the accompaniment of the flute while the performer moved about in a lively fashion to the musical passages.

5. The last stage is represented by a separation of the literary drama

and the old rough form of scenic performance. The literary production continued to develop in a serious direction, while the popular form lived on in the so-called *exodia* (afterpieces), which were plays filled with exuberant clowning and jesting very closely connected (*conserta potissimum*) with the early Oscan Atellans. The historian speaks quite ambiguously at this point. These performances were not acted out by professional players, but by freemen—that is, by amateurs.

Livy's authority, then, clearly meant the *saturae* to be an unsophisticated first step in the development of Italian drama—a loose succession of exuberantly satiric verses, fixed and alternating, some spoken but the majority sung, without any really homogeneous and unifying plot. This source suggested, moreover, that these dramatic *saturae* had evolved from the *versus Fescennini* or something quite similar. They in turn had provided the basis for the Latin literary drama of Livius Andronicus, especially for his tragedies. Finally, the *saturae* had faded away to become afterpieces for these. Theodor Birt had the interesting idea that perhaps the end of Plautus' *Stichus* (683–775) gives us a picture of such preliterary *saturae*.

This is not the place to carry out a full-fledged investigation of the earliest Italian dramatic performances. But we should consider two points: (1) whether such performances, if they existed, did have the name *saturae* and (2) if this is the case, then whether they were of any importance for the history of Latin verse satire as we know it.

Livy's account suffers from a number of errors and downright absurdities. It can be assumed, for example, that the Fescennines are older than the religious performance of 364 B.C. But is there anywhere even a trace of Fescennines performed on the stage? Is there any evidence that the Romans depended directly on actors to produce the Fescennines? Is this at all demonstrable historically? And, above all, it is simply wrong to derive the drama of Livius Andronicus from a popular Italian dramatic performance, whether it be called *satura* or something different. For what Andronicus brought onto the stage were surely translations from the Greek, and it is with good reason that Suetonius calls him an interpreter of the Greeks.[6] What is more, his drama troupe consisted of slaves, while his predecessors, according to Livy's account, were quite clearly exuberant young men of free birth.

How does all of this fit together, then? The attempt to put the drama of Andronicus in a causal relationship with indigenous Italian elements turns out to be, as it has always been considered to be, an obvious invention. And it is surely a patently false invention. But how

did it come about? Apparently Roman scholarship even before Varro's
time had transferred Peripatetic theory of the origin of Athenian drama,
especially tragedy, to the Roman and Italian situation. The Peripatetics,
of course, taught that Greek tragedy had developed from the satyr
choruses. The Italian counterpart to these was to be found in the
versus Fescennini. And so the latter were explained as being the germ
of Andronicus' tragedy. It was a logical, though arbitrary, next step to
give the name *saturae* to the old—at least it was alleged to be old—
scenic performance because in sound this word was superficially like
the name of the satyr play. It is well-enough known that already in the
classical period the word *satura* was believed to be connected etymologically with the satyrs. Vergil's allusion, for example, to Σατύριον,
the old name of Tarentum, with the words *saturi Tarenti* was understood at once by his audience.[7]

And so we may conclude that the designation of an old dramatic
performance in Italy as *saturae,* which is attested by the historian Livy
alone, originated as an obvious and arbitrary conjecture which reveals
itself to be secondary through the plural form *saturae*. As far as we are
concerned, it is simply not acceptable.

Now it is also conceivable, of course, that that Etruscan religious
dance of 364 B.C. which Livy mentions had an Etruscan name which
was unintelligible to the Romans and which sounded very much like
the familiar adjective *satur, satura, saturum* = "full." Livy's account
gives no hint of this, and yet this view has been vigorously defended.
F. Muller-Izn, so far as I know, was the first to put this idea forward,
and he has had quite a following.[8] It is certainly true that in Rome
many of the words and names of dramatic art and practice had been
borrowed from Etruscan. It is also true that in Etruscan there was a
stem *sat-* with a short and long *a*. In this connection it is possible to
point to examples like *Saturnus, Satricum, Saturae palus*,[9] and especially to the proper name *Satura*.[10] B. Snell has even made the suggestion
that *saturae* is connected with the Etruscan *satr, satir* = *orare* (pray,
beg) and that accordingly the Latin *saturae* is explained simply as λόγοι
= *sermones* (talks), although, according to Livy, *impletae modis saturae, descripto iam ad tibicinem cantu motuque congruenti* ("The
saturae [were] full of rhythms and the singing and dancing [were]
now written down and brought into harmony with the flute.").

Muller-Izn further believes that *satura* came to the Latins via the
Etruscans from an Illyrian root which appeared as *satyros* among the
Dorians. It came to the Latins, according to him, by way of the Etrus-
cans as a feminine collective noun for fertility, and the *lanx satura,*

about which more will be said immediately below, is to be understood as the symbol of this whole process of regeneration. It is from here that the origin and name of satire is to be derived. But this could only be considered as a possibility, if there were no way at all of explaining *satura* as being Latin.

Kerényi has followed Muller-Izn's suggestion insofar as he too believes in the old dramatic *satura* and imagines it as being a performance that had gone well beyond the rough improvising and versified skirmishing of the Fescennines.[11] He considers it to be rich in rhythms and accompanied by music and dancing, resembling a kind of vaudeville, but with a Dionysiac character.

Altheim, too, considers the account of the old dramatic *satura* as reliable.[12] He wants to see in it one aspect of the uncontrolled impulsive activity at the festival of Ceres. But he explains the term as coming from the Latin, since he, along with Mommsen, takes *satura* as "fullness," using references in Lucretius and Tibullus[13] to prove his point. In these passages, however, there is obviously a popular etymology at work and the word is no longer correctly understood. Acceptance of this derivation is very difficult, if not completely impossible.

When all is considered, it is certainly conceivable that the name of the Etruscan religious dance which Livy describes sounded like the word *satura*, though what meaning that Etruscan word had we cannot know. A great deal militates against this, but any opinion depends on how far the chapter of Livy (7.2) may be trusted. Certainly it may be objected that Roman verse satire as we know it cannot be connected with that performance either historically as far as its origin is concerned or etymologically with respect to its name. These connections are excluded by its original subject matter and by its general orientation. From its beginnings it is a part of literary poetry, although there certainly may be disagreement as to its quality. But if any kind of judgment is possible, then *satura* stands in no causal relationship at all to popular singing or exchanges in song. Besides, its name can be satisfactorily explained from the Latin. The term is used for the first time in Horace clearly designating the genre[14] and the individual poem,[15] but the word itself by this time had had a long history.

In examining the name, it is necessary to begin with the form *satura*, for spellings like *satyra* and *satira* are relatively late. The change of sound represented here finds a precise parallel in the shift of the name *Sulla* to *Sylla* or in Augustus' fondness for writing *simus* instead of *sumus* which Suetonius mentions.[16] For the Augustan period we cannot exclude the possibility that an etymological connection with the satyrs had its influence on the later spelling.[17]

Diomedes, who makes use of the scholarship of Stilo, Varro, Verrius, Suetonius, and others without always clearly differentiating between the separate contributions of his authorities, gives a choice of several explanations of the word *satura*:[18]

1. *a saturis,* "because in this kind of poetry humorous and off-color things are discussed which are just like the things that the *saturi* say and do." There is room for conjecture as to whether *saturi* here refers to satyrs or to "the satiated," but it is a well-known fact that already in ancient times the name of satyrs was explained as coming *a saturitate* (from fullness). Similarly, in essays *De satura* which stand at the beginning of several of our older Juvenal manuscripts, the following is found: *unde in Liberi patris choro ministri vino ac epulis pleni saturi appellantur* ("And so the attendants in the chorus of father Bacchus filled with wine and food are called *saturi*."), although for *satur* the meaning "drunk" (*ebrius*) that we have to postulate here is not attested elsewhere. On the other hand, some time later the mythological-tragicomical farces were called *fabulae satyricae* which could be included with the Atellan *exodia*. The wildness and lascivity of these were well known.

This explanation, *satura a saturis,* does not warrant our belief, no matter how we look at it. The satire of Ennius does not involve ridiculous or obscene things, and it stands in no evolutionary relationship to the satyr play. But since, as will be shown, Ennius himself used the title or at least recommended it, this wise man of original genius must already have misunderstood the word himself. Again, the etymology *satura a saturis* (*satyris*) presupposes the Peripatetic invention that has already been referred to—that concerning the origins of Latin literary drama and its development from farcical performances to tragedy— an invention that is patently wrong. What is more, an etymology *satura a satyris* in the time of Ennius was, generally speaking, not yet a possibility, as Gerhard in the article mentioned earlier has shown.

2. Diomedes goes on: "Or else *satura* is derived from the plate that was filled with many first offerings from the field and garden and offered to the gods in shrines by people of earlier time. From its full and overflowing contents the plate was called a *satura*." Then follow the two items of proof for this *lanx satura*: Vergil, *Georgics* 2.194 and 2.394.

The scholiast to Horace describes this same plate somewhat more accurately in the introduction to the first book of the *Satires*:[19] "Most people say that satire received its name from the plate which was filled with different fruits of the field and brought to the temple of Ceres. This poetry has also been called satire because in the same way it is stuffed full of many things, in this case to satiate its audience." In the introduction to several Juvenal manuscripts there is a similar statement: *satira dicitur lancis genus, quae sacrificiis Cereris consuevit inferri multis ac variis frugum generibus plena. ad cuius similitudinem hoc carmen satira vocatur, quod multorum vitiorum est collectio* ("Satira is a kind of plate full of many different kinds of fruits that is usually presented as an offering to Ceres. By analogy, this kind of poetry is called satire because it is a collection of many vices.").[20]

3. The third explanation of Diomedes reads roughly like this: "Or else *satura* is derived *a quodam genere farciminis* ("from a certain kind of stuffing") which was filled with many things and called *satura*, according to the evidence of Varro. The following is found in the second book of his *Plautine Investigations: satura* in the vernacular (*vocitatum*) is dried grapes, barley, and pinenuts sprinkled with winehoney. Some people add pomegranates."

The application of Varro's recipe to a hors d'oeuvre or a kind of salad which some scholars make is not a happy one. Also, the word *farcimen* cannot mean "sausage" here as it does in other contexts. It has to be a stuffing in a casing. Mario Puelma Piwonka draws attention to the fact that even today in many parts of Graubünden, a canton in Switzerland, a similar stuffing is made of polenta and raisins and wrapped in linen—a coarse, common food which is called *il plains* (the filling).[21] Here we would find the analogy.

4. Finally, Diomedes says that *satura* can be derived from the *lex satura* which embraced many different items in one proposal because, of course, in satiric poetry also many poems are gathered together. Two passages of Isidorus are usually compared with this derivation of Diomedes.[22] At the same time, a remark of Festus is to the point for meanings three and four.[23] Moreover, there is a reflection of these explanations in the Greek glosses: χορτασία (fullness), κόρος (satiety), δίσκος (dish), τάγηνον (pan), νόμος πολλὰ περιέχων (a law embracing many items).

Explanations two, three, and four of Diomedes have in common the fact that they connect the ideas of abundance and mixture with the word *satura* and that they bring *satura* into an etymological line with the Latin adjective *satur* (full). And so the right approach has been indicated. If the word *satura* is to be explained and understood as coming from the Latin, then we must start from the adjective *satur* and not from the substantive, for the latter is in all probability a secondary form. The adjective *satur*, which is from an Indo-European stem, belongs to a very fertile word family in Latin as *saturitas, saturare, satis, satagere, satias, satiare, satietas,* and other forms show. The stem was even suitable for coining the nickname *Saturio.* This is given to the insatiable parasite in Plautus' *Persa,* and the audience must have understood it immediately. We can add here the title of a lost comedy (*Saturio*) which was alleged to have been written by Plautus and which was apparently named after the main character of the piece, the starveling.

The word *satur,* then, was not a loan word at all, but was itself very much a part of the Latin language. The feminine form of the adjective is also attested early—for the first time, so far as I know, in Plautus' *Amphitryon* (667). Here it has coarse and brutal overtones and is used in the sense of "pregnant." The loutish slave aims it at queen Alcmena, and since Alcmena had been made pregnant by two male partners, the audience would have heard something like "stuffed full with everything possible."

Now to explain the word "satire," the feminine adjective will have to become a substantive. Here we can conceivably go along with Ullman and understand the feminine substantive as a collective plural of the neuter developed in the well-known roundabout way of etymologizing in vulgar Latin (*gaudia = joie*).[24] But it seems to me to be simpler and more natural to explain the substantivizing of the adjective as a shorthand expression in which a feminine noun has dropped out because it was perfectly obvious what it should be. The idea that this noun was *poesis* (poetry) or *fabella* (a tale) is not necessary and, in my opinion, only distracts us in the direction of literature. Diomedes is pointing to something more basic.

Next we can prune away the fourth explanation of the grammarian —the connection with the *lex satura*—for there never was a *lex satura,* but only a *lex per saturam* or a *lex in saturam.* Because there was such a measure that really did consist of a mixture, its designation as a *lex per saturam* obviously presupposes the substantive use of *satura* at this time: "A law put together in the manner of *satura.*" This application of the word is attested as being quite common from the second century B.C. on.[25] The expression finds parallels in phrases such as *exquirere sententias per saturam* (to ask opinions *per saturam*). Pescennius Festus wrote *historias per saturam,* while Seneca's *Apocolocyntosis* appears in one branch of the manuscript tradition as *Divi Claudii* ΑΠΟΘΗΟΣΙΣ

Annaei Senecae per satiram. (*The Apotheosis of the Divine Claudius by Annaeus Seneca per satiram*). There are other examples as well. Enough evidence exists, then, to show that *satura* is well established in Latin usage as a noun-equivalent adjective.

At this point it remains to decide whether *satura* should be taken as coming from the language of religion (*a lance satura*) or from the kitchen language of the common people. The testimony of Varro clearly suggests that in the vernacular the *genus farciminis* which he is describing was generally referred to in short form and, as it were, substantively by using the feminine adjectival form *satura*. The predilection of everyday Latin for such abbreviations is well known. The Roman spoke generally of *merum* (*unmixed* wine), *mulsum* (*honeyed* wine), *Falernum* (*Falernian* wine) with *vinum* understood, and of *calda* (*warm* water) and *frigida* (*cold* water) with *aqua* understood; and he purchased *Cauneas* (*Caunean* figs) with *ficus* understood. *Satura* best belongs in this category. We may, if we want to, imagine *olla* (pot), *patina* (dish), or some such noun as being understood with it, but this is not necessary.

It is certainly possible that in loose colloquial speech the religious *lanx satura* was also abbreviated to *satura*. But this is not attested and is also not probable. And so it is most likely that Diomedes' third explanation is the correct one and that *satura* is taken from the language of the kitchen. If this is the case, then *satura*, like the Italian *farsa* or the French *farce*, would have been the name of a coarse, nutritious mixed stuffing which was well known and well liked by the simple people.

The word then would have undergone a shift in usage and application, and the question is whether it was applied to a dramatic work or to a collection of poems. The title *Satura* which Quinctius Atta is said to have used for a togata and Pomponius for an Atellan may point to the language of the kitchen. The Φακή (*Dish of Lentils*) of Sopater or perhaps also the Atellan, *Placenta* (*The Cake*), might be compared with this. And so might the mime title, *Faba* (*The Bean*), if the tradition is correct. It would also be possible to understand the title *Satura* as being used coarsely in the sense of "the twice impregnated woman," and other titles like *Dotata* (*The Dowered Woman*) and *Munda* (*The Elegant Woman*) might be compared with this.

The *Satura* of Naevius[26] is quite puzzling, if it ever existed at all.[27] If we suppose that it was the title of a comedy—this seems not at all impossible—then it would probably be best to think of the title as being a prostitute's name, Satyra. This does appear elsewhere, and it is certainly possible to imagine Naevius following such a procedure.

Satura is, in any event, a coarse, popular mixed food. The idea of its being transferred to a preliterary farce as a generic name like *Atellana* in my opinion raises serious difficulties. On the other hand, a shift in application to a collection of mixed poems would be simple and perfectly logical. It is clear that Juvenal still understood *satura* in this sense when he described the vices of his times in *nostri farrago libelli* ("the hotchpotch of my little book").[28] *Farrago* was a coarse, nutritious ragout which was a favorite of the peasants.

The person who conceived of this clever coining of *Satura* as a title for a collection was certainly the witty eccentric, Ennius. Not only the ancient grammatical tradition points to him as the originator of Roman verse satire, but so does Horace.[29] Moreover, referring to the *Annales*, Büchner makes the point that in using this title for his epic Ennius was adopting a Roman proper name that was current in another sense,[30] and, what is more, he was using an adjectival form independently.

It is impossible to know for certain whether Ennius titled his collection of personal, well-intentioned poems *carmina per saturam* or more simply *satura*. Perhaps he used this title for the collection only in his oral references to it.

The title *Libri saturarum* does not sound contemporary with Ennius' satires, for *satura* as the label for the individual poem apparently did not appear until considerably later. Moreover, the singular recurred in all periods in a collective sense and as a designation of literary genre. When everything is considered, then, this appears to be the primary use.

The development in application and meaning from the collective *satura* to its use as a designation for individual poems would seem to have its parallels in the development of *Silva* to *Silvarum libri* and λειμών to *Pratorum libri*. Also, *elegia* (elegy) and *iambus* (iambic poetry) first indicated the genre and only later the individual poems in the genre. In the same way πίναξ stood for the individual book and then came to apply to just a part of the book.

With his designation of mixed poems as *satura*, whether it be as a fruit plate or as a mixture, Ennius once more stood in a Hellenistic tradition. For titles like ἄτακτα (miscellaneous poems) and σύμμεικτα (medley) were to be found there. And even more to the point are names like πέπλος (tapestry), κατὰ λεπτόν (subtleties), and Κέρας ᾽Αμαλθείας (Horn of Plenty) which point to a similarly mixed contents.

« III »

The Satires of Quintus Ennius

A FULL appreciation of Ennius and his contributions to Roman poetry, taste, ideas, and values and to the development of the Latin language, meter, and style cannot be undertaken here. That must be left to the handbooks and to other studies.[1]

According to Varro's calculations, Ennius was born in 239 B.C. at Rudiae. The location of this town cannot be known for certain, although the name is usually connected with the present-day Rugge lying south of Brindisi. If this identification is correct, then Ennius would come from the country of the Messapii in southern Italy, a region where there had been a rather thorough mixing of races and cultures. Tarentum is to be rejected as his birthplace.

Ennius seems to have characterized himself as a Messapian,[2] and Silius[3] and the *Suda* confirm this. Moreover, the name "Ennius" itself is apparently Messapian. But the poet himself tells us that there were three other factors that were far more important in molding his personality. At one point in his writings—perhaps in one of his satires—he expressed the idea that he had three hearts, which was his way of indicating that he controlled three literary languages—Greek, Oscan, and Latin.[4] It was logical, then, that Suetonius at a later time should call him a *semigraecus* ("half-Greek").[5]

He is reported to have fought on the Roman side in the Second Punic War, probably in Sardinia. Whether we consider this bit of information reliable or not depends on how much trust we put in the account of the clever and well-read Silius Italicus[6] and in the suggestion made by Claudian.[7] If the information is correct, then the years in question would be those between 215 and 205. There can be no certainty on this point, but it is not at all unlikely. In any case, Marcus Porcius Cato, who was later to become "The Censor," found Ennius in Sardinia in 205. At that time Cato was thirty years old, and in 204 he took Ennius with him to Rome. In spite of what Cicero implies,[8] Cato seems not to have helped him further.

The year 204 was clearly a turning point in Ennius' life. It seems that to begin with he adapted Greek plays, chiefly tragedies, to the Roman stage. He is also reported to have given instruction in Greek and Latin. It is wrong to imagine, however, that this involved instruction in fundamentals, and it was perhaps just this activity that paved the way for his being accepted into the circles of the nobility in Rome.

And so there is mention of his association with Servius Sulpicius Galba, praetor for 188 B.C., and of his connection with Titus Quinctius Flamininus and especially with Marcus Fulvius Nobilior, consul in 189. Ennius accompanied the latter on his Aetolian campaign (189–187 B.C.) as a camp poet. This was a Hellenistic Greek custom as yet unheard of in Rome and something that Cato bitterly censured Nobilior for.

In 184, probably the year of Plautus' death, through Quintus Fulvius, the son of Marcus, Ennius received the Roman citizenship along with an allotment of land,[9] and in all likelihood it was at this time that he took the praenomen "Quintus" from his patron. There is also evidence that Ennius had connections with the elder Scipio and especially with his cousin, Scipio Nasica, about which Cicero tells a humorous story.[10]

The tradition of the poet's statue being found in the tombs of the Scipios and the conjecture that Ennius is the writer of the well-known inscriptions of the Scipios are simply not plausible. And the portrait which was found in that location and alleged to be Ennius can in no way be connected with the poet.

When the names of the Roman nobles with whom Ennius associated are taken together, they are found to be without exception men of enlightened philhellenic outlook. Ennius' feelings about his position vis-à-vis these leaders are indicated by a remark of Aelius Stilo who pointed out that the poet sketched his own portrait in the beautiful lines of *Annales* 234–51.[11]

In spite of his connection with the highest social circles in Rome, the poet lived a fairly simple life as a bachelor in his little house on the Aventine which was also the center of the Roman guild of poets. Report seems to indicate that he had only a single maid,[12] while elsewhere Cicero says: "His attitude to such a modest way of life and his old age was such that he actually seemed to take pleasure in them."[13] Horace mentions the fact that Ennius liked to drink, and a wealth of anecdotes surrounded the poet, as if he was actually an urban character in Rome. His satires could have been the starting point for many of these little stories. His house was frequented by his nephew, the painter and poet Pacuvius, among others, and by the popular comic poet Caecilius who also actively promoted an interest in questions of aesthetics in Rome.

In 169 or 168 B.C., at the age of 70, Ennius died of the gout. He himself had made fun of his sickness in his satires. His grave was pointed out as being both in Rome and in his native city of Rudiae. In all likelihood, the body had been burned in Rome and the urn then taken to Rudiae.

And so Ennius lived at a time when old Rome was undergoing her greatest expansion of power. He experienced the ups and downs of the war with Hannibal when he was old enough to understand what it meant and in all probability took an active part in these events. Then, as Carthage was brought to heel, he watched Rome draw the western part of the Mediterranean basin and a large part of the east under her sway. In Rome Ennius also experienced the beginning of the intellectual life that was to bloom so quickly and with such force. Moreover, he saw how the Roman nobility went about learning the new lessons that were taught by living with subject peoples.

Earlier only the political personality, fostered by a general tradition equal for all members of the nobility, had predominated at Rome. But now for the first time the feeling of an uninhibited individuality was also making itself felt, and from now on in aristocratic circles men began to recognize the values of Hellenism. Their purpose was to identify the realm of the intellect as a separate and autonomous sphere of interest and as something demanding respect and deserving serious study. But at the same time it seems likely that Ennius clearly recognized the dangers involved in too willing a submission to Hellenism.

Into this atmosphere came Ennius, a man with a strong awareness of his own individuality and a poet full of a feeling of creative power. In his vital feeling for life he was a thoroughgoing Hellenist. But in contrast to poets of other and in some cases much older cultures, this Italian did not become absorbed in Hellenism. Quite the opposite; he committed himself to what was Roman and to the language of the Romans. It was in this direction and not toward the Hellenistic world that he turned with his literary efforts, reconciling, promoting, stimulating, elucidating, proclaiming, and inventing. In doing this it was clearly his purpose to use all his powers to provide the Romans with as large and as varied a cross-section of Hellenistic literature as he could and to put it in a form that was at the same time appropriate for them and, at least in part, very demanding and spontaneous. Probably he felt that he in particular had been assigned the task of interpreter, and this is the way Suetonius takes him.[14] But as he carried out his task, his personal style and power made him a pioneer over the broadest areas of Latin literature, and his work actually took on an importance on more than one level.

Ennius was also a Hellenist in that he controlled the greatest possible variety of literary forms. His *opus magnum* was his huge national epic, the *Annales*, written in at least eighteen books. The subject of the poem was the history of Rome from the fall of Troy down to contemporary times. The individual personalities were presented as the bearers of the Roman tradition with special affection and forcefulness. Strongly personal statements were interspersed, in striking contrast to the custom in classical epic and in the great epics of Hellenistic times—at least insofar as we can get an impression of them. Surely Ennius meant his efforts to supersede the older literary production of Naevius, and he found the words to express the challenge.[15]

But he intended to do more. It is not without reason that in the introduction he represents himself as Homer reincarnated. With this remark Ennius not only intended to justify the heroic hexameters that he was putting together for the first time in Latin, but he also wanted to proclaim the serious intent of his poetry. It was meant to have meaning and validity well beyond the present, and as a historical epic it did not avoid comparison with the great sagas and heroic poetry of the Greeks.

In all probability, Ennius had begun to adapt Greek tragedies for the Roman stage well before he turned to the *Annales*. It is obvious that here he felt a special affection for Euripides and probably for the adaptations of his dramas by the players of southern Italy. Ennius' comedies enjoyed less popularity than his tragedies; he could simply not compete with a Plautus or even a Caecilius. It is significant that the drama in Roman dress which Naevius had created earlier was hardly a part of his repertoire. Actually, we have certain knowledge of only one *fabula praetexta*, *The Sabine Women*; the *Ambracia* may have been another. This was possibly an honorary play connected with the capture of Ambracia, the well-fortified city of Pyrrhus, in 189 by Marcus Fulvius Nobilior, Ennius' patron. If this supposition is right, then with this creation Ennius would have brought a Hellenistic custom into the Roman world. For the honorary piece written to lionize the great patron while he was still alive had been in vogue for a very long time in the east.

There are also the remains of a poem in trochaic tetrameters titled *Epicharmus*. Here, using a dream sequence, Ennius put forward precepts of natural philosophy from a Pythagorean point of view. This philosophy of life seems to have had a spiritual attraction for Ennius and there are many indications that his educated listeners were also attracted to it within certain limits.

In the same way the striking double title προτρεπτικός *sive Praecepta* (*An Exhortation or Rules of Conduct*) points in the direction of philosophy. It was probably a call to philosophy—and that in an era when the word *philosophari* meant something like "babbling senseless stuff."

Finally, the ancients had an adaptation of Euhemerus' ἱερὰ ἀναγραφή (*Sacred History*) put together by Ennius, which was probably the first book written in Latin literary prose.[16] This took the form of a fantasy in which a rational explanation of the origin of religious belief was attempted from a point of view that was both antitraditional and patently atheistic. Besides a great deal of didactic material, Ennius' version also contains much irreverence—for example, that involving Venus—and the poet reveals himself once again to be a man of Greek interest in the ease with which he here rejects old, time-honored ideas, as he also did in the tragedies.

Ennius also adapted the *Hedyphagetica (The Pleasures of Eating)* of Archestratus of Gela, one of the many gastronomic works current at the time, this one taking the form of a didactic poem working satirically through its subject matter. Its purpose was to provide information as to where the finest pleasures of the palate were to be found. I do not agree with other scholars who say that this work came from an early period of Ennius' career, for he parodies his own *Annales* in it.

Under the title *Sota* Ennius produced a collection of sotadean verse that was perhaps, at least in part, aggressive, but certainly quite strong. Then we have a few epigrams written in the form of distichs, the first of their kind in Latin, coming probably from late in Ennius' life. And finally there are a few fragments of a piece with the title *Scipio* to which we will return later. Vahlen has collected these shorter works as *Varia*.

And in this connection we must now look more closely at Ennian satire. A collection of four books was known to the ancients. This is well established on the authority of Porphyrion[17] and is not weakened by a comment of Donatus in which the grammarian mentions a sixth book.[18] Whether the division into books goes back to Ennius himself cannot be determined with certainty. Apparently it was known to

Lucilius. Perhaps it is best to imagine Ennius making poems of this kind available to his circle of friends on an informal basis as each was written and keeping copies for himself. He probably referred to them facetiously as *satura*, thinking of coarse, mixed food for healthy people. It is also likely that the whole was made available to the public as a collection only after the death of the poet.

Only very scanty fragments of the satires have been preserved. The collection was made up, as Diomedes indicates, of miscellaneous poems in a variety of meters. Today we can still recognize iambic senarii, trochaic septenarii, dactylic hexameters, and sotadeans. Each book of the collection in its turn contained a variety of poems in different meters; at a later time Lucilius followed this practice in his earlier books. Vahlen has included too much that is doubtful in his collection of the satire fragments. Warmington is more careful, but the autobiographical and anecdotal items need closer study.

If epigram is excepted, Ennius in his satire produced for the first time in the Latin language a poetic form in which the individual could express himself and describe his own experiences in a very personal way. And he could do this with complete freedom, with no restriction of any kind, and in a manner quite different from that of the lyric poet. Earlier Latin poetry did not offer this possibility, for there the individuality of the poet had taken second place throughout to the immediate purpose of the work. That satire appeared as a poetic form of personal expression at precisely the time when the personality of the individual was in the earliest stages of liberation is certainly just as fortuitous as the fact that its creator was a poet who was as thoroughly aware of his own personality as Ennius was.

As far as the content of Ennian satire is concerned, not much in the way of details can be made out. It is quite by accident that we learn from Quintilian that in one of his satires Ennius presented a debate between the two allegorical characters, *Mors* and *Vita* (Death and Life).[19] What they said to each other is not known. But the fact that this poem took the form of a dialogue in which personified abstracts vied in a contest—in an agon, so to speak—is important.

How the later Atellan, *Mortis et vitae iudicium* (*The Trial of Life and Death*), was related to the Ennian theme it is impossible to say, but it is extremely likely that with this satire Ennius was not in a popular Italian tradition, but in a Greek-Hellenistic tradition.

This is suggested by Quintilian who correctly points to the debate between Ἀρετή and Κακία (Virtue and Vice) in Prodicus' allegory of Heracles at the crossroads, a comparison that had become a commonplace well before the time of Ennius. But there is also the well-known debate between Right and Wrong Reason in the *Clouds* of Aristophanes or the corresponding scenes in the *Wealth*. Also comparable is the contest between Earth and Sea in Epicharmus and, without going into detail, it should be pointed out that the popular philosophy of Hellenistic times especially presented a profusion of allegorical abstracts speaking, some of them even in the dialogue of debate. It is most likely, then, that Ennius would have chosen and shaped his subject by following some such model, for he had a special affection for the new and the recent.

Gellius gives a more detailed account of another satire.[20] According to him, Ennius produced a charming version of Aesop's fable about the crested lark. For this he used trochaic tetrameters, a popular meter. The account of Gellius is fairly detailed, and scholars have attempted to find in it quotations from the original poem. But this is hardly convincing, even though there are parallel versions that have survived.[21] The story ended with a *fabula docet* (the moral of the story is):

> Hoc erit tibi argumentum semper in promptu situm:
> Ne quid expectes amicos quod tu⟨te⟩ agere possies. (57–58)
> (And do keep this in mind at all times:
> Don't wait for friends to do what you can do yourself.)

Otto Weinreich treats it in some detail.[22] It seems likely that this fable made up the subject of a complete satire.

A second fable-satire is indicated by the fragment at line 65. There is no clear evidence that this line comes from the satires, although, as C. O. Müller pointed out, it is highly likely.[23] The fragment assumes that scene and situation which Herodotus describes in his first book:[24] Once upon a time, a flute-player was walking along the seashore and was trying to attract the fish with his flute. When they chose not to follow the notes, he seized a large net, threw it out, and brought in a huge catch. As he dragged the net onto the shore and the fish began to wriggle around, he said: "Now look here! You don't have to dance any more now; for when I played the music, you didn't want to come dancing to shore." In Herodotus the lesson is not lacking in pointed political purpose, while in Ennius the moral would certainly have been stated in a far less biting way, if it were stated at all.

And so two fables can be identified in Ennius' satires and perhaps he recounted even more of them. Buecheler, for example, thought that Hyginus' story (220) about *Cura* (Care) could derive from Ennius, but this must remain an open question. Expressed as it was in simple, pleasant language, the fable narrative of Ennius quite naturally lacked topical political pungency. It went rather in the direction of a simple, generally obvious moral—in the direction, then, of the *argumentum* (proof). In attempting to characterize Ennian fable and its purposes in a few words, we could probably cite the words Phaedrus chose in recommending his own fables written some two-and-a-half centuries later: "This little book contains a double dowry, since it lures its audience to laughter and gives the careful reader a lesson for living."[25] The purpose, then, would be to amuse and entertain, but also to provide advice in as clear and direct a manner as possible.

This is, generally speaking, the earliest trace of an independent fable narrative in poetry among the Romans. In the mind of the ancients, the fable belonged among the most unpretentious forms of writing and seemed best suited to influencing the simple, rustic people.[26] Perhaps there is a hint here as to how we should view the mode of Ennian satire and its place in the hierarchy of literature. Moreover, the fable belongs to the thematic repertoire of the later satirists as well. Lucilius adapted the tale of the lion and the fox in a broader context,[27] and Horace followed him with parts of his epistles,[28] but especially with his story of the city mouse and the country mouse.[29]

There can be no doubt that the fable narrative of Ennius is connected with Greek originals. The Greek fable appears in a well-developed form as early as the seventh century in Archilochus. But Ennius preferred the Greek writings of the Hellenistic period. It is now a well-known fact that the poetry of the old iambic poets was stirred to new life in Alexandria during the first half of the third century B.C., and in his *Iambics*, which he wrote late in life, Callimachus quite frankly represented himself as a reincarnated Hipponax. It is not only probable, but almost certain that Ennius knew this popular book.

In this book of iambics, which extended the poetic line running from Hipponax to Phoenix of Colophon in a completely original way, Callimachus had brought in Aesop himself, and, among other things, αἶνοι—the technical term for the Aesopic fable—had their part to play. One of these still survives today in rather long fragments—the contest between the laurel tree and the olive tree[30]—and a second is at least indicated.[31] Callimachus adapted both of these, as we know, using them not in the simple, straightforward way that Ennius did, but for purposes of polemic. This is a fundamental difference between the two poets.

Now other iambic poets of the Hellenistic period also recounted fables.[32] Apart from its occurrence here, it is also found well integrated into the diatribe and related popular writings, to use only one example. We should also not forget the popularity enjoyed by the collection of fables put together by Demetrius of Phalerum not too long before Ennius' time and the importance of the fable in elementary education. And so when everything is considered, we should not go to the extreme of thinking of Callimachus as the only author and the standard source for this aspect of Ennius' satire. It is more likely that Ennius was motivated to use such fables by popular literature or the diatribe and that it is from there that the simple, straightforward approach resulting in a strong, immediately obvious moral is derived. On the other hand, it is surely possible that through the lectures of the Alexandrian poets Ennius learned that fables could also be put into verse. Drawing on both of these sources, then, he was the first poet to let the Latin fable develop within the collective range of the *satura* as a completely individual growth.

The portrait of the parasite (14–19) points to a second theme. In it Ennius put together a piece of real life in all its aspects, and it is not necessary to point out here how infinitely fruitful the portrayal of life became for Roman satire in general. As a matter of fact, the satirists later claimed to be writing poetry that dealt primarily with human existence and served as a mirror of life.

It was also through Ennius, of course, that the autobiographical element became an integral part of Roman satire. The fragment at line 64 is probably taken from a satire: "I never play the poet, unless I'm laid up with the gout" he says there, meaning "when I'm so bogged down that I can't do anything better." This sounds quite true to life, and the self-ridicule is at the same time very pleasant and characteristic. For Ennius enjoyed writing poetry and he was proud of it. Another fragment (63) also has a personal ring to it. Moreover, there is the possibility that Horace drew his information about Ennius the tippler and stalwart drinker from a satire. And the anecdotes about Ennius— for example, the story of his going for a walk with Servius Galba that is found in Cicero[33]—in the last analysis suggest a connection with the satires.

It is important to note in this connection that Ennius represented himself as speaking in the first person in the satires (6) in verses which suggest a Hellenistic model[34] and yet are filled with a pride that is completely personal. In the realm of Latin poetry, the expression of personal feelings by the poet is perfectly familiar to us from the poetry of the neoterics and from verse satire, elegy, and epigram. And to these might be added the self-expression of Varro in the Menippeans. There are precedents for this in Greek literature, but the self-expression of Ennius which appeared here for the first time in a Latin poem, even in its adaptation from the Greek, is something new and completely personal.

If another fragment can be certainly assigned to the satires (10–11), then it is possible to recognize yet another satiric element that is not otherwise clearly identifiable until Lucilius. This is the reference to actual people and events. For these words pretty well have to be related to Scipio's shipping grain.

As far as the form and structure of the satires are concerned, it is clearly established that narration, description, and instruction in a clear and forceful manner all played an important part. But Ennius also chose the dialogue form.[35] The satires certainly also contained sententious material and proverbs.[36]

As far as style in the proper sense of the term is concerned, not too much can be determined. The speech against the parasite (14–19) gives quite a good idea of the kind of language used. The tone is that of informal, educated speech. The portrayal is extremely vivid with each epithet in just the right place and the thoughts arranged in a simple way. *Abligurrire bona* (17: to lap up the goods) sounds like a sloppy turn of phrase—the kind of thing which appears elsewhere in these satires—but it puts the picture the poet wants to get across before the reader's eyes in an abrupt and vivid way. This sort of thing reminds us of Lucilius.

In addition, structural elements of the archaic Latin literary language are used very skillfully—alliteration, doublets, and tricola asyndetically arranged, a three-part antithesis serving as the conclusion of the passage whose elements are again balanced asyndetically (19). Ennius' delight in overflowing expression which works at developing vividness with constantly new turns of phrase also makes itself felt. In addition to such broad strokes—which frequently in Ennius result in a certain verbosity—there is the delight the poet takes in the sound of his language (5; 3–4). As might be expected, this can extend as far as puns and plays upon sounds (59–62). But Ennius can express himself quite differently, even in the satires. His language can fall into a quick and lively pattern (5) or very solemn tones can be heard pervaded by the serious mood of parody (3-4; 66). There must have been a great variety of these moods with the emphasis always on liveliness and never on indecency.

As far as Ennius' methods of composition are concerned, nothing definite can be said. It is logical to expect that there was a tight structure where the subject dictated it—in the debate, fable narrative, and the like. A parallel for this was probably to be found in the *Euhemerus*. Other parts of the satires probably left more of an impression of looseness—the conversation with the parasite, for example.

In order to somewhat broaden this very narrow base on which our knowledge of Ennian satire rests, it has been conjectured that the so-called *Varia* of Ennius, that is the short writings referred to above, had originally been part of the collection of satires. Some scholars, along with Lucian Müller (most recently Fr. Della Corte), would include all of these and others only a part of them. The idea has been defended especially vigorously as far as the *Scipio* of Ennius is concerned. In fact, attempts have been made to be even more precise and identify the *Scipio* with the third book of the satires. Trochaic tetrameters and an awkward hexameter can indeed be documented from this work, so that we have to believe that it contained a number of separate poems in different meters. This was also the situation with the satire books.

In and by itself, a subtitle would probably be possible for a collection such as this. The sixteenth book of Lucilius also went the rounds under the special title *Collyra*, while the first book of Propertius' elegies was called *Cynthia* from the word that begins them. Varro's Menippean Περίπλους II (*Circumnavigation II*) had its own heading Περὶ Φιλοσο-φίας (*Concerning Philosophy*). There are also other examples.

But the habit of the old grammarians of differentiating the short poems of Ennius from his *satura* speaks against assigning the *Scipio* to the satire books. Gellius, for example, at one point makes a citation using the words *Ennii versum . . . ex libro, qui Scipio inscribitur* ("a verse of Ennius . . . from his book titled *Scipio*"),[37] while later this same authority refers to *Ennius in saturis* ("Ennius in his satires").[38] And Nonius in particular cites the third book of the satires, but never the *Scipio*. The usual practice seems to have been to refer to the individual book which had its own title but which was part of a larger work by using the main title. And so we find something like *Lucilius in satur-arum decimo sexto* (Lucilius in the sixteenth book of his *Satires*) and not *Lucilius in Collyra* (Lucilius in his *Collyra*).

It seems to me that one of Horace's odes[39] provides especially strong evidence against including the *Scipio* in the collection of satires. For Ennius can be represented as a glorifier of Scipio on the basis of his *Annales* or a personal collection of poetry, the *Scipio*, but hardly on the basis of his four books of satires—least of all by Horace! So the idea that has the most to recommend it is that the *Scipio* was an independent collection of poems and is to be kept separate from the satire corpus. If the idea that the *Scipio* preceded the *Annales* turns out to be right, then it would provide another argument for separating it from the satires, for, as a collection, the latter can only belong to a period of the poet's literary production when he had already mastered the hexameter.

In the same way, the Ennian *Epigrammata* must be kept separate from his satires. Any appeal to the form of Lucilius' Book 22 as showing a connection proves nothing. The epigrams there surely do not belong to *satura* in the narrow sense. The same may be said about the hint at epigrams found in Varro's Menippeans.

The bold and very provocative book of Mario Puelma Piwonka takes all of this into account.[40] But Puelma includes the rest of the short writings of Ennius—that is, everything that is left of the *Varia* with the exception of the *Scipio* and the epigrams—together under the *genus saturae* (genre satire) and draws broad conclusions from them. In this *corpus saturarum*, then, prose also would have been of frequent occurrence, and Ennius would no longer be the creator of Latin verse satire. This, in spite of the fact that Horace, for example, labels him the originator in a passage which in my opinion has been best explained by K. Büchner.[41]

It is also certainly possible to trace thematic connections between the *Varia* of Ennius and the Roman verse satire, as, for example, between the *Hedyphagetica* and Horace's satire in which Catius gives his lecture on food.[42] But is it conceivable that, in about the year 169 B.C., and especially in Rome, something like a complete collection of small works edited by the author himself at the end of his life should be in existence?

And are not the ancient citations of title better understood if we imagine that Ennius wrote his *Epicharmus*, his *Praecepta*, and whatever other individual *Varia* there were as separate pieces and made them available to a wide reading public in this form? In the same way, the individual pieces of his *Satura* were first circulated and only after the poet's death were collected, divided into four books, and made available to the general public. In this case it is entirely possible that

Satura as a title for the whole collection goes back to a half-serious coinage by the poet himself who with it summed up this group of poems so widely different in content and metrical form but at the same time of so very personal a nature as a "medley." In any case, it is advisable to differentiate between the so-called *Varia* and the *Satura*.[43]

Within these limits, then, the *Satura* of Ennius represents a collection of miscellaneous individual poems in different meters. Its subject matter was not clearly fixed and in matters of style there was clearly quite a bit of leeway. What held it together and gave it a unity was purely and simply the forceful and distinctive personality of the poet, and this aspect of satire adopted by Ennius became standard for his successors. In Lucilius, satire serves to a great extent as topical criticism, while in Horace it is more contemplative and aims at the *emendatio sui* (improvement of himself), out of which, if we understand correctly what the poet says, an *emendatio* of the reader can also be expected. Again, satire bears witness to the educational experience of a Persius or, as in the case of Juvenal, it is simply a means of venting one's indignation. But no matter what form it took, Roman satire at all stages of its development served as the completely personal expression of the opinions and feelings of the poet writing it.

In the satire of Ennius there is as yet no trace of the tones of polemic; it was hardly Ennius' purpose to expose any specific person by publicly mentioning his name. On the other hand, moral instruction probably played a greater role than the fragments indicate. Without doubt many elements of theme and form, which later appeared more clearly and better developed in the satire of Lucilius, had started here. It is naturally no longer possible to ascertain in detail to what extent Lucilius was indebted to his predecessor. Moreover, there were many individual characteristics of Ennian satire that were derived from Greek models. We may accept the fact that the profusion of literature from Greece, that was at the same time didactic, moralizing, and entertaining, had a strong influence on Ennius—especially the diatribe, the Cynic debate, and the mime, but also Latin verse comedy and many others. There is also a good possibility that Ennius was influenced by the Hellenistic iambic poets like Phoenix of Colophon, and it is quite likely that he owes a great deal to the iambics of Callimachus. For these collections also comprised a series of separate, individual pieces in a variety of meters; they too had been conceived of as being very personal, and they moved on a stylistic level which was said to have been close to actual speech with its great variety of shading; their manner too was sparkling and lively and rich in humor. And, what is more, Ennius probably owed quite a number of individual motifs to these collections.

But in spite of all this, there is no reason to see an evolutional connection. For there are dissimilarities, and clearly significant ones, which are more than just a reflection of a basic difference in poetic personality. And while iambics are a well-established poetic form as far as the Hellenistic poets are concerned, Roman satire in Ennius' hands, quite to the contrary, is clearly *in statu nascendi* (in the process of coming into being).

In any event, Scevola Mariotti's suggestion that with his satires Ennius meant to create a Latin counterpart to the Callimachean iambic poetry seems to me to be far too bold. We are not yet in a position to say with certainty that a unified conception was basic to Ennian satire from the beginning. Nor can we know whether these poems which appeared at different times and without forethought were meant to be more than occasional expressions of personal thoughts and feelings put into an attractive form. And finally we cannot get away from the judgment of Horace that Ennius' satires were a creation which was alien to the Greeks[44] or from Quintilian's assertion that verse satire was a purely Roman development.[45]

In later times the satires of Ennius were clearly overshadowed by the poems of Lucilius, so that apparently even a Roman as knowledgeable about early Latin literature as Cicero did not read them any longer. Whether the fragment on the ape (69), for example, which is found in Cicero's *De natura deorum* (1.97), comes from the satires is uncertain. There can be no doubt that a man like Varro knew the collection, and even the grammarians looked into it from time to time. In general, however, they belonged among the curiosities of literature until they, like other inheritances from the past, were again sought out by the archaists of the second century after Christ and read again for linguistic, stylistic, and especially antiquarian purposes. And so, except for Gellius, it is mainly the grammarians who have preserved the scanty remains on which our knowledge is based.

« IV »

Gaius Lucilius

ENNIUS' nephew, Marcus Pacuvius, whose dates are placed between 220 and about 132 B.C., carried on the Ennian satiric tradition without interruption. It was primarily as a poet of the stage that he earned his reputation, but it is attested that he also wrote satires. And he wrote them in the contemplative manner of Ennius and not yet in the aggressive style of Lucilius.[1] Not a single fragment has been preserved. And though Pacuvius probably struck out in no new directions with his satire, still it is very important that the fledgling tradition of writing satiric poetry in Rome was put on a firm footing by him, so that when Lucilius began to write, he already had at least two worthy predecessors and a tradition covering two generations that he could look back to.

Mention should be made here more in the way of a note of a few chance references which show clearly how different elements contributed to the development of this satiric tradition which becomes clearly perceptible again only with Lucilius. The private letter written in verse, for example, is an important subtype of Roman satire. Here we learn from Cicero that Spurius Mummius, the brother of the destroyer of Corinth, sent letters containing humorous verses to his friends while he was serving in camp.[2] This happened about fourteen or fifteen years before the first satires of Lucilius were written. These letters were certainly never published, but were preserved in the family archives. Lucilius would surely have known them, since like him, Spurius Mummius belonged to Scipio's circle of friends. By sheer accident, then, it is possible for once to recognize here an element which probably had its importance for the history of Roman satire.

Moreover, it should be remembered that the brief, generally anonymous lampoon, especially the political kind, led a vigorous life in Rome and that the political pamphlet had been a part of Roman literature since Cato's time. It had gained a special importance in the struggle for domestic reform, and there can be no doubt that such political squibs had their influence on Lucilius.

At the same time, the farce in poetic form was very much in evidence in Rome. Lucilius mentions the *Lex Tappula* (Tappulan Law),[3] for example, which was a poem of Valerius of Valentia in which the poet, surely following a Hellenistic model, had drawn up a set of regulations for drinking which parodied the Roman legal style. By some stroke of fate, the introduction to this comic piece has apparently been preserved for us,[4] although the relationship between Valerius' poem and the inscription is not yet by any means clear. There may have been many more examples of this kind of thing; passages like the legal parody at the end of Plautus' *Mercator* (1015–26), for example, make this probable.

In spite of such writings which, indeed, to a large extent had no literary pretensions, the ancients insisted categorically that Lucilius first gave Roman satire its particular character. Lucilius lived in an era of the strongest moral, social, and political pressures. The complicated system of conventions under which the old Roman life ran its course had tottered; the struggle for the welfare of the state began to develop into the struggle of party leaders. This was the time that paved the way for the civil wars and dictatorships.

And so it seems understandable that Lucilius did not hide his convictions and that he took satire, which had been passed down to him as a medium for expressing personal feelings, and put it to use as a weapon. From this time on the ancients felt this aggressiveness to be the most significant characteristic of satire. In contrast to his predecessors, they said, Lucilius took Roman satire, as Aristophanes had taken old comedy earlier, and imbued it with a new mood of attack. Like the Greek comedian, Lucilius brought out into the open especially the mistakes of the people and the classes that made up the political leadership, and he did this with an almost reckless candor. He established satire as a poetry of conflict, as topical "battle-writing," which was not at all anonymous and which contained great personal pungency. But we should certainly not for this reason connect Lucilian satire in a causal way with the old Attic comedy as Horace did;[5] it is quite certain, however, that Lucilius first gave satire a direction which it did not have before his time and which it was destined never to give up completely.

Lucilius established the subject matter, spirit, style, and principles of satire anew so definitely that Horace was able to call him the *inventor* ("discoverer") of satire, in spite of all the respect felt for Ennius.[6] At the same time it should be emphasized that Lucilius' palette was a great deal richer. Certainly many of his poems served the purposes of personal attack, but others merely aimed at providing advice, warning, or commentary or else they were meant only to amuse and entertain without allowing polemic any great latitude. And very often Lucilius just told a story in a simple and straightforward way as Ennius probably had before him.

To be sure, not a single complete poem from his abundant literary production has come down to us; nor has any index of his poems survived. In all, there are about 1300 verses extant which are by no means always complete and for the most part are totally out of context.[7]

The praenomen and family name of the poet are known for certain by his own testimony and through that of other authorities. His name was Gaius Lucilius. His place of birth was Suessa Aurunca, a town situated in the border district between Latium and Campania at the foot of Mons Massicus.[8] The year of his death is also well attested. Under the year 102 B.C., Jerome, drawing on Suetonius and probably indirectly on Varro, makes the following observation: "The satiric poet Lucilius dies at Naples and is buried in a public grave." This sounds authentic, and in the fragments of the poet that have come down to us there is also no chronological reference later than 107 or possibly 105. Moreover, in his dialogue *De oratore*, which is set in 91 B.C., Cicero has the participants speak of Lucilius as if he is deceased.

Jerome gives 148/7 B.C. as the year of Lucilius' birth, which can hardly be correct. Perhaps an error already existed in Suetonius. Lucilius enjoyed a close friendship with Scipio, who was born in 185 B.C., and behaved with him as with an intimate,[9] so that there could not have been a difference in age of forty years between the two of them. Moreover, Velleius Paterculus tells us (2.9.4) that Lucilius served in the campaign at Numantia as a member of the cavalry and began producing his satires after that. And so he necessarily would have been a soldier when he was barely fifteen years old and would have applied himself to poetry while still a minor. Finally, Horace, who is one of our most reliable sources, puts forward the idea that Lucilius was still composing poetry when he was a *senex* or old man.[10] Accordingly, the poet must have lived to be at least sixty years old. In order to remove these inconsistencies, Moritz Haupt made the oral suggestion that per-

haps the chronicler confused the consuls of the year 148/7, Spurius
Postumius Albinus and Lucius Calpurnius Piso, with those of the year
180, Aulus Postumius Albinus and Gaius Calpurnius Piso, and that
accordingly the year 180 is to be taken as the poet's birthdate. As attractive as this conjecture is, it is not without its problems, and Cichorius
recommended an estimate for the birthdate that falls between the other
two—about 167 B.C.

There is every probability that, as Cichorius proved in opposition to
Marx, Lucilius was a Roman citizen and not a *socius nominis Latini*
(Latin ally). If he were the latter, he would not at all have been able
to associate with Scipio and his circle of friends on even terms. And he
would not have been able to attack the opponents of Scipio and his
political views with such pungency and frankness. And besides, Lucilius
had a brother, as he himself mentions, and the brother had senatorial
rank and consequently had held public office. The brother's daughter,
Lucilia, married Gnaeus Pompeius Strabo and in the year 106 gave
birth to Pompey who was to become the triumvir.[11] The poet himself
probably remained a bachelor.

It is possible that Lucilius' father, whose name may have been
Marcus, had already held a curule office. The family undoubtedly had
considerable wealth, and Lucilius was certainly a member of the equestrian order. With this position he could move as a social equal in circles
of the nobility of Rome. It seems worth noting that Lucilius was the
first Roman poet of rank for whom poetry was an expression of his
personality and not just an amusement. With this came the revelation
of what was clearly a new point of view and a reappraisal of intellectual
pursuits by the Romans, for the older Latin poets had all belonged to the
lower social strata.

As a landowner, Lucilius led a completely independent life. He
owned estates in the vicinity of Suessa Aurunca and on Sicily and probably also in southern Italy and perhaps on Sardinia. A comment of
Cicero accords with this, for he says that the poet made enemies because he let his herds graze on the *ager publicus* (public land).[12]

Lucilius owned a palace in Rome that had been built originally for
Demetrius, the Seleucid prince, and besides this he probably had at
least one other townhouse, this located in Naples. Horace refers to this
considerable wealth and to the earlier satirist's respected social position,[13]
and Lucilius' own statements tally well with this. Lucilius' spirit of
independence also manifested itself in the fact that he never held
public office in Rome. And so the general circumstances of the life he

led seem to suggest that Lucilius should be looked upon as a man of the world and not as a person with an outspoken poetic nature.

The fragments of his satires that have been preserved provide the only evidence there is that he enjoyed a first-rate education. He obviously mastered the Greek language and knew Greek literature thoroughly. More than once he translated a passage of Homer into Latin verse, apparently for his own pleasure (1254), and he applied detailed criticism to the *Cresphontes* of Euripides.[14] And not only are Greek epic and Greek drama always present for him, but he was also familiar with much less common material such as Archilochus (698, 699), whom few people in Rome read before Horace, and also Aristophanes, Pherecrates, Teleclides, Euclid, and, of course, Demosthenes, Plato, and many others.

He often ridiculed Hellenistic philosophy, but he was certainly familiar with it and it influenced his satires to a very great extent. We even know that he also maintained personal connections with Greek philosophers. As a result, Clitomachus, for example, the head of the Academy in Athens from 127/6 to 110, who was a Carthaginian by birth, dedicated one of his writings to Lucilius.[15] The satirist perhaps thanked him in a satire for doing this. Lucilius also spoke of Carneades 214/3–129/8 B.C.) with respect (31) and seems on the whole to have taken a position closest to the Academy of all the philosophical schools.[16]

The fragments of the satires that have been preserved for us also reveal such an accurate knowledge of Athenian cultural life, Greek practices and conditions, Greek maxims, and even of Greek art, that the hypothesis putting Lucilius in Athens for some time, probably for educational purposes, cannot be rejected. It is entirely possible that on this occasion he also came to know the great port of Delos. Here is evidence once again of a completely personal move, for travel like this for educational purposes, which many young nobles undertook in Horace's time, was still the exception in the middle of the second century B.C.

Lucilius was just as well read in Latin literature—in the older writers as well as in his contemporaries. And he challenged it with the same freedom that he challenged Greek literature. Horace attests to his criticizing his great model Ennius,[17] and at the same time the fragments clearly show his arguments with Pacuvius and Accius,[18] his knowledge of Caecilius and Terence, and probably his quarrel with Afranius.

Lucilius' friendship with the younger Scipio and his membership in his very narrow circle of friends were of the greatest importance for the story of his life. It is entirely possible that this connection went back to the poet's early youth, for the estate of Scipio, Lavernium, must have been located in close proximity to Lucilius' holdings at Suessa Aurunca. Then, when Scipio took command at Numantia in the year 134, Lucilius served under him as an *eques* or cavalryman,[19] probably in the *cohors praetoria* (Praetorian Cohort), and this friendship lasted right to Scipio's death in 129 B.C. Whether Lucilius had already fought with him earlier in Spain against Viriathus and the Lusitanians is uncertain.

Out of this friendship with Scipio came a variety of friendships and enmities for the satirist. We know, for example, of his friendship with Rutilius Rufus, Manius Manilius, Quintus Fabius Maximus, and also with Gaius Laelius, Junius Congus, and other members of the Scipionic Circle. It is also likely that he himself became acquainted with the important Greeks that came and went. After Scipio's death a closer tie with Gaius Sempronius Tuditanus seems to have developed. But the poet's circle of friends must have been really quite large; this can be gathered from dedications of individual poems, for example, and from occasional incidental comments.

But the crowd of Lucilius' enemies and adversaries was far greater. First of all, there was the large group of political and personal opponents of Scipio, among whom were Quintus Caecilius Metellus Macedonicus (censor 131 B.C.), his son, Gaius Caecilius Caprarius, and his son-in-law, Gaius Servilius Vatia. Then there were Tiberius Claudius Asellus and the Pontifex Maximus, Publius Mucius Scaevola (consul 133 B.C.), a leading opponent of Scipio, as well as the brothers Papirii Carbones, Lucius Cornelius Lentulus Lupus, the leader of the Senate from the year 131 on, Lucius Aurelius Cotta, perhaps Appius Claudius Pulcher, and many others. These were the *primores populi* ("the most illustrious of the people") with whom, Horace tells us, Lucilius carried on a running battle.[20] The motives which guided the satirist in these struggles of his were probably for the most part less objective than personal, for he apparently found nice, sympathetic things to say about Tiberius Gracchus who was a bitter enemy of Scipio's politics.[21]

There were also probably personal motives behind his attacks on other members of the Roman nobility who cannot be shown to have felt any opposition to Scipio's political views. Aulus Postumius Albinus was one of these, and it is possible that in attacking this man Lucilius meant to strike out at the coterie of philhellenes in Rome.

In addition to these, there was also the circle of his literary enemies. We are especially well informed about his quarrels with Accius, the tragedian, grammarian, and apparently somewhat arrogant arbiter of taste. The point of departure of the dispute with Accius could have been literary, but it could also have been a matter of politics, for it is not unlikely that Accius' *Brutus* had been directed against Scipio. Lucilius was certainly the attacker here, but Accius fought back. Lucilius apparently also engaged in a running quarrel with the comic poet, Afranius. It is actually attested that the satirist once brought a suit against an actor because he attacked him in a libelous manner by name from the stage.[22]

The ancients had thirty books of Lucilius' poems, representing the literary production of his lifetime. This was a surprising achievement which can be explained not just by the satirist's remarkable creative power, but also probably by the very great ease with which he produced his poetry and by his occasional neglect of details, a habit which Horace censured so bitterly and certainly not without reason.[23]

Varro refers to an edition of the satires made up of two parts, the first of which included books 1–21.[24] But there are convincing reasons for our assuming a tripartite division, according to which the whole collection was divided into books 1–21, 22–25, and 26–30. The oldest of these three collections comprised books 26–30 and contained poems written shortly after the war at Numantia (about 132/1 B.C.) and in part still in the lifetime of Scipio (before 129). The latest chronological reference (671–72) points to the year 123. Lucilius had prefaced the collection with a poem of introduction, so that there can be no doubt that he himself collected books 26–30 and published them after the poems had become generally known earlier while circulating individually.

There can be no certainty about the title. Lucilius speaks of his works as *poemata* (1013: "poems") and *ludus ac sermones* (1039: "playful conversations"), while the grammarians cite them as *satirae*. Undoubtedly Lucilius wanted to make a point of recalling Ennius in his title, but there can be no agreement as to whether he published his writings under the collective title *Satura*, which would have designated the poetic genre, whether he called them *Libri saturarum* (*Books of Satires*), or whether they had some other title. A designation *schedium* (extemporaneous poetry), which some have thought of, cannot be supported.

It is not unlikely that Lucilius also published books 1–21 himself. To limit this collection to books 1–20 would contradict the evidence offered by Varro. The fact that no fragment has been preserved from book 21 may be explained from its position at the end of the corpus. The tradition in the case of other authors would offer parallels for this. A fragment (578) which Cichorius wanted to explain as a farewell to poetry does not provide sufficient basis for such a far-reaching conclusion.

Finally, there are books 22–25 about which we are very poorly informed. As Cichorius surmises with probability, they could have been published posthumously from Lucilius' estate. They also contained pieces of poetry which did not allow the designation satires, as, for example, the epigrams. Apparently in the copy which Nonius used these books had been combined with books 1–21, while books 26–30 balanced this large corpus as a special collection.

When they are viewed as a whole, it becomes clear that the arrangement of the satires is based on a metrical scheme. Books 1–21 contained hexameters only, while 22–25 (besides hexameters?) were made up of distichs. Books 26–30 were polymetric and actually were arranged in such a way that a clear development of the poet can be made out. His earliest books (26 and 27) contained trochaic septenarii only. This was the popular verse form which Ennius had also used readily in his satires. In books 28 and 29, in addition to trochaics, there were poems in iambic senarii and dactylic hexameters, just as in Ennius' fragments. The thirtieth book contained hexameters only, the verse form, then, that Lucilius himself and like him the later Roman satirists retained as the only meter suitable for satire.

It is not known who arranged this complete edition. But it was probably already extant in Varro's time. Now there is evidence that philological activity with the text of Lucilius began very early. Suetonius mentions two men from the circle of friends of the poet himself who busied themselves with his writings—Vettius Philocomus and Quintus Laelius Archelaus.[25] It is entirely possible that the first complete edition of Lucilius goes right back to them.

The next step in the tradition follows immediately after this. From the circle of Pompey the Great, who was the grandnephew of Lucilius, Valerius Cato, a student of Philocomus, Pompeius Lenaeus, a student of Archelaus, and Curtius Nicias are said to have turned their attention to interpreting the poetry of Lucilius with the approval of other scholars. The old interpolated verses prefaced to Horace's Satire 1.10 (*Lucili quam sis mendosus*, etc.) point to a revised edition of Lucilius done by

Valerius Cato. From this time also probably came the first collections
of glosses on Lucilius as well as the first commentaries. The use of
these is attested still for the times of the Emperor Tiberius.[26] The early
empire had editions of the poet with critical marks, an indication that
the text was also used in the classroom. In this connection, Probus of
Berytus and his school come to mind immediately.

Well before this time, probably as early as Horace, there were anthologies of Lucilius' satires and probably also collections of witty say-
ings, which are reflected in Macrobius, for example. Preparatory work
on the life of the poet seems also to have existed, and we meet its influence early in Varro, Nepos, Atticus, and Velleius, then in Suetonius,
and finally in Jerome.

Just as the satires of Lucilius had many commentators and editors,
so they did not lack readers. Partisans of the national Roman literature
like Cicero, Varro, and Asinius Pollio had referred to Lucilius. The
classical movement in literature, especially Horace, had set itself in
opposition to him. But already in the Flavian period we hear again of
people who admire Lucilius,[27] until the old satirist enjoyed a rebirth
in the era of the archaists. Independent knowledge of Lucilius can be
found in Cicero, Varro, Asinius Pollio, Horace, Vergil, Persius,
Petronius, Seneca, Pliny, Martial, Quintilian, Juvenal, the archaists,
and a few other authors. There are no sure indications that Lucilius
was read beyond the second century after Christ, for Lactantius, whom
we have to thank for several quite lengthy fragments,[28] probably drew
these from a moral anthology.

The citations of the grammarians are to be distinguished from
these sources to which we owe connected and coherent quotations. The
grammarians were not concerned with continuity of sense, but their
interest lay in glossing points of grammar. A large number of these
citations go back to Verrius Flaccus, but he was by no means the only
scholar who concerned himself with the language of Lucilius. We
still see this in the different ways of quoting that the extant grammarians use, for in doing this they were following their authorities. The
great majority of the fragments of Lucilius by far have come down to
us through Nonius, with others preserved by Festus, Charisius,
Diomedes, Priscian, and the scholia literature, as well as by Macrobius
and several others.

The extraordinary difficulties of interpretation or, for that matter,
even of reconstruction are obvious. Only very seldom has a continuous
piece been preserved comprising more than three verses; the great ma-

jority are just short fragments lifted from their context. Quite often the individual fragment resists a significant meaning when taken by itself; it seldom allows a reliable supposition about the context. Moreover, as Marx suspected, the order of the individual fragments within the limits of the separate books cannot be ascertained from the grammatical tradition.

But in spite of this, it has been possible in many cases to cluster several fragments of one and the same book in groups. Only very seldom can such groups then be assigned with confidence to one or several individual satires. For the structure of the Lucilian satire seems to have been loose and often desultory, so that the poet was able to change tone and scenery within the same poem and to mix quite disparate subjects together. Without doubt analogy is a great help in attempting reconstruction, especially comparison with the satirists dependent on Lucilius. Combining fragments is essential, but this device also has its limits.

If we go a step further and ask about the precise content of the individual books, we are once again subject to the caprices of the ancient authorities doing the selecting. From books 21 and 24 no quotation at all has been preserved, and so nothing can be said about the content. The sixteenth book is said to have had the subtitle *Collyra* and to have dealt with Lucilius' lady-friend of that name.[29] But not a single one of the fragments that have been preserved refers in any way to this. We would have just as little reason for concluding on the basis of existing fragments that there was a polemic against Accius in book 10, but its existence is attested by the ancients.[30]

The length of the individual poems seems to have varied considerably; in general we should probably not imagine them as being very long. From the different meters preserved, for example, it follows that books 28 and 29 contained at least three, but probably more individual poems. On the other hand, it is often assumed that the first three books are each devoted to a single topic. For books 1 and 2 this may be correct, and there is the parallel in Juvenal's sixth satire. But as far as the third book is concerned, Porphyrion knew that it also contained an attack on Accius. Of course, none of the fragments that have come down to us points to this, so that no real certainty is attainable on this point.

Comparatively speaking, the majority of the fragments that have been preserved come from the oldest collection—that is, from books 26–30. As has already been mentioned, Lucilius began writing immediately after the Numantine campaign when the political position of Scipio was the subject of very lively dispute. The earliest poems were clearly meant only for the narrow circle of friends (592–96) but quickly became well known (e.g., 1013), and in the year 123 or shortly thereafter (671–72), Lucilius himself published this first collection. He had prefaced it with a programmatic poem, and it is with this satire as a starting point that Lucilius' conception of his poetic personality and his satiric poetry should be traced—though the search should not be limited to this satire alone. Verses 587–96 in particular belong to this poem. Horace's Trebatius satire[31] may be brought in for comparison, since the concern here is the same as it is there—the vindication of a writer's satiric poetry by showing its intrinsic value and describing the natural disposition of the poet. The situations are further comparable in that in both cases satiric poems had been written earlier that had led to personal attacks on the poet. Horace also probably followed Lucilius in various matters of detail in his poem. In this connection the differences between the two satires need not come into the picture.

The introductory poem in Lucilius, as in Horace, probably took the form of a dialogue. Just as Horace said that satiric poetry was the kind which best suited his personality, so well before him Lucilius had clearly given voice to the same idea, though in a more boisterous way (622). In this connection, he spoke of his inability to write an epic about Augustus, and a remarkably similar feeling is to be found in a fragment of Lucilius (621) containing a request for an epic lament over Popilius' defeat (138 B.C.) and a glorification of Scipio's deeds. So here, as in the case of the Horace passage, the speaker seems to have advised against satiric poetry and to have recommended a different, more respectable subject. Probably Lucilius here weighed epic against satire and came to the conclusion that, while epic was indeed something attractive, it did not suit his talent.

Now also in book 26 he made a number of nasty comments about tragedy. This is suggested by one fragment in particular (597–98): To stir up pity, tragedy would bring onto the stage people who were in the most horrible misery—in this case a woman *neque inimicis invidiosam neque amico exoptabilem* ("neither hateful to her enemies nor longed-for by a friend"). And there followed mocking parodies of tragic passages from Pacuvius and Accius. Thus at least the possibility exists that at this point Lucilius also contrasted his satire with tragedy. For the purpose of his satire was to perform a very real and topical function, that is to create joy and happiness for friends and pain for enemies.

If this suggestion seems logical, then Lucilius could have defended

the value of satire in opposition to other *studia* (pursuits) as well—
history and philosophy, for example—in the context of this same poem.
It should be stressed, however, that all of this is in the realm of possibility only, for Lucilius might also have spoken about these things
in a second satire of book 26 rather than just in the introductory poem.
But his point of view and his opinion are perfectly clear: he attacks
tragedy as its popular representatives wrote it and explains their work
as psychagogy with which an attempt was being made to ensnare the
unthinking masses (588–89). As far as he himself is concerned, Lucilius
insists the judgment of the people is a matter of indifference; he wants
neither the tasteless mob nor the well-educated arbiters of taste like
Manius Manilius and Persius as his readers, but friends of average
learning, like the young Junius Congus or Decimus (not Gaius) Laelius
(590–96).

If this represents a correct interpretation of these fragments, then
they too would have their counterpart in Horace,[32] who with the same
precision describes the circle of friends with whom approval lies as far
as he is concerned. And so it is clear that a satire was intended to be
primarily a poem of an exclusive nature serving the pleasure of the
narrow circle of friends. And this idea appears in the later satirists
down to Persius.

Well then, where does the value of satire lie? In a programmatic
piece in the thirtieth book (1014) Lucilius defined his poems as *facta
saeva* ("savage actions") and as *tristia dicta* ("gloomy words"). They
were meant to be of use to friends on a completely material level
through advice and admonition; they also had as their purpose to harm
mutual enemies. The fragment on the duties of a friend (611) is perhaps also apropos in this connection. In book 26 Lucilius also treated
other *studia* in the same critical way as he had tragedy. But here once
again it must remain an open question as to whether he did this
within the framework of the introductory satire. The analogy of
Horace's first epistle tends to bear this out. Fragment 624 is, in my
opinion, certainly to be related to philosophy, not to the writing of
history and so probably are fragments 625 and 626. Here Lucilius is
disassociating himself from having *tranquillitas* (peace) as a personal
goal, and in two later fragments (628, 629), if we along with Marx are
interpreting the words correctly, he turns against the ideal of the wise
man. For in his strong feeling of self-assurance he wants to be as unlike the wise man as possible (630). Moreover, philosophy seems to
him to serve no real purpose. Another fragment (631) suggests that

here Lucilius represented philosophy as idleness, while man was born for activity.

Satire, on the other hand, has a really useful purpose (632). If another fragment may be included here (633–34), then he went on to say that, as soldiers when they attack a city are intent only on seizing the enemy, so it is his intention to make bodily attacks only against his enemies in order to destroy them.

Also in book 26 Lucilius spoke about rhetoric and the writing of history. But it is no longer possible to know whether these themes stood in any connection with his program. In contrast to Horace, however, Lucilius sought to justify his poetry not by referring to his literary predecessors, but by emphasizing its quite obvious usefulness. In his time satire was still by no means a recognized literary form but was still definitely in a state of evolution.

Also, Lucilius did not, like Horace, deny the fact that it was his intention to harm others, and he did not say that the proof of the legitimacy of his poetry lay in its artistic value. Quite to the contrary, he obviously put less value on artistic purposes as opposed to the real and practical power of his satire.[33] But Lucilius and Horace are certainly in agreement on one point: it was purely personal motivation that made them decide in favor of satire, with Horace first taking an ironic, but then a completely serious approach,[34] while Lucilius never employed that irony.

Lucilius spoke rather frequently about his conception of satiric poetry in the twenty-seventh and twenty-ninth books, and especially in book 30. There we see him in the midst of battle, for "he attacked the leaders of the people and the people too tribe-by-tribe and was obviously fair to virtue alone and her friends."[35] Naturally Lucilius was fully aware of this aggressiveness; to some extent, his satires must have been out-and-out political polemics. And so he represents himself (1033) as a man who knows the *maculae* ("blemishes") and *notae* ("marks of disgrace") of others and who pursues his opponents and their burdens right into their hiding places (1034) and exposes them in public. Yet, his poetry *will* give insult and disgrace (896) while it brings people's shortcomings to light and publicly names the names of those who are being described (920–21).

It naturally follows that if he broadcasts the sins of the senatorial rank abroad (e.g., 690), he will have to defend himself against criticism. He was accused of jealousy (704–05) and meanness (821–22, 1026); he was charged with writing out of malicious pleasure and spite (1015,

1030) and with getting enjoyment from gossiping and from things that were none of his business (1016–20). On the other hand, he used satire as self-defense;[36] he emphasized the fact that his satire applied to his circle of friends only. But this is not entirely true, since Lucilius was aware of its reverberations (1013) and took pleasure in this. Besides, as he says, satire could bring honor as well as disgrace (1021 and frequently elsewhere)—honor to the honest people (1084), disgrace to the degenerates (1288; cf. 1326–38). And so he attempted to combine ethical and topical purposes, and this is the way Horace understood him.[37] Accordingly, Lucilius said, his poetry did not serve as gossip (1015), but had as its purpose to uncover the truth which so many people posing falsely as men of honor had to fear (1034; cf. 1228–34). And no one could with justification accuse him of getting malicious pleasure out of it.

In book 26 he spoke not only about his poetry, but about his personality as well. Whether he devoted a whole satire here to this subject as Horace did[38] cannot be known with any certainty, but it is entirely possible. In this case there are three fragments that would belong to such a satire (671–72, 675, 669–70). The self-confident verses which Nonius has preserved for us (671–72) must have stood at the beginning of the discussion: "To become a tax-farmer in Asia, a pen-pusher, instead of being Lucilius, this I do not want, and I would not take the whole world in exchange for this one thing." And so he wants no title, no appointment, and no giant job. He wants to be Lucilius; that is worth more to him than anything else. When he speaks of "Lucilius" here, he means not just the poet, but the whole man, and this is somewhat different from Horace's point of view. His wealth is part of this and so is his carefree life in the grand style. His culture also belongs here, for he does not want himself abused (649; cf. 1241) as an *inlitteratus* ("ignorant person") and an *idiota* ("uneducated man"). Above all, there are his freedom and independence, and his superiority which exercises a candid criticism of all injuries and makes fun of pride of rank, greed, covetousness, prodigality, and other delusions. Lucilius took delight in this free individuality of his, and his writing is just a small, though certainly essential, part of it.

In his poems Lucilius spoke of himself often and willingly, so that Horace could actually compare them with poetic daybooks.[39] And their greatest charm must have been the fact that the person of the poet was always prominent in the poem. Thus a detailed review of the personal observations of Lucilius would take us too far afield here.

Instead of this, a brief survey of the contents of the individual books may suffice.

In book 1 a meeting of the gods was described as they deliberated over the death of Lucius Cornelius Lentulus Lupus. It perhaps came from the year 123 B.C., and the content and arrangement of the satire can be easily made out. Not only did Lucilius ridicule a dead opponent of the Scipionic party with the greatest animosity, but at the same time used this poem to parody an epic council of the gods[40] and a meeting of the Roman Senate. Seneca made use of this satire in his *Apocolocyntosis*, and Martial also read it.

Book 2 was an account of a lawsuit brought by the Epicurean, Titus Albucius, against the Stoic, Quintus Mucius Scaevola, who was the son-in-law of Laelius and well known to Lucilius. The poem was written in 119 B.C. at the earliest, but probably before 117. Lucilius seems to have reserved his own judgment, as Horace did in his Satire 1.7, which is related to this one in theme.

The third book was written in the form of a letter, in which Lucilius described a trip which took him first by land to Capua and then by ship from Puteoli to Sicily. This was the first poetic diary in Latin that we know of. As Porphyrion emphasizes, Horace in his *Iter Brundisinum* (Journey to Brundisium) produced a poem that was meant to be competitive with this.[41] Even before Horace, Cinna had probably modelled his *Propempticon* (Poem of Farewell), which was addressed to Asinius Pollio, on this poem of Lucilius. The tradition was then carried on through Caesar, Valgius, and Persius right down to Ausonius and Rutilius, though certainly not in satiric form. It is possible that there were other poems besides this in book 3.

The fourth book contained several satires. Two longer fragments deal with a gladiatorial contest. Besides this, Lucilius is said to have attacked prodigality here, though none of the fragments that have been preserved point in this direction.[42]

Book 5 brings fragments of a letter of quite a personal nature which the poet addressed to a friend from his sickbed; he spoke to him, at least in part, in a very familiar way.[43] Its content may remind the reader of Catullus' poem 38 and of one or other of Horace's epistles. In other fragments of this same book, however, a thoroughly playful mood comes through in an account of a rustic meal which was at the same time probably rather pitiful. It is possible that one of the participants related a piece of history from the Ligurian war of the year 180 which Ennius had probably also described in the seventeenth book of his *Annales*. There is also discussion of things grammatical in the fragments. We might with some caution assign the book a date some-time after 118, perhaps about 116.

Book 6 contained a discussion of a slave holiday which fell on August 13. As a second theme, it is possible to recognize an attack on a miser who was portrayed very vividly. Finally, the book seems to have contained a political satire in which the shortcomings of the nobility were censured. It is entirely possible, however, that Lucilius put the coarse criticisms that we read here in the mouth of a popular leader, perhaps his enemy Gaius Memmius, in order to give him a solid rebuff at the end.

Book 7 contained erotic material, probably pictures of the dissolute life of the playboy world in Rome. But Lucilius also spoke here of his own παῖδες καλοί (pretty boys) and at least touched on the theme of Horace's Satire 1.2. In this book there is also a very personal judgment passed on the question of marriage (282–83). Another group of frag-ments involves recollections of the war in Spain.

The eighth book also had erotic material as its subject matter, and the descriptions, at least in part, are quite drastic. Later satire avoided the personal love-affair as a motif, but it was taken over by lyric and elegy in particular. A comparison with Juvenal's sixth satire can il-lustrate his objective approach and his different point of view.

In book 9, which was apparently in the form of an epistle, literary, aesthetic, grammatical, and orthographical questions as well as prob-lems of poetics were treated with precise knowledge of Hellenistic theory. The book was directed against Accius primarily.

Book 10 is also said to have contained a polemic against Accius and against new-fangled literature as well. Other fragments are part of a description of a particular battle. This book is said to have inspired Persius, who quotes it, to write his first satire.

In book 11 there was much of political-historical interest. In all likelihood it contained a series of stories and anecdotes and probably also the description of a law case in which a member of the nobility with a bad reputation had become involved. The book might have been written between 116 and 110.

From the twelfth book only a very few fragments have been pre-served, some of which show a strong personal coloring. Apparently Lucilius had much to say here about his family circumstances.

In book 13 Lucilius turned to attack the extravagance of the table, perhaps using the *cena* (banquet) form, which he chose quite often. The rest of the fragments will not fit together logically.

Book 14 brought recollections of the war in Spain, with at least part of the book appearing in a very lively dialogue form. One fragment (474-75) probably referred to sumptuary legislation.

In book 15 Lucilius expressed himself on mythology and its incredibility and also on the unreliability of dreams. Other fragments, in which Lucilius speaks of his people, horses, and the like, lead in a purely personal direction. Still others deal with the high cost of living, the behavior of a married woman toward her husband, and many other things.

The sixteenth book is said to have had the special title "Collyra," which was the name of a sweetheart of Lucilius and was taken from the content of the book.[44] Since not a single fragment that has come down to us gives any hint as to the subject matter, Cichorius conjectured that the subtitle belonged to book 21. In the extant fragments, there is mention of a question involving marriage law (519-20); a snob (522-24), a spendthrift (530), and an annoying questioner (537) are attacked; there is also a reference to Lysippus' colossal statue of Jupiter (525-26). Another fragment deals with the winds (527-29) and still others with agriculture (531-36). No logical connection between all these fragments can be made out.

Book 17 dealt with heroines. Penelope, for example, was depicted in conversation with Eurycleia, a hint as to the form of the piece. Philosophy also came up for discussion. The book perhaps falls in the year 108.

As far as book 18 is concerned, nothing certain may be said. At the same time, the remains of book 19 suggest no real continuity. The comparison with the ant (561-62) seems to point to a serious, protreptic purpose.

In the twentieth book Lucilius described a famous banquet given by the clever herald Granius.[45] The satirist is supposed to have given an account of this meal once again in book 21, this time as one of the participants. The parallel for this might be found in Horace's *Cena Nasidieni* (Banquet of Nasidienus),[46] and Juvenal carries on the tradition in Satire 5, although this is different, since it is much less personal, and the *cena* has become almost a general theme. The date of composition of books 20 and 21 probably falls somewhere around 107 B.C.

Book 22 contained a collection of epigrams in distichs with one fragment (579-80) apparently serving as the introductory piece. With the epigrams that had been collected in this book, Lucilius clearly meant to provide a literary memorial for his servants and farmhands— a fine, early evidence of Roman humanity. It is impossible to get any picture at all of books 23-25.

Book 26 was introduced by a programmatic poem which has already been discussed. Whether the fragments of this same book which contain a criticism of the tragedies of Pacuvius and Accius and an argument with philosophy, rhetoric, and historiography belong to the same satire cannot be ascertained. In another poem Lucilius probably spoke about himself, perhaps including suggestions regarding the proper way of living.

A number of fragments (678–86) may be assigned with certainty to a single satire in which Lucilius, the opponent of marriage, directed a lively and very personal attack against the marriage legislation of Quintus Metellus Macedonicus (censor 131), making use of arguments drawn from popular philosophy. And then there is a series of fragments which are part of a dialogue between the poet and a young friend, probably a budding historian, while other fragments have prodigality, ambition, and greed as their subject matter. Still others treat questions of medicine and philosophy, and finally there are two fragments (667, 668) of a purely personal nature. How all these themes are to be assigned to individual satires in book 26 is vigorously disputed.

There can be no doubt that book 27 contained a number of satires. The remains of a political piece are clearly recognizable; this contained an attack on the sins of the senatorial rank marked by topical sarcasm. Other fragments involve practical philosophy, while still others contain references to friendship, honesty and genuineness, and false values. A fourth group treats the theme of courtesans and maidservants.

The different meters show that book 28 was also made up of at least three satires and probably more. A poem containing a dialogue between an older and a younger man about questions of practical wisdom was written in trochaic tetrameters. At least two poems were in iambic senarii. One was a banquet laid in Athens with philosophers in attendance, during which a follower of Epicurus was probably refuted by an Academic. Quite a bit from the school history of the Athenian Academy was also brought into the discussion. The action of the second iambic poem took place in Rome and involved a description of the storming of a house, probably a house of prostitution, in which Lucilius himself took part. Finally, the book also contained at least one hexameter poem, though its content can on the whole no longer be made out. One fragment from this (794) probably includes ridicule of Accius, while in another (800–01) there is mention of examples of time-honored nobility. Lucilius seems also to have spoken about his slaves here.

There also seem to have been several satires in book 29. In a trochaic fragment (810) a blasé woman is speaking, and this whole piece may have been a description of the poet's liaison with the courtesan Hymnis. Other trochaic fragments refer to questions of how to live correctly and of practical philosophy. It cannot be determined with any certainty whether Lucilius adapted the *Hymnis* of Caecilius in another trochaic poem in this book as Cichorius supposes. There can be no doubt that several fragments are clearly reminiscent of comedy, and it is a fact that Lucilius did quote Caecilius on occasion.

Some of the iambic fragments belong to the high-spirited description of the storming of a house which contains reminiscences of a passage in Terence's *Eunuch* (771–816). One of the participants parodies Odysseus as he is saving himself from the hellish experience with the Cyclops (836). The verses alluding to Hannibal's being outwitted by Claudius Nero at Canusium in 207 perhaps belong to the same poem (823–27). But this was probably not the only iambic poem of book 29, for we hear a *puer delicatus* (effeminate boy) speaking in this meter, while other iambics have a philosophical content. There was perhaps only a single satire written in hexameters. This, like Horace's Satire 1.2, dealt with questions of sex, probably in the form of advice to a friend.

Book 30 contained several satires in hexameters. At the beginning there was probably a dedicatory poem to Gaius Sempronius Tuditanus (consul 129), as Cichorius has surmised with some justification. Whether the extensive group of fragments which have literary polemic as their subject matter is to be included in this poem or whether they belonged to a second satire in which Lucilius was vindicating his poetry must remain an open question. Other fragments suggest a description of war experiences in Spain, as well as a variety of amusing stories. Here, for example, a reprimand is given to an old slut; there was also a description of a banquet with quite beggarly trappings; in a strongly mimetic poem Lucilius spoke about the relation between man and wife, and so on. Besides these pieces, the book seems to have contained a purely political satire. Here, too, Lucilius recounted the fable of the lion and the fox in the tradition of Ennius and anticipating Horace.

When we glance back over this summary of the topics of Lucilian satire, it becomes perfectly clear that its subject matter is almost unlimited; it is far more varied than the themes of the later Roman satir-

ists. The depiction of personal life and the description of specific experiences and specific life situations with unparalleled frankness
played a large part, and Horace's words[47] are borne out completely by
the fragments which have been preserved. Here also belongs the portrayal of the society in which the poet moved—the portrayal of his
friends and especially the Scipionic Circle.[48] At a later time Horace
carried on this tradition when he spoke of Maecenas and mentioned his
friends. But this was subject matter that Juvenal avoided completely.

Lucilius spoke of his times with the same frankness and so sharp-
ened satire as an instrument of criticism as far as both time and society
were concerned. Compared to what Ennius had done, this was an important innovation. Lucilius pilloried universal faults and human types,
but also individual people, especially the leaders of the government.
But at the same time, he gave his opinions to the people as a whole
whenever he thought it right.[49] As he did this, it was clearly not so
much philosophical principles and beliefs that guided him—for Lucilius
never represents himself as a moralist—but rather his fierce temper-
ament. He saw how the usurer swaggered about behind the mask of
an honorable man and his anger overflowed (1228–34).

Moreover, themes of a general nature had an important place in
the satires—questions of how to lead a proper life and how to control
one's life—themes which everywhere presupposed Hellenistic popular
philosophy. Lucilius, of course, preferred to link these to a real event
and prove his point by using concrete examples from the present. He
was not philosophically inclined, and yet he was fully conversant with
Hellenistic philosophy—not only with the ethical teachings of the
various schools, but also with physics, dialectic, and the philosophy of
language. In these matters he did not adopt a dogmatic point of view,
and it is against this background that his comments on the Roman
folk religion and superstition are to be read and understood.[50]

In addition, there was the broad field of literary criticism. Lucilius
expressed himself in considerable detail on matters of rhetoric, poetics,
aesthetics, grammar, and other similar topics. His criticism shows the
greatest independence and intellectual freedom as well as a very accurate knowledge of Hellenistic theory. In this Lucilius was a forerunner of Horace's literary epistles, not only in externals, but also in
the seriousness and forcefulness with which he undertook the discussion of these things and even conscientiously pursued seemingly
unimportant questions involving semantics or even orthography. It is
possible to see here how, next to his polemical-critical purposes, the de-

termination to work effectively through instruction took on a completely separate importance.

And so Lucilian satire represented in the most varied way the poet's
tool for the expression of his personal opinions—especially his personal
criticism and, in particular, criticism of the contemporary scene. Besides
the intention to ridicule, to quarrel, to advise, and to warn, the sheer
pleasure that the satirist took in telling stories and in creating lively
narrative, whether as anecdotes or as fresh and amusing descriptions,
must have been obvious in the words he used. If the satires of Lucilius
were preserved for us, then we would have in them an absolutely priceless document of a universal vividness and colorfulness.

The form of Lucilian satire was as varied as its content and its
ever-changing aspect. A great deal was put together in dialogue form,
while other poems gave the appearance of being lectures, meditation,
instruction and warning, or letters. Many even made use of a fantastic
scenery much like that which appears again in an isolated instance in
one of Horace's satires.[51] But the main attraction of Lucilian satire
was its energy and the directness of the poet. The high praise that
such competent judges as Cicero and Varro bestowed on Lucilius—
on his genius, but also on his style—shows this to be the case. Varro,
for example, declared the poet to be a model of *gracilitas* ("plainness").
In contrast to this there is the sharp censure by Horace which is strongest in his Satire 1.4, softened certainly in Satire 1.10, and best balanced
in Satire 2.1. But even Horace, of course, gives recognition to the
ingenium ("genius") of the old satirist,[52] and he portrays Lucilius as
the real inventor of the satiric form of poetry, even though Ennius had
gone before him.

But Horace criticizes the form of Lucilian satire and the lack of
attention to literary artistry that he finds there. Indeed, he does not
deny that Lucilius brought an advance over Ennius in the formal aspects of satire,[53] which is, after all, clear to us even today. But Horace
censures his predecessor's great verbosity and prolixity, as well as his
loose versification and the poetic dissonance that it produced. He finds
fault also with Lucilius' mixing Greek words and turns of expression
into his Latin verse and also criticizes him for his hasty production and
for the uneven product that resulted from this. He even expressed his
disapproval of the satirist's alleged purpose—the rousing of uncontrolled laughter at any price. Even during his lifetime there had been
attacks on Lucilius' satiric poetry, and he had defended himself against

them. These, however, had never involved the form, but only the content, tone, and intention of the poet.

As he developed this polemic, Horace was speaking in his own defense. The basic form of the Lucilian hexameter was the verse of Ennius. Through the neoterics it had been fundamentally changed and polished so that actually as far as euphony and arrangement are concerned, Horace's verse represents a far more advanced stage of development. Moreover, the language of Horace is quite different from that of Lucilius. Lucilius' was the language of life; with complete impartiality he took the striking expression from wherever he found it, whether it was proper or not. And so in his poetry the vocabulary of educated language stood next to out-and-out jargon. Moreover, he did not hesitate to coin the striking expression himself. In Horace a rather long process of linguistic development, which had as its goal a rigorous purification of the literary language, came to its conclusion. Now the perfect form of expression is attained by the most economical and most selective means. Such a purity had to reject the swelling fullness of expression of a Lucilius. It also had to attack the mixture of Greek and Latin which Lucilius had presented as a faithful reflection of informal colloquial speech.

We are not in a position to pass judgment on Lucilius' composition which Horace censures, but general considerations suggest that the later satirist's criticism was not without foundation, as even individual passages seem to have lacked a careful and thorough shaping. This may still be seen, for example, in the most extensive fragment of Lucilius that has been preserved (1326–38).

It is quite probable that the literary satires of Lucilius stimulated and influenced the grammatical and aesthetic criticism of the succeeding generation. Quintus Valerius of Sora, a younger contemporary of Lucilius, who in a poem of polemic set himself against Accius,[54] should be mentioned in this connection. Again, the verses of Volcacius Sedigitus and Porcius Licinus are hardly imaginable without this great predecessor. Certainly in all these poems it was not, strictly speaking, a case of the poet writing satire, and the general observation should be made that between Lucilius and Horace Roman satire in verse form did not find an authoritative representative. On the other hand, there was developing, probably in the first third of the first century before Christ, a second kind of Roman satire to which we must now turn our attention.

« V »

Varro's Menippeans

THE outward characteristic of this new type was the mixing of prose and poetry—the prosimetric style, as this literary form has been called since the twelfth and thirteenth centuries. The person who introduced it into Latin literature was Marcus Terentius Varro (116–27 B.C.), the friend of Cicero and Pompey and Rome's greatest scholar and encyclopedist.[1] Varro called this collection of new pieces which he put together *Saturae Menippeae* (*Menippean Satires*), and through the title he no doubt meant to emphasize both the connection with Lucilius and the difference between their conceptions of satire. The designation *saturae* characterized these writings as works of a critical nature. Their model, however, was reported to be not Lucilius, but the Cynic writer Menippus of Gadara, a Hellenized Syrian who had been active in the third century B.C. And so Quintilian remarks with some justification that this form of satire is in reality even older than the Lucilian.[2]

The catalogue of Varro's writings in Jerome contains mention of 150 books of Menippean satires. Not a single satire has survived complete and none can be reconstructed in detail. What we have consists of about 90 titles and nearly 600 fragments. These have been preserved mainly through the old grammarians, especially Nonius, while a certain number have been added by Gellius, Macrobius, and others. Since the majority of the fragments that appear in these authors are selected from a purely linguistic point of view, there are difficulties of arrangement and reconstruction that are quite similar to those which are encountered in dealing with the fragments of Lucilius' satires. In Latin only Seneca's *Apocolocyntosis* provides a clear idea of the nature of the genre.

To begin with, Varro probably published his Menippeans one after the other as separate pamphlets, so that each of them also had its own title—some of them a Latin one, some a Greek one, and some both

53

Latin and Greek. As far as we can see, only one satire, *The Circum-navigation* (*414-19*), comprised two books; Book Two was subtitled *On Philosophy*. The superscriptions go back to Varro himself. The satirist then collected these pamphlets and provided the collective title *Saturae Menippeae*, which is explicitly attested by Aulus Gellius.[3] We also have Varro's reason for choosing this title, for Probus remarks that Varro is called *Menippeus* ("Menippean") not after his master who lived long before him but from the intellectual connection (*a societate ingenii*), because he too embellished his satires with highly varied poetry.[4] Cicero goes a step further and has Varro mention "those well-known old writings" that had imitated Menippus but were not direct translations of his work.[5] According to Cicero, Varro had included much that was amusing in these, had added a good deal from his deep-est philosophical feelings, and had made frequent use of dialect.

As Cichorius has pointed out, Cicero's statement on the date of composition allows us to determine with some precision that in all probability Varro wrote his Menippeans between 80 and 67 B.C.[6] How-ever, there are no certain chronological references that extend later than this. To be specific on this point, *The Three-Headed Monster* (*556*) which alluded to the first triumvirate, was apparently not a satire at all, but a prose writing of a different kind. And Cichorius explained other chronological references more correctly than his predecessors who wanted to put Varro's Menippeans, in part, substantially later. A more accurate chronological arrangement of the individual satires is possi-ble only in the case of especially favorable circumstances. But, gen-erally speaking, it may be said that the Menippeans appeared as a collection before the years of stress and strain in which the opposition between Pompey and Caesar developed. Accordingly, their direction is not at all markedly political, but their intention is predominantly moral, and they have an ethical reform of the ruling class as their special purpose.

With the Menippeans, then, it is not a case of their being what might be properly called youthful writings, for Varro was between thirty-five and fifty years old when he wrote them. They substantially predate his great philosophical works, and this was important. They were the product of a period of his life when Varro was busy mainly as an officer of high rank and an elected official. They were also put together without much in the way of literary resources.

What caused Varro to choose Menippus as his model was certainly the κυνικὸς τρόπος (the Cynic manner), that is, the art of making a moral purpose clear in a witty way. For a general orientation on this Cynic style we should look at the lively essay on Diogenes written by Eduard Schwartz.[7] Strictly speaking, Cynicism is not to be defined as a true philosophical movement; rather the Cynic's purpose was a practical reform—even a revolutionizing of life. He wanted to lead his fellow men to reflect on their existence as human beings, and he did this in the briefest possible way, using a humorous and drastic approach. He usually preferred to use his own example rather than employ a system of hard and fast philosophical teachings.

As he did this, he was completely undogmatic and made reference to a very few principles that were immediately and generally obvious. He did not occupy himself with speculation or systematic dialectic; quite to the contrary, his total attitude was one of hostility to culture and education. Moreover, he did not turn to a public that was interested in things intellectual, but mainly to the broad mass of the population; whoever wanted to could listen to him.

His purpose in all of this was completely practical: proper conduct and control of one's life. He began from the proposition that men should live according to nature, which is, above all, to be without any pretensions. For that man is happiest who is without wants and renounces all desires, which came into existence only subsequent to creation through the agency of man himself. And so the Cynic's ultimate purpose was to free man from all of the bonds in which he found himself entangled—from the bonds of religion, state, society, family, and above all convention, for all of this was not in harmony with nature and was mere pretense. In this way man was to be an individual again and completely independent. And, most important of all, he would be brought back to his natural freedom which even the wild beast enjoys and perhaps also the barbarian who is not yet so strongly bound by culture or, as the Cynics taught, is not corrupted as the civilized man of the Hellenistic period had been.

The dog with its modesty, its free and easy ways, and its tendency to bite was openly adopted as a model. In making this choice the Cynic was showing his preference for starting from the realities of everyday life. This was his point of departure for his criticism against time and circumstance. And his criticism, of course, was basically negative, for in that culture and tradition he saw something that was plainly destructive, something that only diverted people from true worth.

Accordingly, the subject matter was inexhaustible, and the form in which the themes appeared was always amusing, startling, and frequently fantastic. The precise wording was generally both comprehensible and fresh, showing in addition a preference for the paradoxical. The gnomic element also played an important role. But the lecturing and the form this took were always kept on an extremely personal level. The Cynic liked to refer to his own person, for he was certainly no anchorite and no preacher of repentance, but a man who sought out men in order to make human activity laughable and to present it as folly and not as sinfulness. Whoever listened to him was expected to laugh and through this laughter to come to the serious acknowledgment of the vanity of mankind.

Originally the Cynic's diatribe was meant only for the immediate audience. Diogenes, the real founder of the sect, had left no writings behind, although there were certainly many witty tales and anecdotes told about him. It was only in the following period that the diatribe was established as a literary form.

Certainly for Varro, Menippus was only the name representing the whole genre, for Menippus himself was looked upon by the ancients not as a Cynic—quite the opposite, his way of life was completely contrary to the Cynic manner of living, as the biography in Diogenes Laertius,[8] for example, shows—but rather as an especially successful literary propagandist for Cynicism. Nothing any longer remains from his thirteen books, to be sure. But a reasonable picture of his kind of writing may be gathered from several pieces of Lucian, whose independence should certainly not be underrated, and from other works such as Julian's *Caesares*.

It is hardly possible to imagine a greater contrast than that presented by Menippus and Varro. On the one hand we have a Hellenized Syrian, a one-time slave, a man without a country, a cosmopolite, and a completely free thinker who certainly succumbed to all the conventions of the civilized world, but at the same time laughed at them and ridiculed them as a man who preached complete freedom and an uninhibited individuality. On the other side is a Roman from a most distinguished family, a descendant of the consul defeated at Cannae, himself a high state official and a field-officer, a man with a broad education, who was without doubt completely familiar with the modern enlightenment but who himself held with conviction to the traditional beliefs of his class and proudly characterized himself as an old-fashioned gentleman (167). He was also quick to express his unqualified approval of the state (235), the citizen community (507), worship of the gods (265), the laws (cf. 264), the time-honored customs (303), the family unit (238), and duty toward friends—in short, the collective canon of Roman virtues and duties—and in addition took pride in scholarship, learning, and philosophy. Moreover, Varro spoke to a different audience than the Syrian did. Menippus directed his attention to the lower classes in the large city and all who flirted with them, while Varro spoke to people of his own class, to distinguished Roman citizens whom he wanted to make aware of certain shortcomings privately which could not be denied and which he could observe at close range in his circle of friends. And so he turned to men for whom the basic idea of the individual was something entirely foreign and in whom, moreover, he could assume the existence of values and beliefs identical with those which he himself defended. In this atmosphere Varro strove for reform, but a revolutionizing purpose was certainly far from his thoughts.

With these different views of life and with these different purposes, personalities, and audiences, Varronian satire had to become something quite different from the Menippean diatribe, and our emphasis here will have to be on the differences which were caused by the transplantation of the form to the Roman atmosphere as well as on the additions that Varro made to his Cynic prototype.

It was not through the title *Saturae Menippeae* alone that Varro himself went about making a point of his connection with Menippus and the Cynic sect. He did this also through a profusion of individual satire titles—*The Cynic (82)*, *The Horse-Dog (220–21)*, *The Dog-Teachings (230)*, *The Dog Judge? (231)*, *The Dog Pleader (231–32)*, *The Burial of Menippus (516–39)*, *The Water [Drinking] Dog (575)*. In addition there are many clear allusions in the satires themselves.[9] There are also many reminiscences that may be pointed out in matters of form, theme, and content as well as in general purpose and specific beliefs.

Like Menippus, Varro wanted to put forward the serious as a joke in his satires in order to move his listeners to consideration of the real value of life.[10] The purpose, then, was at the same time to amuse and to provide something of use for life (cf. 340). Like the Cynics, Varro behaved as an observer and supervisor of men as he carried out his purposes; a comment in *The Endymions* brings this home (105). Only it will become clear that Varro was not striving at all for the reform of mankind, but for the reform of Roman society. The conviction that much rot existed on the contemporary scene was common to the two of them, as is obvious with this conception of the problem. Both

therefore wanted to stimulate criticism of their times, Menippus in a
rather biting way and Varro more good-naturedly. Varro believed that
in each field of corn there were also weeds and in each bad crop there
was also something good (241).

But common to the two of them is the call for simplicity. The
Cynic justified this with the appeal to nature and the natural equality
of men. In Varro, too, the idea of nature played an important role; he
too saw in men perfected through nature the model worth emulating
(208). Like the Cynic, he also spoke of the natural equality of all men.
Whether king or working-man (205), all had drunk mother's milk
(261), all had human features (289), and all had the predisposition toward *virtus* (71: "virtue") which a man came by only with a certain
amount of real effort and trouble.[11] The realization of this natural talent
and disposition was the only thing that led to contentment and happiness
(22, 316). Varro, however, did not feel, as the Cynic did, that the root
of all the trouble lay in the simple possession of property, but in the
consequences of this—in greed and prodigality especially and in the
instability that accompany these (78). The evidence for this struggle
is manifold: avarice appears as drunkenness (30), as confusion of the
senses, as illness and madness (126). In the same way he criticized
prodigality which cannot be checked by laws (252), gourmandizing
(137), and the other sicknesses that accompany civilization and close
men's eyes to the true values. Just as what is yellow and what is not
yellow appear alike as yellow to the jaundiced man, so healthy men
and raving men both seem mad to the madman (148). Varro may certainly have found similar thoughts in the Cynic writings, and these
must have contained many of the positive precepts that Varro liked to
insert in his satires: a person should drink sweet water which does him
good and eat onions which make his eyes water (250); for the hungry
man an agreeable dish is as valuable as the fish market of Naples (160);
and with special reminiscence of Cynic teaching there is, for example,
fragment 316.[12]

In Varro's Menippeans the personal point of view that is continually stressed was a Cynic characteristic.[13] So was the process of argument which used the evidence without any deductive detour,[14] the
humorous tone and the pleasure taken in attack,[15] the bright-colored
scenery that was so frequently fantastic, and so on. But the characteristic that in the eyes of the ancients provided the most obvious link
between Varro's satire and the diatribe of Menippus, at least as far as
externals were concerned, was the prosimetric form. To what source

Menippus' use of this is to be traced, whether to popular Greek forms, as they are reflected perhaps in the piece which has the contest between Homer and Hesiod as its subject, or, as is more likely, to semitic models, and whether the Menippeans were related directly to these or via certain intermediate stages, or again whether there exist connections with the mime—all of this is still disputed. It is also uncertain what proportion of the satires the poetic parts in Menippus filled, what forms they took, and how important they were. Probably the base was prose and the poetry was embellishment.

Varro seems to have looked at it in basically the same way, and yet the distribution and form of the poetic parts suggest that Varro showed considerable independence. For the poetic interludes—which, it should be pointed out, were not just inserted in passages that were elevated or full of parody, but frequently served as narrative descriptions pure and simple—are evidence of an extreme richness of form and of a confident control of meters of the most varied, difficult, and modern kind for which the Latin language had still not developed any style of its own. And so Varro did not use the naturalized recitative meters alone—that is, the dactylic hexameter, the distich, and iambic senarius, as well as the trochaic septenarius and other old Latin long verses including the sotadean—but he also put to use in a very masterly way the meters which had been newly introduced and which, strictly speaking, became palpable only in the neoteric poets: the limping iambus, the hendecasyllable, the glyconic, and the ionic. Varro went well beyond his original in his partiality for polymetry, for in all likelihood Menippus had employed only the hexameter and certainly the iambic trimeter. Wilamowitz has suggested quite plausibly that the profusion of verse forms and Varro's complete mastery of them go back to his study of textbooks on metrics.[16] It is likely that the different characters of the individual metrical forms were discussed there (cf. 57).

But Varro's independence of Menippus extends to his basic scheme of viewing the world around him. The Cynic with his call to modesty and his rejection of anything cultural was appealing to the principle that man should live according to nature. By contrast, Varro presented the Romans' ancestors as the concrete example of a proper and ideal life in conformity with nature. So in Varro the idea of the *maiores* (ancestors) directly replaces the Hellenistic concept of φύσις (nature). And indeed not only does the satirist appeal to past times where examples are always ready and waiting,[17] but he also refers to the conditions which he experienced himself as a youth. He does this both in the *Logistorici* (*Discussions from History*)[18] and in other writings —for example, the *Ulysses and a Half* (460–84).

Now, while the Cynic radically rejected every convention and every custom with his call to nature, since all of this of course was the late and transitory creation of man, Varro subjected to his criticism only that which in his time deviated from the ideal *mos maiorum* (ancestral custom). Someone might call this a romantic bias on Varro's part, but this adaptation of a Greek ideal to the world of Roman thoughts and ideas leads to far-reaching consequences. From this position Varro formulated his criticism of the times, revealing a preference for the antithetical, as he balanced the past against the present and then passed judgment.[19] And as a result his satire acquired a second positive, advisory function. *The Sexagenarian*, for example, was based completely on the opposition between past and present (485–505). There the narrator was a man who had fallen asleep when he was ten years old and had slept for fifty years. Now he had returned to Rome, and in the meantime everything had changed (491). It is quite important here that not just anyone at all is doing the narrating, but a Roman and that he did not measure the conditions that he came upon by some abstract ideal, but by the world of the Romans' forebears. Moreover, the narrator is sincerely interested in the corruption as a Roman patriot, not simply as a moralist.[20] What he misses are three cardinal virtues of old Rome (495) which have no real equivalent on the Greek side: *pietas* (duty), *fides* (trustworthiness), and *pudicitia* (modesty).

It is clear that Varro then arranged his description of the decay of basic morals by using a tight arrangement—in family life (496), in the life of the state (497), in the realm of law (498, 499), in private life (501, 502). That Varro then adds a special seasoning to this appeal with his self-irony is a nice touch. He appeared personally in this satire and had someone say to him "It isn't right of you, Marcus, to accuse us while you ruminate your old rubbish again" (505).

As in this case, criticism of the times taking the form of an antithesis between old Rome and contemporary Rome was a leitmotiv of many of Varro's Menippeans. We need only look for antithetical combinations like *tunc . . . nunc* (then . . . now). In *The Double Marcus* there is the following observation: "Our grandfathers and great-grandfathers, though their words reeked of garlic and onions, were nevertheless noble chaps" (63). Here he turned against the luxury of banquets and against effeminacy, as well as the corruption of provincial administration (64), avarice, and the dangers of shifts in society resulting from the growing prosperity of the slave population (66). Varro did not see in the slave a human being above all else, as perhaps the Cynic did. But that a freeborn man should run after a slave who has become wealthy was in his eyes a scandal that would not have happened among his ancestors.

The Old Man Teacher was also based on the contrast between past and present. In earlier times, Varro says here, religion was sacred and decorum ruled in all things (181). And once again this antithesis was illustrated from quite different perspectives. One fragment (186) turns against excessive refinement and another (187) against the gay life of the younger generation who gained their experience with women so early. A little later (190) the ideal Roman matron is presented, and the beautiful ladies of contemporary Rome with their idle ways, love of finery, their flirtations, and their feeble resistance to their suitors are obviously contrasted with her (192). There is also an indignant comment about a slave rebellion (193), which is probably an allusion to the revolt led by Spartacus in the years 73-71 B.C. Moreover, there is criticism of gluttony, a favorite theme of Varro who knew his Romans well, especially as it is seen in the import of luxuries from abroad (183). Varro also speaks against luxury in domestic furnishings (197), and opposes the corruptibility and indifference of the state officials (196).

The *maiores* appear again in *The Burial of Menippus*, a satire which contained a eulogy of Menippus on the occasion of his funeral feast. Here the old, practical, modest habits are contrasted with the ostentation of modern homes (524). The *Ulysses and a Half* was conceived of in an especially personal way. Here Varro contrasted his own youth with the depravity of contemporary times. This much-discussed piece was written about the year 71. Similar opposition between the past and the contemporary scene can be shown for the *Agathon* (6-14), the *Manius* (247-68), and other satires.

The variety involved in this juxtaposition must have been very great. The Roman element has come through in Varro even where at first it might not have been thought possible. In the *Prometheus* (423-36), for example, Varro introduced a dialogue between Prometheus and Hercules in the Scythian wilderness. Here it was shown how practical man had been made, and then the line of thought probably ran to the satiric description of what men had accomplished with their talent that was so practical—they carouse, they need beds encrusted with ivory, they are wildly effeminate, and so on. The impression left by this is that the discussion involved the general deterioration of mankind. But even here there is a doubling back to Rome and reality, for in one fragment (435) there is the observation that people live in shadows and in a pigsty; the Forum is like a pigsty and most people there are like pigs (cf. 70). The Forum, then! And even in this satire, with mention of the Forum we would be in Rome once again.

Rome or the Republic was mentioned in other satires as well (53, 82, 456), and reference is made to Roman or Italian places (330, 421, 511). Italian landscapes figure as examples (17) and native customs are touched on—the tradition of the wedding poem (10), the songs of the vintners and seamstresses (363). Latin poets are cited by name and also anonymously, and reference is made to the language of the old Romans (320) or to their laws. Then again personalities well-known in the city are mentioned—the actor Amphion (367), for example, or the robber chief Agamemno (570). In short, Varro was very careful to emphasize in every way possible the fact that he did not want to promote criticism of culture in general but criticism of a particular time—life and society in contemporary Rome.

He must have gone into particulars with gusto as he levelled his attacks. The luxury of the banquet, drunkenness, gluttony, the preference for imported gourmet items were the things in particular to which he returned again and again—in *The Double Marcus* (52-55), in the satire *On Foods* (403-4), in *The Measure*, which was an appeal to moderation,[21] and in which once again past and present were contrasted, in *The Perfume on the Dish of Lentils* (549-51), and elsewhere. Ostentation was also a favorite theme, whether it was in the furnishings of private houses,[22] in clothing (313), in utensils (7, 197, 212?), in sacrifices, or in burial of the dead.[23]

What Varro was censuring in these things was above all moral damage, effeteness (369), and vanity. He was also against the damage to a person's health (especially *The Festival of Minerva*) and general well-being (513). And last but not least, he laughed at the importance which men put on externals while disregarding the important things. Varro describes such impulses as mere foolishness (198) and childishness (279, 283) and as making up a life of fancy and illusion.[24]

What is missing is insight and judgment. He who has no understanding of this, Varro says (382), mistakes an ordinary oyster for
one containing a pearl and takes glass as being emeralds. But insight
into true worth can be gained only through effort. "If of all the effort
that you have put into seeing that your baker bakes good bread you
had devoted only one-twelfth to philosophy, you would long ago have
been a morally good person. But this is the way it stands now: whoever knows that baker is willing to buy him for 100,000, but as far as
you are concerned, no one, if he knows you, is willing to buy you for
even 100." [25] For, according to what Varro teaches, only the real values
guarantee inner freedom and harmony. In this context the satirist could
be called a moralist. And he becomes one again where he ridicules the
vanity of the fashions and fashionable amusements of his time, especially in the satire which he seems to have called *Baiae?* (*44*) after
the fashionable spa. He turned to attack the modish elegance of the
young men just as he did the overly elaborate hunting costume of the
young women. He had no use for the extravagant tastes that prevailed
among those who owned slaves or horses, and in an original satire
titled *Meleager* he lashed out with great wit and forcefulness against
the sport of hunting which the younger Scipio, following the example
of the Macedonians, had introduced to the Romans.[26]

As he criticized luxury and extravagance, so Varro also had much
to say about avarice, the other principal evil of the time, using a variety
of approaches. To be sure, he was not at all a political person and in
his Menippeans he avoided attacks on political personalities of the time.
But in a whole satire with the perplexing title *Flaxtabula* (*175–80*) he
dealt in detail with the abuses of the Roman provincial administration.
He must at least have touched upon the same theme elsewhere—in
The Double Marcus (*64–65*), *The Old Man Teacher* (*196*), and the
Poppa's Papia (*378*), for example. A fragment of the last mentioned
satire (*377*) suggests a reference to the corruption of the courts, and
another fragment, where he mentions a very special, sly, speculative
maneuver, shows how clearly he saw through the intrigues of the
businessmen (*37*).

But his criticism of the times is by no means limited to the themes
that have been mentioned. For example, Varro acknowledges the old
religious ties for his own person throughout the satires. Fragment 265
reads like this: "The respectable citizen should obey the laws, honor
the gods, and put only a small piece of meat in his frying-pan." [27] Varro
is of course too enlightened to feel any fear at bad omens or to tremble

before the angry look of a haruspex (558). Similarly mythology for him
is just a poetic game;[28] at best it can be taken as allegory (470). But
what he rejected out of hand was superstition and the obtrusive activity of foreign cults that were spreading in Rome. And so the pom-
pous display of the orgiastic religious celebrations with their provocative
music disgusted him, and he expressed his disgust clearly in *The Furies*
(117–65). Another satire seems to have had the title *Sarapis*;[29] in *Apollo
the Liar* (438–39) he also spoke of foreign rites. In all of this he probably saw not just a sickness of current fashion but probably also a moral
danger. At the same time it is also possible to assume that the basic
mistrust of the foreigner that the Roman was inclined to feel right
from the beginning was being expressed here.

Varro attacked philosophy and education just as infrequently as he
condemned or laughed at real religious feeling. He considered his
Menippeans as in reality being popular philosophical writings;[30] he
called truth a foster-daughter of Attic philosophy (141) and was constantly stressing, both explicitly and implicitly, the extremely high
value of training and education.[31] Moreover, as far as content was
concerned, Varro owed an immense amount to Hellenistic philosophy
and he was clearly aware of this. Over large stretches of his work he
was especially dependent on Hellenistic ethics, not only for thematic
material, but also for his point of view. He was himself a moralist and
could rely on the interest of his contemporaries when he turned to discuss questions which bore directly on the conduct of life. His observations on individual vices like envy, ambition, conceit, snobbery, on
quite general topics such as the nature of man, the rule of reason, the
attainment of moral perfection, conduct, eternity, and also on casuistic
questions such as marriage and bringing up children, self-education,
suicide, and many more—all of these are conceivable only on the as-
sumption that Hellenistic philosophy played its part.

And Varro was proud of this philosophical education of his. The
same goes for the part of his training which can generally be called
rhetorical. In *The Lyre-Listening Ass* especially he spoke in detail
about literature, taste, aesthetics, and music, while in the *Parmeno*,
related subjects were dealt with right down to the fine points (385–99).

On the other hand, Varro did attack the disreputable representatives
of philosophy, the fashionable philosophers with their pretentious public appearances and their greed (419); he attacked sophistries and
educated snobbery. More than once he chose the milieu of the philosophic debate in order to show that there the argument was often about

trifles. This he did in the *War of Words* (242-43) and in the satire with a title full of parody—*Trial of Arms* (42-43). Again, in *Shadow-Boxing*, he severely criticized the arrogance of the false philosophers (506-10). Frequently he also spoke about the different dogmas, as in *The Funeral of Menippus* (516-39), *On Sects* (400-402), *Ulysses and a Half* (esp. 483-84), *Asses Praise Asses* (322-25), *Prometheus*, and elsewhere as well. The freedom and candor of judgment in these cases are quite striking. And so in his Menippeans with their purely practical purpose Varro shows little respect for dialectic in which he himself was so thoroughly trained. Much that it contained was represented here as mere hair-splitting. In this context even the paradoxes were rejected, generally perhaps in fragment 122 or specifically, as in the paradoxical picture of the Stoic wise man (245).

Physics was valued as a remedy against superstition (231), and so were the theorems of human nature and its practicality or the doctrine of nature as the universal teacher (242, 526). But where Hellenistic physics rose to metaphysical speculation, it did not escape the Roman's ridicule. The reference to the Stoic idea of the gods (583), for example, deserves a reading!

Next to this colorful content, a special charm of Varro's Menippeans clearly lay in their form and composition. It is possible to imagine a great variety of scenery full of fantasy.

What Varro wanted to say was often held together by a story within a story, frequently a common one. The reader may find himself, for example, at a banquet, where each participant expresses himself quite freely. In the *Serranus* (450-59) everyone was obviously waiting for the election results and in the meantime things came up for discussion that had nothing at all to do with the election. This reminds us of Varro's dialogue on agriculture.

In *The Funeral of Menippus* the occasion for the discussion is the funeral banquet, while in *The Furies* it is a procession of Attis fanatics. In another fragment (144) the discussion involves a rhetorical demonstration which reminds us of the situation at the beginning of Petronius as we have him; in the *Manius* (255-56) the people have dug up a box full of books and bring them to Varro. Another fragment (276) comes from an account of a trip, a second (520) refers to a walk, while yet another (346) sounds exactly like a phrase from a letter. This everyday scenery was certainly very bright, diverse, and entertaining.

The account was frequently presented in the first person. There can be no doubt that the dialogue element had a large part to play, and, besides the diatribe, the dialogues of Heraclides, who was even quoted by Varro (81, 445), might be considered as having an influence here.

Now and then Varro employed a mythical or mythological scenery. This can be seen best in his *Prometheus*,[32] but it is found in other satires as well. Finally, there was much in the form of sheer fantasy. In *The Slave of Marcus* (269–87) someone made a flight through the air, as in the *Icaromenippus*, while in *The Sexagenarian* a man returned to Rome after sleeping for fifty years. There are other examples as well.

And in Varro the greatest array of characters appears. On one occasion exactly 300 Jupiters without heads appeared (582); the deity Tutanus spoke (213); heroes made their appearance—Hercules in conversation with Prometheus, for example—as did abstractions like *Infamia* (123: Disrepute), *Veritas* (141: Truth), *Existimatio* (147: Honor), *Metamelos* (239: Repentance), and creatures of fantasy, too (291). There were also people of earlier and contemporary times—even people whom Varro knew personally—such as Titus Albucius (127), Romans and non-Romans (378), freemen, freedmen, and even slaves (513, 514). And Varro himself frequently appeared.[33]

In view of the pleasure Varro took in bright scenery, a multitude of actors, and dialogue, connections with the drama are not surprising. The satirist himself draws attention to drama, whether through a title (e.g., *Trial of Arms*), quotations,[34] parodies,[35] speech of the theater,[36] or even an explicit remark (e.g., 304). It is perfectly clear, then, that there are strong influences from dramatic literature and practice. And yet it seems wrong to connect Varro's Menippeans with the drama, as Hirzel wanted to do.[37]

Such a variety of material and form is matched by the many various modes of expression that the satirist uses. Varro reveals himself in his Menippeans to be a master of widely different styles. The prose parts for the most part reproduce the colloquial idiom of the educated just as it appeared before its impoverishment through the classicistic movement. The sentence structure is generally simple and somewhat periodic, while the word order is free and natural and the choice of words is striking. Very frequently Greek words and phrases are sprinkled in, as was common in the spoken language. A lively freshness, vividness, humor, and unerring aim are the hallmarks of this old Latin prose. One feature of the liveliness, for example, is Varro's ever-ready ability to create new words. In one fragment (353) the *cinaedici* ("erotics") and the *scaenatici* ("theatrics") appear along with the *comici* ("comics"). Elsewhere a *longurio* ("beanpole") blocks the view (562), Varro calls himself a *libellio* (256: "a notary"), or he speaks of a *senex derisissimus* (51: "a most mockable old man"). And word monsters are found not only in the titles and in the poetry (e.g., 97), but also in the prose sections (291). Part of this power to coin words consists of a readiness to put a Greek expression into Latin.[38] The satirist's delight in words reveals itself further in the frequent wordplays[39] which are augmented by Varro's well-known predilection for etymology.[40] In his hands these sometimes degenerate even to puns.

The effect of this language drawn from real life was unusually vivid, especially in the profusion of its metaphors,[41] and Varro did not reject the lively expression even when it was coarse (267, 332), free and easy (104, 262), or even decidedly indecent (282, 331?). The numerous comparisons from everyday life also contributed to this vividness.[42] In addition to these there are the interesting comparisons with animals which had their prototype in the diatribe.[43] Comparison can also serve as drastic, apodeictic criticism, as in the fragment where Empedocles teaches that men are born out of the earth, like weeds (163). This can also serve as terse and pithy characterization (e.g., 207).

Vividness through brevity seems especially characteristic of the style. Fragment 292 might be noted in this connection, or the description of the Roman matron in 190 (*ne aduratur!* = "to see that [the pot of mush] doesn't burn!"). The many proverbs, which Varro likes to use also as titles, are also part of the popular coloring of the speech in the satires, as are alliterative phrases like *purus putus* (91: "clean and clear"), *viget veget* (268: "he's lively and enlivening"), and last but not least a sentence tempo that often runs along in an allegro.[44] But in all of this popular coloring of language Varro avoided using grammatical mistakes, as they were ridiculed in the Atellans, for example.

Whenever he used an elevated style, then Varro displayed all the magnificence of the old Latin literary prose. To a large extent this was based stylistically on the old legal language (e.g., 543), and the polish can be attributed to the agency of Asianism, as Norden has correctly emphasized.[45]

The style of the poetic sections is of at least the same scope, for Varro reveals an exceptionally confident feel for the moods that the individual meters could produce and for the ethos of the actual situations which his verse is serving. In his Menippeans it is possible to find spoken verses which can be barely distinguished from colloquial speech.

Then again there are passages of emphatic pathos, real or burlesque, as well as broad, easy-going characterizations,[46] artistic descriptions (370–72), iambic septenarii in an almost vulgar tone, ionics full of gaiety (87), passages like the praise of wine (111), and many others.

Finally, as far as the construction of Varro's Menippeans is concerned, we can only resort to conjecture, for we have information about the arrangement of only one satire, *You Don't Know What Late Evening May Bring* (333–41). This is preserved by Aulus Gellius.[47] As might naturally be surmised in the case of a person as methodical as Varro, the satire was precisely structured throughout. The satirist was here dealing with the banquet and in particular with the proper number of guests and the planning and execution of the meal itself. At the outset, he also made use of the twofold division according to persons and things which had been reformulated again and again since the time of Aristotle. This was recognized by Norden as the backbone of the so-called eisagogic schema,[48] and its great importance for the arrangement of ancient introductory treatises over a very broad spectrum can be clearly demonstrated.

The banquet itself was treated from four points of view: *homines* (people), *locus* (place), *tempus* (time), *res* (things), categories which appear also in Varro's treatise, *De lingua Latina* (*On The Latin Language*).

Varro seems to have followed a similarly sharp, almost pedantically precise arrangement in other of his satires as well. We have a fragment from the satire *The Will* (541) which reads: "I now come to another form of will which is called a 'natural' one." Different kinds of wills must have been mentioned, then, and we are reminded almost instinctively of the division of theology also advocated by Varro[49] in which he separates out the *genus mythicum* (the mythical kind), *physicum* (the natural kind), and *civile* (the civil kind). With the phrase *venio nunc* ("I now come") Varro points in an almost pedantic way to the fact that he is going on to a new item. The same transitional phrase appears again in the satire *The Maenian Law* where Varro deals with questions of marriage (239): "I now come to the widow who gets married again" (*ad biviram venio*). Clearly the discussion before this involved the *univira* (woman who has had one husband), and before that the *virgo* (unmarried woman), and so on. Here too, then, a strict, systematic arrangement is suggested.

Finally, mention should be made of several, certainly less clear indications which point in the same direction. A systematic arrangement seems likely for the satire *On Foods*.[50] In the first book of *The Circumnavigation* (414-16) the organization had perhaps already been presented through the subject matter. It is significant in this case that Varro seems to have put particular emphasis on the tabular nature of the piece through his style.[51] It is possible to find a stress on arrangement from other turns of phrase as well.[52] This strong desire for order was probably to be found right down through the individual parts of the satires and can be recognized in sharp divisions within some of the fragments.[53]

« VI »

Satire at
the End of the Republic

QUINTILIAN does not mention any successor to Varro in the field of Menippean satire. But when Roman satire is taken as a whole it is very important that a second form had been developed by Varro with extreme brilliance. Just as the essence of Lucilian satire was to be found in its purpose of offering criticism of the times filled with polemic and political point, so the hallmark of the Menippeans as Varro wrote them was criticism of the times with a moral-philosophical basis. The influence of this Menippean perspective on Horace's satires can be clearly traced, especially in the second book of the *Sermones*. On the other hand, a full development of the Menippean form assimilating the reckless spirit of attack of Lucilius, and the subsequent use of the type as a political pamphlet, were both natural and obvious. Even to-day in Seneca's *Apocolocyntosis* we have an example of this kind of thing close at hand, and here the writer has carefully emphasized his dependence on both Lucilius and Varro. And so connections between the two forms do exist, and it is possible to show that in all likelihood such connections were already present in the period of the decline of the Republic.

Horace names only Varro of Atax "and a few others" as his predecessors in the field of poetic satire after the time of Lucilius,[1] and he obviously did not attach any real importance to them. Varro was from Atax in Narbonese Gaul and lived between 82 and 37 B.C. His principal claim to fame lay in the area of epic poetry, but he also had experience in elegy and epigram. He is to be noted as a man who reflected the modern tendencies of his time, as a Roman Hellenist who had studied his Greek models thoroughly and who was skilled in matters of versification.

Varro of Atax seems not to have been a really original poetic personality in this. Nothing has survived from his satires. It has not yet even been ascertained whether he followed Lucilius or Ennius more closely in them. General considerations seem to suggest that he carried out certain refinements in form.

It is just as difficult to get a picture of the poetic satires of Varro of Reate. The ancients had four books of these, and they were quite separate from his collection of Menippeans.

Mention might be made of Sevius Nicanor who comes from a somewhat earlier time and who is mentioned by Suetonius.[2] He seems to have written in the time of Sulla, and Suetonius says that among other things he also wrote a *satura* in which he remarked that he was a freedman and had two cognomina. Then Suetonius adds two hexameters written by him which are put together according to the old, preneoteric versification. He was following the example of Lucilius, then, in speaking about himself and the details of his life and even mentioning his name. Varro presents us with yet another follower of Lucilius in Lucius Abuccius[3] who was a very learned man *cuius Luciliano charactere sunt libelli* ("whose little books are Lucilian in character"). It is impossible to say with any precision when these satires were written.

The contemporaries of Lucilius had already realized that aggressiveness—the pleasure in personal attack—was the most obvious characteristic of his satire. And so it soon developed that each and every poem of conflict and dispute containing a personal edge could be called a *satura*. Toward the end, in the chaotic decades which preceded the fall of the Roman Republic, it was possible to characterize invective quite simply and plainly as *satura*, whether it was written in verse or in prose form. Pompeius Lenaeus, the freedman of Pompey the Great and the executor of Lucilius' estate, wrote such a satire against Sallust[4] in which he deluged his enemy with the most atrocious insults. The tone of attacks like these may very well be seen in the late rhetorical invectives which were forged in the names of Sallust and Cicero.

The satire which Trebonius wrote in 43 B.C. against Antony[5] was probably no more polite than Lenaeus' pamphlet. This was a poetic invective, the tone of which was determined by Trebonius' *iracundia* (anger) and Antony's *turpitudo* (immorality). It is significant that Trebonius justified his frankness by referring to Lucilius, and so the pamphlet must have been conceived in his manner.

There can be no doubt that at this time, during these years of continuing revolution, there was much more of this kind of thing than what we learn of by chance. But all of these satires clearly served the purposes of the immediate struggle only, and it is hardly possible that any poetic value was attributed to them. And so for us they have been lost. It was Horace who called Roman satire back from this line of development.

« VII »

Horace's Satires and Epistles

IN his works Horace has left behind a comprehensive picture of his life, including both his activities and especially his thoughts, such as is found in no other Latin poet. By way of biographical material, there are several other accounts from antiquity, especially the fragment of the first-rate Suetonius vita. This was prefaced to the manuscripts of Horace's works at a fairly early time and was also probably known to Porphyrion.

Quintus Horatius Flaccus was born on December 8, 65 B.C. at Venusia—in Apulia, then, not far from the Lucanian border. He died on November 27, 8 B.C. in his fifty-seventh year, probably in Rome. He was the son of a freedman, so that the poet's origin cannot be determined. He himself felt that he was a descendant of the Sabine border population of his birthplace in southern Italy. Horace's father seems to have come into prosperous circumstances in the country towns as a *coactor auctionarius* (auctioneer's clerk). He then moved to the capital and there provided for the training and the very thorough education of his son. From here Horace went to Athens to study at a time when Cicero's son, Marcus, as well as Bibulus, Messalla, and other young Romans of the upper classes were studying there. At that time this was by no means the usual thing to do, and for a man of Horace's rank it was something quite unique. This may have been about the year 45. Horace mentions philosophical studies with moral and dialectical emphases as belonging to this period, and he recalls them with pleasure (*Epist.* 2.2.43-45).

Caesar was murdered shortly after this, and in the fall of 44 B.C. Brutus came to Athens and rallied the young men with his call to freedom. He must have been immediately drawn to Horace, for in the war against Antony and Octavian Horace was a tribune of a legion, although he was at the time only twenty-one or twenty-two years old,

73

of low station, and not at all interested in things military. And so a very strong personal respect lay behind the appointment.

In the period that followed Horace was probably with Brutus in Asia Minor, among other places. How he stood the test of the war is uncertain. After the defeat at Philippi in 42, he returned to Italy, probably at the beginning of 41, and we find him in Rome after the amnesty which followed the peace settlement of Brundisium in the next year. The property of his father had in the meantime been confiscated and so Horace bought a clerical position in Rome with what money was left and became a *scriba quaestorius* (treasury clerk).

His first attempts at Latin poetry appeared at this time after earlier efforts in Greek (*Sat.* 1.10.31). The personal acknowledgment that *paupertas impulit audax / ut versus facerem* (*Epist.* 2.2.51–52: "straitened circumstances forced me to be bold and write verse") should certainly not be taken literally. The observation is not without irony and even has its parallels in Greek literature. But it is a fact that his occupation as scribe and secretary did not satisfy Horace. In any event, he at that time frequented the gatherings of poets in Rome, and his earliest writings were meant for this small circle. It is noteworthy that Horace did not follow the Alexandrian models as contemporary fashion dictated, but took the old classical writers as his standard. From the beginning, then, his literary line was well established.

Early in the year 38 B.C., two men from these literary circles with whom he remained close friends throughout his life, Vergil and Varius, who was already well known by this time, introduced Horace to Maecenas, and nine months later, probably toward the end of 38 or at the beginning of 37, the latter accepted him into his innermost circle. Horace describes this vividly in one of his satires (1.6).

In his earliest poems, Horace occupied himself with two poetic forms at the same time—the so-called epodes and the satires. With his iambics, which were later designated epodes by the grammarians, Horace meant to compete with Archilochus (*Epist.* 1.19.23–25). But while he adopted the verse form and the fire of his Greek predecessor and imitated him in many a verbal form and embellishment as well, he took his subject matter from contemporary Rome. In the poems of Archilochus, which since Hellenistic times had been collected under the title *Iambics,* the ancients saw the epitome of biting invective directed against specific contemporaries with names named. Horace also followed this rule, though not in all of his epodes.

Horace's iambics were also meant to serve the particular purpose of personal attack, and, as the law of the genre required, the tone was often violent and even purposefully coarse. The fact that Horace busied himself with iambic and satiric poetry at the same time was probably what caused his satire to become something quite different from that of Lucilius right from the first. Horace took over several elements from the old satire in his epodes and gradually excluded these from his satires more and more—personal attack on individual men of high rank and especially themes that were topical-political.

The seventeen epodes which have been preserved probably represent a selection which Horace himself made for the purpose of an edition. It may be taken as certain that the collection appeared shortly after the Battle of Actium, probably in the year 30 B.C. Individual pieces, however, were written substantially earlier, and as a matter of fact the iambics may be divided into two periods of production. Epodes 16, 4, and 7 appeared before Horace's entry into the circle of Maecenas— between 40 and 38 B.C., then. The second period of Horace's epode writing falls a good seven years later, about 31/30 B.C. There was an interval between as the fourteenth epode shows, and it was essentially in this period that Horace's satires were written.

Horace published two books of satires, both after joining Maecenas' circle. Between the appearance of the first and second books there had been some public criticism of these poems, as may be gathered from the first satire of the second book. Some people had found fault with Horace's aggressive attitude, while others criticized the professed feebleness of his satires. The second book, then, appeared after the first book, for it contains a quotation from the first book,[1] and in style, composition, and content it is quite different.

The ten satires of the first book probably represent a selection made by Horace himself for purposes of publication. Originally the idea of a collection and publication seems to have been far from the poet's thoughts.[2] Quite to the contrary, the poems were meant primarily for the poet's circle of friends and were separate efforts (*Sat.* 1.5.104). But as such they also made their way into the public eye. This follows especially clearly from the fourth satire of book 1. Then Horace decided on publication. Following the example of Vergil's *Eclogues*, he put ten poems together in a collection. Also like the *Eclogues*, these ten poems divided into two halves, in the same way as the epodes and the second book of the satires did later, with Satire 1.6 representing a new beginning, so to speak. The introductory poem contains the dedication to Maecenas, while the tenth satire forms the epilogue with the last verse serving as a subscript which Propertius imitated later (3.23.23). The hypothesis of a double edition of the first book of the satires, whether it was done by Horace himself or whether it came from his estate, is insufficiently attested and is to be rejected.

Maecenas is mentioned in seven satires of book 1 (1, 3, 5, 6, 8, 9, 10), all of which appeared in the year 38 or later. Of the three satires that remain (2, 4, 7) the earliest is probably Satire 2, since of all Horace's satires it stands closest to the style of Lucilius. It reflects the Lucilian character especially strongly and it is also tied to a real event, as satire commonly was with Lucilius. The language has already been much refined and obscenity, though it is intended, is certainly not promoted as it is in several epodes. At the same time, Horace names a disproportionately large number of Roman men and women, some of them from the upper stratum of society, for at that time, as was still the case when he wrote the fourth satire of book 1, Horace considered personal attack as the essential characteristic of Lucilian satire. Certainly the supposition that the mention of Maltinus was aimed at Maecenas (*Sat.* 1.2.25) is not acceptable. As far as subject matter goes, Satire 1.2 is probably modelled on the twenty-ninth book of Lucilius, and so it comes from about the same time as the sixteenth epode—that is, from 40 or 39 B.C.

Satire 1.7 may also belong to this early time, though this supposition is by no means certain. Marked as it is by an unrestrained exuberance and impudent irony, the poem is modelled in subject—but only mildly so—on Lucilius' second book and probably with better reason is explained as a counterpart to the *nugae* (trifles) of the neoterics that correspond to it in content. Satire 1.4 was written later than 1.2 which is quoted there[3] and perhaps also later than 1.3. In any case, it presupposes several of Horace's satires as being known. It is certain, however, that Satire 1.4 is earlier than 1.10 in which it is quoted twice.[4]

The chronology of the seven Maecenas satires is a matter of dispute. The fifth satire of book 1 allows an absolute date, since the poem presupposes the journey of Maecenas to Brundisium which he undertook early in 37 B.C. with the purpose of ironing out certain differences that had arisen between Octavian and Antony.[5] The *terminus post quem* follows from this. Apparently Satire 1.8 was written soon after Horace's acquaintance with Maecenas began, and Satire 1.3 leaves a generally early impression, while the first satire is probably the earliest satire of book 1.

It is not possible to put together a chronology of the poems. The question of the exact chronological order has to take into consideration not only development of language and style, but above all the development of the satiric form from invective in the Lucilian mode to an organ of self-projection.[6]

Since the second book of satires appeared later and the earliest chronological reference in it relates to the year 33 B.C., the years 37–33 are taken as the time during which the first book was completed. If the friend mentioned in the last satire of book 1 (1.10.86) can be identified with certainty as Lucius Calpurnius Bibulus, Horace's fellow-student and comrade-in-arms, who was engaged at Alexandria serving Antony and did not return to Rome until 35 B.C.[7] but who is mentioned by Horace as being among those present, then the year of publication of the first book of satires would have to be sought between 35 and 33 B.C. It is quite likely that this estimate is right. Certainly book 1 of the satires was the first poetic work that Horace published. The attempt of Witte to establish a date with the help of Vergil's First Georgic is not convincing, for it is not known precisely when the end of Georgic One (512–14) which Horace is said to be imitating in his first satire (1.1.114–16) was written and it is not even at all certain that he was attempting an imitation.

Satiric poetry was especially well suited to Horace's poetic disposition, as he himself admits.[8] And so there was no interruption at this point either; the second book followed the first book without any delay. In the meantime Maecenas had given Horace his farm, the *fundus Sabinus* (Sabine farm), and by doing this had helped him fulfill his heart's desire. This seems to have been in the year 33 or shortly before. Horace spoke often of this farm of his.[9] To the amazement of others, he did not view this property as a sinecure at all, but he visited his country estate often and with pleasure. Also between the publication of the first and second books of the satires the association between Horace and Octavian developed, probably through the agency of Maecenas.

The aedileship of Agrippa which fell in the year 33 B.C. provides a *terminus post quem* for the composition of the second book, for there is a reference to this in the third satire (*Sat.* 2.3.185). In the sixth satire (*Sat.* 2.6.51–56) there seem to be references to the events after the Battle of Actium which took place on September 2, 31 B.C. (*Sat.* 2.9.31). The parody of the oracle also fits this (*Sat.* 2.5.62–65). Finally, Satire 2.7 presupposes Satires 2.3, 2.2, and 2.6, so that it is possible to conclude that the second book of satires was published in 30 B.C. about the same time as the epodes.

Eight poems are included in this book in a two-part arrangement, as Friedrich Boll recognized (Satires 1–4 and 5–8), and they were meant for publication from the start. The humorous concluding satire balances the prologue poem. The relationship between the two halves will be considered in more detail later.

Horace's satires are referred to uniformly in our manuscripts as *sermones* (conversations). This evidence should be taken as reliable, even though Horace spoke of the genre as *satura* (*Sat.* 2.1.1) and at one point even designated the individual poems *saturae* (*Sat.* 2.6.17). On the other hand, he himself calls the satires *sermones*,[10] as Lucilius had already done in passing.[11] Horace also gave this designation to the epistles, which belong to the same literary genre (*Epist.* 2.1.4), or to both (*Epist.* 2.1.250). In addition there is the explicit evidence of Porphyrion[12] as well as that of Suetonius.[13] I cannot see anything in Satire 1.4.42 that militates against this idea. It would be much more likely that Horace would carefully avoid *satura* in the title because at that time it was loaded with connotations of personal invective and Horace's satires did not have this as a purpose. It is also possible that the poet wanted to designate a part of the whole as *sermones* as he later treated a second part of *satura* in the *epistulae*. The word *sermo* in this case could be interpreted as the Latin equivalent of διατριβή (diatribe). *Saturae* may have been the title of the edition of Probus (see below) which also perhaps designated the iambics as *Epodon liber* (*Book of Epodes*) and the letter to the Pisos as *Ars poetica* (*The Art of Poetry*). For the sake of convenience, in what follows reference will be made to Horace's *sermones* and to his satires without distinction.

The first satire of book 1, the poem of dedication to Maecenas, involves two themes—human discontent with one's given lot and avarice. The two main ideas are indeed connected with one another by a hinge (envy), but an organic unity is not established. The poem is particularly rich in lively pictures and scenes. On the whole, Heindorf's judgment is valid: "Horace would hardly have become the favorite of all witty men of the world of all succeeding centuries with his satires, if he had written them all in this tone and spirit." It is quite certain that Horace is following a Greek treatise in the essentials of his criticism. The twenty-first speech of Maximus of Tyre especially provides points of contact. But Horace saturates everything with Roman colors.[14]

Methods of sexual gratification make up the theme of the second satire, which was a motif that had appeared in Lucilius more than once.

In the third satire of book 1 the poet issues an invitation to tolerance; he speaks here of his own shortcomings as if he wants to educate himself by means of the poem. This is an early example of Horace's use of tact in his function as a teacher.

In the fourth satire Horace presents a vindication of his revision of Lucilian satire, and the tone is heavily polemic. With the *Iter Brundisinum* (Journey to Brundisium) in the fifth satire he entered into competition with the *Iter Siculum* (Journey to Sicily) of Lucilius. The poem reads like a forerunner of the literary epistle.

The sixth satire is probably the most personal of the whole book; it is an expansive, free-wheeling, apologetic piece. Horace speaks here of his origin and his development, of his relationship with Maecenas that is based on human and humane values alone, and he affirms his commitment to a life amid peace and quiet. By contrast, lines 12–44 sound like a concession to the pugnacity of Lucilian satire.

The seventh satire is an account of a lawsuit before the tribunal of Brutus in the year 43 B.C. It amounts to a recounting of a *bonmot*. The eighth satire represents an exception, inasmuch as Priapus, the god of gardens, is the speaker. As if in an expanded *Priapeum* (Priapus poem), Horace has him describe an experience which he had one night in the garden of Maecenas on the Esquiline.

In the ninth poem the satirist portrays an everyday experience as Catullus does in one of his poems (10); it is a satire about a prattler. In the tenth satire of book 1 the poet once again takes up the criticism of Lucilius that he had put forward in the fourth satire. Here he softens and limits it considerably and develops the artistic pretensions from his own poetry.

With the first book of his satires Horace represented himself as carrying on and revising Lucilian satire, for he saw in Lucilius the greater founder of the art of writing satiric poetry, the man through whom Roman satire developed beyond Ennius to receive its general and binding generic formula. And according to ancient custom, Horace again and again indicates his dependence on Lucilius right down to the last of his epistles, not only *expressis verbis* (by direct statement), but also through numerous reminiscences. He praised Lucilius for his talent and for his power, for his frankness and intellectual agility, for his charm, his biting wit and ridicule, as well as for his pleasantness, his culture, and his cleverness and common sense. But Horace criticized his irregular verse, his verbosity, as he did his deficiencies in composition generally. In addition he censured him for his negligent use of language, especially the mixing of scraps of Greek in his Latin verses. All of this, as Horace said, was the result of his method of composition which was too hasty and which, conditioned by a false pride, exhibited a lack of artistic conscience. Moreover, Horace kept away from the malice and sharpness of Lucilius. It has already been shown in outline how Horace wanted to carry on the Lucilian tradition and in what ways he was out to modify it.

What attracted Horace to satire was first of all something universal —its very personal character, its delight in criticism, and its comprehensiveness. The subject of Lucilian satire had been human life, even his own, in all of its shadings. This was an inexhaustible theme that lay closer than any other to the heart of Horace (*Sat.* 2.1.60), the constant observer and realistic commentator. Similarly man stood at the center of old satire, which had held the mirror in front of him with complete frankness and had passed healthy judgment on the nature of right and wrong. Horace, whose strength lay in criticism, as he well knew, accepted this task, and the road that Lucilius had followed became Horace's also. Through the portrayal of the wrongheaded person what was right should become clear. This process might involve wit, jesting, or even an opinion expressed with pungency, but it was always carried out in such a way that it could just as well be part of a conversation.

What Horace missed especially in Lucilius was real meaning and artistic value, and so modification and revision of Lucilius' style coming from the changed spirit of a more exacting time seemed to him to be necessary. Horace had to carry through his claim against two strong and hostile groups. First there were the blind admirers of Lucilius, who in the tradition of a Cicero and a Varro recognized the vigorous old Roman *ingenia* (geniuses) as they had been, and, full of national pride, saw in them the proper counterweights to the advancing Hellenism. How firmly established the group was—and how successfully they even resisted the attack of the classic poets—may be gathered from Vitruvius or Velleius Paterculus.[15] On the other hand, Horace sharply criticized the "sons" of the neoterics for whom art meant a pure product resulting from diligent application of artistic rules. Over against both of these the poet laid down his own claim quite clearly. In contrast to contemporary fashion, his goal was a Roman literary language which could be placed beside the Greek on an equal footing; his aim was art with a worthwhile spirit and content, not *nugae* (trifles), but art in a form which was the ultimate in perfection. Firmly and without compromise he raised art from the level of artificiality and loose dilettantism and declared it to be a serious area of life, and he described the artistic conscience—he was the first to do this in the Latin language—as a real power (*Sat.* 1.10.72-77). In this Horace saw the modern lesson (*Sat.* 1.10.67-71), and he was the first to express the thesis to which he along with Vergil, Varius, and several others subscribed. It is like a formulation of Goethe: Content brings the form with it; form is never without content. The purpose that his friends had already achieved at least in part in other areas—in comedy and tragedy, in epic, and Vergil in the *Georgics* (*Sat.* 1.10.40-45)—this was what Horace was trying to achieve as a satiric poet in conformity with his natural inclination and talent.

The formula seemed to have been well established by Lucilius. It did not demand of the poet, as Horace taught, the venerable inspiration, but referred satire, as it did comedy, to a more modest level. According to this formula again satire moves on a plane somewhere between inspired poetry and prose,[16] and as a matter of fact the general level of Horatian satire does lie below that of the epodes which in turn fall below the odes. The satiric style, however, had a number of very different shadings at its disposal and as a whole rose considerably above the style of the mimes of Laberius, for example (*Sat.* 1.10.5-6). In qualifying satire in this way Horace as a satirist also wanted to be a poet, a poetic shaper of urbane discourse which extended from small talk and the brief account of an event all the way to substantial conversation about the complicated art of living. This comes through clearly in a number of satires,[17] and later generations interpreted Horace's purposes in this way.[18] At that time Horace had not yet revealed his capacity for writing odes.

While it had been Lucilius' intention to achieve real and visible results with his poems, Horace's satires strove after artistic worth; they were meant to be *bona carmina* (good poems), *carmina recte scripta* (poems written correctly). And so it followed that the censure alleging a malicious and slanderous purpose which his enemies brought against him did not affect Horace. He stood up to these attacks with great seriousness and with emphatic outspokenness. But the change in purpose of Horatian satire brought with it other changes, too—in tone and content and in the point of view and the spirit of his satire.

Horace's satires at first sight seem much poorer in subject matter than those of Lucilius. For both poets, of course, the question of the relation of man to society is primary and both prefer to devote their

attention to social, cultural, and human questions. But topical themes
(with the exception of those involving literature or man), especially
political themes, the bold mixing of the poet in the great and small
events of the day—these had little part to play in Horace and finally
disappeared completely. The times, as Horace rightly judged, dis-
allowed criticism in a Lucilian manner and the specific wishes of
Maecenas probably worked in the same direction. Instead of this the
questions of how to live a proper life and how to control and direct
life were much more important for Horace than for Lucilius. Horace's
service was to open up philosophy for satire in the sense of a practical
art of living. We can follow this educational experience as it gradually
acquires greater and greater power over him, and it would be quite
wrong to regard philosophy in his case as a substitute for political
polemic which was no longer possible. The philosophical experience
was real in Horace.

At a later time, as he looked back over these earliest writings of his,
he at one point characterized them as *Bionei sermones*, as talk, then,
in the style of Bion (*Epist.* 2.2.60), and in doing so he was referring to
an author whose name must have been familiar to his audience. A
brief biographical sketch of Bion has been preserved for us by Diogenes
Laertius,[19] and his personality left a clear impression on popular philosophical literature. We get to know him there as a man who without
defending a real philosophical dogma knew how to deal with questions
of life in a witty and attractive way in discourses that were generally
understandable. And so it was that Eratosthenes could say of him with
complete justification that he had clothed philosophy in the gaudy
garb of the prostitute. Like the Cynics, though without their strictness,
he ridiculed human foolishness and inconsistency and also criticized
human society in order to lead people to knowledge through laughter.

When Horace refers to discourses of this kind, it may be assumed
that he became familiar with them not only from literature but also
from life. In Athens there were enough popular philosophers of this
kind and in Rome, too, popular philosophical propaganda had gained
considerable ground so that Horace could even laugh at an opponent,
Plotius Crispinus, who published such tracts in carelessly versified
form.

How very much Horace was committed to the diatribe in his satires,
as he at the same time refined its style and deepened its meaning, has
become increasingly clear since the appearance of Heinze's dissertation
mentioned earlier,[20] so that today the fact of *imitatio* (imitation) seems

almost immaterial. If Horace brought the philosophical discourse into satire as an essential motive, then he felt it to be a deviation from what Lucilius had done. Through this satire took on a meaning and importance in a universal, human sense. Several of his poems could actually have quite general titles applied to them.

Another divergence from Lucilius consisted in the fact that, while Horace probably wanted to laugh and to laugh out loud just as Bion and the followers of Bion had, he did not want to wound as Lucilius had. Instead of this, Horace's satire took on an educational function, as the poet represented it, through observation and precise description with the ultimate purpose of understanding and perfecting oneself. And finally in this kind of discourse that was both serious and humorous, Horace probably felt that there was a connection with the Greek in that here the personality of the person directing the conversation was the most important element, even more essential than the actual subject.

Now Horace's satires of course became something quite unlike diatribes in the usual sense. *Philosophia* was for the poet a means of grasping personal experience and using it to come to an understanding of the multi-faceted world and the human heart. With this he renounced the impulsiveness and directness of Lucilius. Certainly he saw human weaknesses and the perverse follies of society no less sharply than Lucilius did, but he saw them differently—as universal human foolishness and not as the coarseness of especially depraved individuals who belonged on the rack. Accordingly his purpose was not, as Lucilius' had been, to expose and exterminate scoundrels, but his aim was knowledge and through this the understanding of life and men as they really were. And so Horace is no censor and no emotionalist or declaimer, but he knows how to tell the truth with a smile, almost like a joke, from a position of great inner strength. For though there is a lot he understands and smiles at, his point of view is undeviating, and he knows also how to condemn harshly and very pungently when there is a need for it.

His approach to the phenomena of life was therefore dialectic. He saw the polarity of human *vitia* (shortcomings); they represented deviation from the natural precept of moderation and mean. He also saw their complex character so that for him life was something to be expressed in an infinitely richer fullness and differentiation than it had been for Lucilius. In this sense understanding assumes a great inner liveliness and sensitivity and also a strong power of reflection, especially a vivid, disciplined insight into oneself, which was characteristic of Horace to an especially high degree.[21] It is primarily this power of reflection that raises Horace above things as an observer and a critic. It gives him his great flexibility and superiority, and it is the source of Horace's special brand of humor and his sense of irony that is almost always present.

And so in his satire Horace, unlike Lucilius, rejected the adoption of so many subjects. But what he did formulate he knew how to comprehend in considerably greater depth and with far greater precision. Horace did this as an educated, thinking soul, not as a philosopher. As a thoroughgoing bibliophile he certainly read and used a great number of philosophical writings in all of which, significantly enough, his reliance on Cicero is quite limited. But he is no dogmatist and he is not committed to any particular school. Probably in the 30's the Epicurean philosophy was closest to his heart as it was for Vergil, though in quite a different way, and as a result there appeared in the first book of his satires many sarcastic comments on the paradoxes and the street-preachers of the Stoic sect.

As in content, so in metrical form Horace's satire at first sight appears much less rich than that of Lucilius. It makes use of the hexameter alone, and this is based on the polished rules that both Lucretius and with even more finality the neoterics had developed. But the poetry shows how unceasingly and how perceptively and successfully Horace worked all his life on the continuing refinement of his satiric verse in order to make it the most tractable and the most euphonious vehicle for the stylized *sermo* (conversation). Heinze's introduction to his study of the satires (see below) is the shortest and the best account of Horace's verse that exists today.[22]

In the same way it is possible to follow step by step the conscientious and serious way in which he worked at his artistic language. His purpose was a purity and vigor with a view to achieving the greatest power of expression by the most economical means—this in contrast to Lucilius' luxuriant fullness of style. The disciplining of the language through good taste, which was an enemy of all artificiality, led to a balance and precision of expression that all later Roman satirists recognized as classical. Horace's satiric language sounds free and easy, and yet it is very difficult to fully penetrate its concentrated thought. It also presupposes a host of fundamentals that are, at least in part, obscure. The progressive formulation of Horace's language has become clear to us in very many details, but the challenge of putting together a comprehensive comparative poetic grammar for Horace has still not been met.

Finally, the poet's masterful skill is revealed in matters of composition. Here too Horace showed his great power in limiting and arranging his material. In contrast to the prolixity of Lucilius, he knows how to carry the thoughts through with a precise shading or how to break them off at the right moment, as in a full-fledged conversation. As a true leader of the conversation, Horace only seldom aims at exhausting his topic. With apparent casualness, which is by no means without a purpose, he prefers to let the talk flow from one concern to the other. In this way, like an experienced persuader, he accomplishes his artistic purpose with an alternation of feeling, fantasy, carefully formed observation, thoughts, and opinion. The result is the stylized illusion of smoothly flowing speech making up a refined conversation.

Horace's production was not hasty and was hardly voluminous, and he himself considered this to be a first priority. Certainly because of it he probably had to listen to many a reproach even from his friends.[23] But the modest volume of his poetic production was explained by his conception of literature which demanded quality and diligent application to the artistic side. This was the thought which Horace put at the beginning of his second book of satires. There he made the point that his satires were meant to be poetic creations that were aesthetically valuable—*bona carmina* (good poems). This same poem also conveys the clear impression that Horace's poetic position has now become established in contrast to what it was when he wrote his earlier literary-critical satires (1.4; 1.10). He is writing in what in the meantime has been recognized as an artistic *genus* (genre). Moreover, the poet himself has developed, and so the second book of the satires differs quite markedly from book 1 in tone and in the breadth of human horizon, although the same artistic form and for the most part similar themes are involved. On a purely superficial level, what catches the eye is the fact that the epic ornament has disappeared and the urbanity of the style has grown. But even more noticeable is the fact that almost all of the poems of book 2 are put together as dialogues with a preference for the kind where Horace engages personally in a discussion with his partner and usually plays the recipient who allows himself to be taught. The general observation may also be made that Horace has consciously strengthened the dramatic power of his poems in the second book. Only the first and sixth satires are put together somewhat differently.[24] In the second book of the satires Horace the dialectician is much more to the forefront than in the first book. Corresponding with this is the fact that irony, in which the boundaries between the light and the serious so often become blurred, plays an even more prominent role here.

Consequently, the dialogue form as it appears in the second book probably represents a further departure from Lucilius and assumes an even more searching interest on the poet's part in popular philosophy. In this connection, there remains the task of showing whether this book is to be understood, among other things, as a discussion with Menippean satire and if so, to what extent this is the case. The preference for general questions about life stands out more strongly here, and in spite of all the strangeness of the teaching and its popular advocates, Horace now considers a detailed discussion with the Stoa as something necessary. It is as if in the meantime he had recognized the earnestness and the moral power of its dogma. Horace now seems to be walking along the road that continues on to some of the odes (1.34; 2.2). The philosophic art of living has for him become his most personal concern. On the other hand, personal polemic in the second book becomes more and more an accessory item and for large stretches it has disappeared completely. Certainly there is still a great deal of real polemic here, but as far as personal attack is concerned, the second book no longer offers anything to compare with Satire 1.2, with the polemic sections of 1.4 and 1.10, or with the Canidia satire (1.8). Horace is satisfied now with casual sarcastic remarks.

Satire 2.1 takes the form of a private talk that Horace has with the old jurist Trebatius about his poems. It is a question of self-justification, but on a far more literary level than it was in the two satires of book 1 (1.4; 1.10), where the poet still had to protect himself against hostile feelings that were quite real. Horace in the meantime had been successful with his poetry, and so the tone of the poem is quite confident and easygoing.

In 2.2 Horace reports to his friends a discourse of his compatriot Ofellus on true simplicity as contrasted with the prevalent luxury of the table. It is worth noting how the views of Ofellus in essence mingle with those of the poet. The composition is very artificial and is meant to leave an impression of lazy informality.

Satire 2.3 is the longest poem of the book and is straight dialogue. A character named Damasippus descends blustering on the poet who has retreated to his farm at the time of the Saturnalia. Damasippus, who as a merchant had gone bankrupt, has been converted by a certain Stertinius to the Stoic doctrine of salvation, and now Horace portrays him as recounting the discourse of Stertinius in all its detail (*Sat.* 2.3.38–299). At the center of the discussion stands the Stoic paradox that all men with the exception of the wise man are fools, a theme which Varro had taken up in his *Eumenides*. That this piece is based on a Greek tract follows not only from the content but also from the emphasis that is placed on the arrangement which is carried through with an almost pedantic accuracy. Horace wants to be taught at last where exactly his own foolishness lies. Damasippus' answer is blunt and coarse and filled with generalities, and Horace with apparent impatience breaks off the conversation. Certainly the poet here, as earlier in Satire 1.9, meant to present a certain human type which at that time was quite familiar in Rome—in this case the tactless proselytizer. And yet the talk of that bankrupt businessman who poses as a freshly made wise man contains so much that is serious and even thoughtful that a conflict arises for us as it did in Satire 2.2. Horace knew perfectly well, then, that neither the thing that should be rejected nor that which is worth approval presents itself clearly and simply, but that quite to the contrary life is a great spectacle made up of a mixture of patterns and shapes. The σπουδαιογέλοιον (mixing of humor and seriousness) is revealed here in a completely unexpected light.

The counterpart to this poem at the corresponding point in the second half of the book is Satire 2.7. This is a lecture on virtue which the poet has his slave Davus present. Like Damasippus, he too has his wisdom from a second source—in this case from the doorman of the Stoic Crispinus. The theme is freedom, and it is discussed from the strict, Stoic point of view.

In the fourth satire of this book Horace lets himself be initiated by a certain Catius in the secrets of gastronomic pleasures and in the proper preparation of a refined banquet. Once again there is a closely knit combination of seriousness and ridicule. The poem is also related to the piece just mentioned in that Catius owes his knowledge to an informant. The idea has been put forward that in this satire it may have been Horace's intention to have a joke with Maecenas himself, but this cannot be proved nor is it very probable. Here too the subject is a theme from popular philosophy— περὶ ἐδεσμάτων (on foods)—which

was also treated in Latin; Varro had dealt with it several times already
in his Menippeans.

In the second half of the book Satire 2.8 corresponds to the fourth
satire. This is the account by a friend, the comic poet Fundanius, of
the banquet which Nasidienus Rufus had given for Maecenas and his
circle of friends. The social framework is quite different from that in
Petronius' *Cena Trimalchionis* (Banquet of Trimalchio), although it
is not improbable that Petronius imitated this in matters of detail. Here
Horace has presented a lively picture of a facet of life using a traditional subject.[25]

The fifth satire of book 2 is especially interesting because this is
the only place where Horace has presented a real and serious subject
in fantastic dress. Since it was not possible for him to declaim on the
mean habit of legacy hunting, he shifted the scenery to the under-
world. The comic effect of the poem is overwhelming, and an influence
from the Menippean tradition is very likely. And so Odysseus consults
the wise Tiresias in the underworld, asking him how he can find
prosperity again. He gets the categorical answer: only through legacy-
hunting. Then follows the appropriate detailed advice as the hero listens
reluctantly. The main attraction of the piece lies in the fact that this
advice given by Tiresias is shot through with a Roman coloring.

Satire 2.6, which is Horace's poem of rejoicing over his farm, is
a high point in his satiric poetry. It ends with the story of the city
mouse and the country mouse recounted by the worthy peasant Cervius.

The composition and compilation of the first three books of the
odes fall in the next period; they were completed in the year 23 B.C.
Only after this, in the so-called *intervallum lyricum* (hiatus in his lyric
production), that is between 23 and 17 B.C., did Horace turn again to
satiric poetry—this time in the form of epistles, the first collection of
poetic letters in the Latin language. The title *Epistulae* is attested unan-
imously by the manuscripts and also by the indirect tradition, and it
is confirmed by the nature of the collection.

The first book of the epistles includes twenty poems. It exists today
in the same state in which it was given to the public by Horace himself in the fall of 20 B.C., not long before his forty-fifth birthday. It is a
product of the early *Pax Augusta* (Augustan Peace), as is clear from
the poem which serves as an epilogue (1.20). The oldest datable epistle
of the collection (*Epist.* 1.13) presupposes the publication of the first
three books of the odes. And so it follows that the years 23–20 were

the time of composition of book 1 of the epistles. From the point of view of Horace, then, who grew old early, the collection was a late work.

The second book includes as its first poem the great literary epistle to Augustus, which with good reason might be dated to about the year 14 B.C.; this is Vahlen's date. Timewise the second literary epistle is earlier. It is addressed to Florus, a younger friend of Horace who belonged to the literary circle of Tiberius. Vahlen has very convincingly pointed to the year 18 as its date of composition.

The epistle to the Pisos, which on the authority of Quintilian and others we usually call the *Ars poetica* (*Art of Poetry*), though not with complete justification, is not dated with certainty. This great open letter possibly appeared in the *intervallum lyricum*, that is between 23 and 17, the latter being the year of the *Carmen saeculare* which ushered in a new flowering of Horatian ode writing. By this reckoning it is reasonable to put the *Ars* in the period before Vergil's death and so perhaps somewhere around 20/19 B.C. In my opinion this estimate seems much more probable. A considerably later estimate is certainly possible, according to which the work was composed in the last years of Horace's life and was perhaps not published until after his death. It has certainly not been possible to detect any traces of incompleteness. It cannot be ascertained whether the *Ars poetica* originally belonged to the corpus of the second book of the epistles or whether it went the rounds from the start as a separate circular letter. The grammarians cite the letter to the Pisos both as a separate work, that is as the *Ars poetica*, and also as part of the *Epistulae*.

Horace's epistles belong to the same literary genre as the satires. Porphyrion attests to this[26] and Horace himself suggests it.[27] Moreover, considerations of meter, language, and style show that the basic rationale is the same in both. It is just that with the epistles Horace has perfected his mastery of the art still further.

Also according to ancient theory the epistolary style most closely approximated the tone of conversation. The differences between the epistles and satires, then, are to be explained essentially by the development of the poet as a person and much less by the newly chosen framework. All of the letters were addressed to correspondents some distance away, in part to men with whom we are well acquainted from history. Now since a group of these epistles contained quite individual characteristics, it was earlier thought that it was a case of their all being real letters. For some of the epistles this may be true, but poems like Epistles 1.13 and 1.14 were not conceived as real letters but as fictional ones, even though they were obviously based on real situations. Even a missive as personally conceived as Epistle 1.7 can only have been written after Horace's relationship to Maecenas had become clear. In the same way the outspoken philosophical letters like 1.2, 1.6, and 1.16 are to be understood as open letters in poetry and not as real letters.[28] The same is probably true of the literary epistles. Linking the objective with the personal is, in fact, a characteristic of Horace's poetry. All in all, the collection of epistles leaves the impression of a broadly ranging correspondence. This was surely part of Horace's purpose and is to be compared with the universal content of the first three books of the odes. The principle of arrangement has not yet been worked out in detail.

The purpose of the first book of epistles is to draw attention to the value which accrues to man from directing his attention to things of the intellect. After editing the first three books of the odes, Horace felt that as an artist he was unproductive. He was resolved to bid fare-well to pretentious poetry and instead to follow the summons of phil-osophy which bade man to make the most of his last chance for self-education, in order in this way to be ready to leave the stage of life well equipped and with decorum. Horace is fully aware of the fact that the decision for *sapientia* (philosophical wisdom) needs boldness, but he also knows that this way, once it is begun, leads to a life that is happy and free. In the first book of the epistles he presents this struggle and striving of his not as a wise man, but as a man who knows what is necessary. As he had done earlier, Horace here aims for the educa-tional effect by speaking of himself again and again quite candidly and without any vanity at all.

The theme that appears over and over again is the use and control of real life through the intellect (e.g., *Epist.* 1.1.19). Here too Horace is sworn to no particular philosophical school and even guards against any dogmatism (*Epist.* 1.1.14–18). Of course he does not deny his special preference for the teachings of Epicurus even here (*Epist.* 1.4.15–16), but he also does not refuse recognition to other dogmas, so that even the Stoa finds its place in this educational structure.[29] Any attempt to deduce from this a conversion of the poet such as has been read into Ode 1.34 would certainly be wrong. Philosophy was for him still only an especially broad base—philosophy as the art of living. Horace put it to use in his own personal way as an artistic character.

In the first book of the epistles much self-consciousness, resigna-
tion, and depression lie beneath the surface, but there is also a great
deal of human feeling. This is the work of a man who himself lives
a retired life. Amid the wealth of maxim and all the brilliant worldly
wisdom that is found here, Horace keeps speaking more and more in-
timately, with the warmth that is peculiar to men who are no longer
quite young. So this belongs to the most mature work that has come
down to us from Horace.[30]

Just as a common theme runs through the first book of the letters
and is essential to it, a theme that accompanied Horace throughout his
life—man and *philosophia*—so a main idea of fundamental importance
also runs through the second book including the *Ars*—Roman poetry
and its educative function. Horace, who obviously knew Hellenistic and
Roman aesthetic theory very well, developed this too in his very personal way. In Epistle 2.2 the thought still echoes clearly with philosophic
overtones, but even here the theme of "poetic art" is dominant. This
was a subject with which Horace had busied himself so intensely all
along and it was one that had already appeared in the last epistles of
the first book.[31] Mommsen called the second book of epistles the most
charming and most delightful work of all Latin literature.

In Epistle 2.1 Horace speaks to the emperor about the current condition of poetry in Rome. He defends poetry as a province of life
with its own special value and its own legislation and justifies its claim
through its educational force. The epistle to Florus (2.2) again takes
up Horace's renunciation of lofty poetry—actually of poetry in general.
It describes the literary life in Rome in lively scenes, and against this
background Horace in a central section formulates the demands which
the genuine poet had to comply with. The letter reaches its climax in
the defense of Horace's own life decision—to live no longer for art but
to strive after ethical insight.

At one time for almost a century the letter to the Pisos was flatly considered to be a book of statutes for poetry-writing on the authority of
a Boileau. Real philological activity with the work belongs to much
more recent times. Caught up by the old interpretation that Horace
meant to produce a systematic theory of poetry, scholars took exception
to the apparently planless composition which resulted from the epistolary
form and sought to correct it by vigorously attacking the text. The
nineteenth century in particular offered several such violent modifica-
tions of the text. Research into the composition of this epistle was put
on a new and solid basis in the year 1905 through the efforts of Eduard

Norden,[32] who recognized the principle behind the organization of this work in the so-called eisagogic scheme. This article formed the basis of many studies, some of them very useful, which tried to solve the problem of composition with increasing precision. Norden's conclusions at the same time opened the way for a second line of inquiry: the connection of the *Ars* with Greek theory and the problem of sources. Porphyrion had named Neoptolemus of Parion as an important authority for the *Ars poetica*. Now Chr. Jensen succeeded in extracting several sentences of this author from the remains of Philodemus' work on poetics[33] and with this discovery the question of sources moved to the forefront of subsequent inquiries. These received their fullest rebuttal in the edition with commentary by A. Rostagni (Turin, 1930), who rightly pointed to the predominantly Peripatetic basis of the dogmas which Horace put forward in his *Ars*. The problem of origins was then advanced considerably through new efforts.

On the other hand, Otto Immisch in 1932 widened the perspective by showing in a shrewd and scholarly way that Horace had not intended to present a complete system of poetic theory, but that he was dealing with chosen parts or selections, as suited the epistolary nature of the work.[34] Immisch wanted to explain Horace's choice as coming from the poet's regard for the relevance of the questions discussed for the Roman poetry of his time. Most recently Friedrich Klingner has attempted to understand and to explain the Roman work in its purpose, structure, and plan as an artistic production in and of itself alone.[35] Before him Lotte Labowsky had already tried to do the same kind of thing in her Heidelberg dissertation.[36] W. Steidle's studies on the *Ars poetica* of Horace are strongly influenced by Klingner without losing any independent value because of this.[37] All four points of view have produced important findings, but they still seem to leave considerable room for future investigation.

Our text of Horace is, generally speaking, well transmitted. We have about 250 manuscripts, the oldest of which comes from the early ninth century. The variant readings of ancient or medieval origin are by no means few, but almost always somewhere in the manuscript tradition the right one is to be found. It just has to be tracked down. It is remarkably seldom that a verse appears in two basically different forms that are at the same time apparently of equal value.[38] The text of Horace is not preserved nearly as well as that of Vergil where the words are well established over hundreds of verses at a stretch. Critical conjecture should not be given up completely in dealing with Horace's hexameter poems,[39] even if a Bentley's joy in conjecture is no longer sanctioned today.

The extensive manuscript material was made available, thanks to the efforts of O. Keller and A. Holder especially, which came to fruition in the apparatus of their great edition of Horace (vol. 2, Jena, 1925). While well-known scholars of our times have generally given way and have shown no interest at all in pursuing the history of the manuscript tradition, Friedrich Klingner has very recently gone beyond Keller, Christ, Vollmer, Leo, and others with good success in an attempt to bring order to the profuse tradition.[40] He seeks to show that two ancient editings of the text, Ξ and Ψ, formed the main basis for the Horace tradition of medieval times and that the derivatives of these offered various contaminations of these two versions. And so it is advisable to use the word "class" only *a potiori* in the case of an author who in medieval times was as widely read as Horace. And certainly this holds not only for the satires but even more for the epistles which were especially popular because of the wealth of maxims that they contain. For text criticism Klingner recommends logically and with full justification an eclectic method.

While Klingner's research is done precisely and is filled with good ideas, he is probably content with a minimum of the knowledge that is safely attainable. It is entirely possible that more than just two exemplars of Horace were transmitted in our medieval tradition, for even in antiquity, as, for example, the indirect tradition shows, the mixing of texts was the customary thing. Also the different order in which the individual books of Horace's poems appear in the manuscripts can be taken as pointing to more than only two ancient recensions. And finally Klingner himself believes, and rightly so, that in the *Blandinius Vetustissimus*, which is now lost, there can be seen a third ancient editing of the text, though only in scant traces. For it is a proven fact that this third manuscript alone or almost alone contained the correct reading in a whole series of passages, and these were not at all based on correct conjecture, but were drawn from the direct tradition.[41] And so it might also be possible that the obvious mixture of texts found in group Q, which in several cases seems to outdo the Ξ and Ψ traditions in originality, also belongs to antiquity. Similarly it is impossible to get rid of the impression that in comparison with Ψ the *Vaticanus Reginensis 1703* contains material of value that goes back to antiquity, especially in matters of orthography. Perhaps new man-

uscript discoveries and fuller collations can complete the picture which
Klingner has traced along these lines, for good readings are found even
in codices that are not very well known or which have been ignored
by research.[42] Is it a matter of conjecture in all cases like this, or is
there a tradition reflected here that is at least in part genuine, while
elsewhere it has been obliterated?

The historical stages of the Horace tradition should be sketched
here only briefly. Horace himself had prophesied with easygoing ridicule that his works would one day serve as lecture material for school
boys (*Epist.* 1.20.17–18). And this did happen, certainly not immediately as with Vergil, but as early as the first century after Christ. It is
questionable whether already in the Augustan period Quintus Caecilius Epirota dealt with Horace as he did with Vergil in his school.
But as far as the elder Seneca, Velleius Paterculus, and the schoolboys
in Pompeii were concerned, he clearly was not yet considered a classic,
though he probably was by Quintilian, Tacitus,[43] and at a later time
Juvenal.[44] From this very early period come the forgeries under Horace's
name which Suetonius mentions in the vita—the *elegi et epistula prosa
oratione quasi se commendantis Maecenati* ("the elegiac verses and
the epistle in prose [written] as if he was recommending himself to
Maecenas"). It is likely, too, that a few interpolations were made in the
text at this time—for example, the eight spurious verses at the beginning of Satire 1.10 (*Lucili quam sis mendosus*, etc.), which certainly did not have Heiricus of Auxerre as their author as Vollmer
believed, but originated in early times. Moreover, a series of word
variants goes back to this early period, as the citations of Seneca the
philosopher and Quintilian show.

Unless the tradition is completely misleading, the text of Horace
was subjected to scrutiny by the grammarians from the first century
after Christ on. The most notable achievement here was Valerius
Probus' edition of Horace from the last third of that century. It was
provided with critical marks which were used for oral interpretation
of the poet, and this edition also probably contained variant readings.
There was no commentary. The reconstruction of this edition is the
most important intermediate task of the *recensio* (recension) which
goes from the manuscripts right back to antiquity.[45]

At that time too the practice of writing commentary on the text
grew out of the activity in the schools. In the time of Domitian, Aufidius
Modestus and Claranus were busy as explicators of Horace, while in

the time of Hadrian there was Quintus Terentius Scaurus who probably wrote commentary on part of Horace's writings. Then in the second century there probably existed an authoritative commentary on the whole of Horace, perhaps by Helenius Acron, based on the text of Probus.

Of the exegetic material on Horace that has survived there are the following:

1. The commentary on his collected works by Pomponius Porphyrion from the third century which was written from a grammatical-rhetorical point of view, but very important statements on subject matter are also preserved here—for example, those about specific personalities—which were based on earlier specialized treatment of these subjects.[46] Moreover, Porphyrion provides evidence of a series of text variants[47] and in different places he goes against the evidence of the bulk of the manuscripts to give a correct reading.[48] The work, of course, no longer exists in its original form. Porphyrion is usually cited according to the edition of A. Holder (Innsbruck, 1894).

2. Of far less value but also indispensable are the critical comments which since the fifteenth century have been attributed to Acron and which have been preserved in at least two main styles as marginal scholia in the Horace manuscripts.

They depend in part on Porphyrion and they also presuppose the Vergil commentary of Servius. It is uncertain what the relationship is between these comments and the Horace commentary which Jerome mentions[49] and whether they contain anything that is genuinely Acron's. In spite of the general interest in trivia that they exhibit, they do provide several variants.[50] The authoritative edition of these so-called pseudo-Acronian scholia is that of O. Keller (Leipzig, 1902/4) which has the satires and epistles in the second volume. The contributions of E. Schweikert and P. Wessner in particular have brought further advances. Today the work of H.J. Botschuyver is to be used along with Keller's edition.[51]

3. Finally, before the Horace scholia are completely researched, the expository material of Jacob Cruquius must be taken into account; this was part of his edition of Horace which appeared from 1565 on (the satires in 1573). Cruquius still had access to those manuscripts, among others, which belonged to the Benedictine abbey on Mont Blandin near Ghent, founded by St. Amandus, and which were subsequently lost in the destruction of the abbey in the year 1578 by the

Anabaptists. Not everything that Cruquius published as commentary
is by any means ancient. It is also probable that many of his comments
appear again in other manuscripts that are still extant.

The Horace tradition developed without any break at all from the
first century after Christ to the end of antiquity. The poet belonged to
those authors most frequently read from the time of Seneca and Persius
to that of Venantius Fortunatus. Even in the Greek-speaking world he
apparently did not remain completely unknown.

That editions of Horace were still being put together in the sixth
century is clear from the subscript of Mavortius (consul 527) which
appears in several manuscripts. But it is not possible on the strength
of this to reconstruct the text of Mavortius' edition—and besides, it
probably contained only the lyrics. But the loss is only a minor one.
Scholarship since Bentley has moved well away from his opinion:
Flaccum ex Mavortii recensione hodie habemus ("We have Horace
today from Mavortius' recension."). Probably the edition was only one
among many and it was the work of a dilettante.

In the Dark Ages, the Horace tradition probably lay fallow. Certainly a limited knowledge of the poet was kept alive even then through
glossaries, anthologies, and the grammarians. I would not dare to give
an opinion as to whether Bede and Columban had a first-hand knowledge of the poet.

The rediscovery of the poet was clearly due to the efforts of the
circle around Charlemagne at the end of the eighth century. Our
manuscript tradition begins shortly after this, at the beginning of the
ninth century, and it does not break off again. Horace was widely read
in the schools already in the tenth century, and once again in the
medieval period his works were more than once subjected to commentary and glossing. As L. Traube's introduction to his *Aetas Vir-
giliana, Ovidiana und Horatiana* makes clear, the influence of the poet
was most far-reaching in the later Middle Ages and this development
continued in the Renaissance. In more recent times Horace has definitely surpassed in popularity even Vergil who, however, was master
of the whole medieval period.[52]

Only a very few examples of the many editions and the extensive
ancillary material on Horace can be mentioned here. The literary histories, the Pauly-Wissowa article by Stemplinger (16.2336–99), as well
as the surveys of the literature[53] provide more complete material.

Horace was edited early in Renaissance times, first between 1470 and 1473, probably in Italy. Immediately after this there followed the first editions of Porphyrion and of the pseudo-Acronian scholia (1474 and 1481). The interest in Horace was strong and widespread. In the sixteenth century Lambinus' great edition of Horace with commentary (first published, 1561) was a distinguished achievement. It was marked by an excellent knowledge of Roman literature, sophistication, and good taste. Lambinus contributed much parallel material and a good deal of explanation. The edition of Jacob Cruquius (1565 and the years following) provided access to new manuscript material. It is especially valuable for the information it provides about readings from the *Codex Blandinius Vetustissimus* which is now lost.

The commentaries of Jan Dousa and Daniel Heinsius (1612) should just be mentioned in passing. Also from the seventeenth century comes the French translation by Dacier (1681). Early in the next century the edition of Horace by Richard Bentley appeared (first published, Cambridge, 1711); this was an epoch-making achievement, since in it an attempt was made for the first time to put together a text established on genuinely critical principals with the use of new manuscript material (among this, the old *Harleianus* δ). Relying on a remarkable knowledge of language and his fine critical powers, Bentley broke in a fundamental way with the old principle of fidelity to each and every letter. The text was provided with long text-critical notes, and though we today have again become much more conservative in dealing with the text, Bentley's Horace advanced our understanding of the poet's language to an extraordinary degree. He contributed nothing at all by way of aesthetic interpretation, although this probably goes without saying for Bentley. The whole thing was topped off by an index of words that was revised by Zangemeister in 1869.

The appreciation of Horace's poetry in Germany began with Wieland's translation of the epistles (1782) and satires (1786) with commentary. A passage from Goethe's talk about Wieland of February 18, 1813, on the congeniality of the two poets might be added here: "He was closely related to the Greeks in taste and even more so with the Romans in spirit. It was not that he had allowed himself to be overpowered by a republican or patriotic zeal, but as he only imitated the Greeks, so to speak, he finds among the Romans people who were really like him. Horace behaves in much the same way; a genius and a man of the court and the world, Horace is an intelligent critic of life and art." Later Herder and Friedrich Schlegel in particular promoted a deeper understanding of the poet's work.

From the next period mention might be made of the tasteful edition of the satires with commentary done by L.F. Heindorf (first published, Breslau, 1815), the interesting and forceful edition of Hofman Peerlkamp (Amsterdam, 1863), as well as that of Karl Lehrs (Leipzig, 1869). A. Kiessling's edition of 1886 brought a very important development. Kiessling was the first to make extensive use of Greek literature for purposes of interpreting Horace; he was also an expert in Greek philosophy. Today his commentary exists in a version extensively revised by Richard Heinze whose masterly accuracy is well known.[54] The first-rate edition of Plessis-Lejay with commentary should certainly be used along with this (5 ed., Paris, 1912). Also very useful within its own limits is the school edition with notes edited by Krüger-Hoppe (17 ed., Leipzig, 1923), and so is the selection done by K.P. Schulze (Berlin, 1895).

As far as critical editions of the text are concerned, that of O. Keller and A. Holder should be mentioned before all others.[55] Vollmer's edition is based on this (*ed. maior*, 2 ed., Leipzig, 1912), while that of Fr. Villeneuve, which is the most popular French edition (Paris, 1927–1934), is more closely connected with Lejay. Of the Italian editions those of N. Terzaghi (Milan, 1939) and E. Romagnoli (Bologna, 1939) might be mentioned.

A critical pocket edition which in every respect stands high in scholarship is now that of Fr. Klingner (Leipzig, 1939 [2 ed., 1950], from it the *ed. minor*, 1940). The pocket texts without commentary of Haupt-Vahlen (5 ed., Leipzig, 1908) and of R. Heinze in the *Bibliotheca Mundi* series of the Inselverlag (Leipzig, 1921) are very good.

There is a survey of the numerous translations of Horace into German in R. Newald, *Deutscher Horaz in fünf Jahrhunderten*.[56] The oldest translation of the satires comes from Jac. Roth (Basel, 1671) which had already been preceded by A.H. Buchholtz' translation of the *Ars poetica* (Rinteln, 1639). Wieland's translation of the satires and epistles has already been mentioned.[57] The translation by J.H. Voss might be added here (Cologne, 1822).

A very accurate, though somewhat wordy rendering of the satires and epistles into prose was done by Hermann Röhl (Berlin, 1917). The translation by C. Barth (4 ed., Berlin, 1914) reads agreeably, though it is perhaps better described as a paraphrase. In the thirties there appeared the translations of R. Schöne (Munich, 1934) and K. Schönberger (Munich, 1938).[58]

« VIII »

Seneca's Apocolocyntosis

IMMEDIATELY after Horace's death there was apparently no successor working in poetic satire. There *is* the information in a fairly unclear note of the scholiast on Horace that Julius Florus wrote satires just as he also put together an anthology from the satires of Ennius, Lucilius, and Varro. This was the younger friend of Horace to whom the poet had addressed two of his epistles[1] and who was a member of the poetic circle around Tiberius. But it is impossible to get any picture of his literary activity. The importance of Horatian satire for other literary genres may certainly be detected early, but no noteworthy representative of poetic satire itself appears again until the reign of Nero when Aules Persius Flaccus wrote. Before turning to a discussion of his work, however, we should first consider briefly the development of Menippean satire, for the only example of this genre in the Latin language that has been preserved for us, the *Apocolocyntosis* of Lucius Annaeus Seneca, comes from the beginning of Nero's reign.[2]

In the great majority of the manuscripts the title reads *Ludus Senecae de Morte Claudii Neronis* (*The Joke of Seneca on the Death of Claudius Nero*) or something like this, while in the old manuscript from St. Gall it is *Divi Claudii* ΑΠΟΘΗΟΣΙΣ *Annaei Senecae per saturam* (*The Apotheosis of the Divine Claudius by Annaeus Seneca Through a Satire*) with the *subscriptio* (subscription) reading much the same. Neither of the two forms can be original, and certainly the words *per saturam* cannot come from Seneca. Cassius Dio alone offers evidence for the real title, *Apocolocyntosis* (60.35.3), for the lampoon of Seneca against Claudius that the historian mentions has since the time of Hadrianus Junius been quite correctly identified with the satire that has come down to us. The suggestion that antiquity was familiar with two different pamphlets of this kind must be rejected.

The title should clearly parody an *Apotheosis* (deification) or *Apathanatisis.*[3] Accordingly, it was suggested that in the pamphlet Claudius must have been changed into a pumpkin instead of becoming a god and that this incident was described in a passage at the end of the piece that is now lost. But perhaps the part of the text that has fallen out after chapter 7 contained clarification of the title. This idea of a lost ending has been reiterated rather often since Boxhorn's time (1636), but it can be taken as having no support today. Rather, it seems most likely that the joke lay simply in the title. Like the word *frutex* (bush = blockhead), so also "pumpkin" in ancient times seems to have been a term of insult for the blockhead or idiot,[4] as it still is in a number of modern languages. And so the title simply meant that after his death Claudius remained the same fool as he had been when he was alive, and the hypothesis of a loss at the end of the satire—which, incidentally, the subscriptions and, above all, the structure of the piece militate against—seems unnecessary and wrong.

Seneca's authorship has also been questioned. The point has been made that, among other things, the philosopher composed the eulogy which Nero delivered for his adoptive father, Claudius, from the funeral platform.[5] And so it did not seem reasonable that he could have written a pamphlet full of scorn and hatred against Claudius at the same time as the *laudatio funebris* (funeral eulogy)—at which, by the way, the audience laughed when the speaker turned to talk about the *providentia* (foresight) and *sapientia* (wisdom) of the deceased. Besides, this was the same man for whom he had expressed the greatest respect just a few years earlier in the *Consolatio ad Polybium* (*Consolation to Polybius*) and elsewhere, too.[6] An attempt was made to strengthen this case by discovering contradictions between the *Apocolocyntosis* and statements of Seneca found elsewhere, by noticing differences in style between this piece and Seneca's philosophical works, and also by explaining away as an impossibility the idea that Rome's leading statesman should in this way have attacked the deification of Claudius which had just taken place. And, last but not least, the silence of Quintilian, Tacitus, Suetonius, the younger Pliny, and Juvenal about the pamphlet was used as an argument against its authenticity.

Today all of these objections can be considered as dispensed with. In part, they contradict facts that are quite irrefutable, as, for example, the consistency in language and style between the *Apocolocyntosis* and the philosophical writings and tragedies of Seneca. And it is in the hands of just such a scintillating personality as Seneca—and he was already recognized as such by antiquity[7]—that the simultaneous composition of a eulogy and a lampoon on Claudius is a distinct possibility. Besides, it is attested that he never gave up his personal hatred of Claudius[8] and a remark of his in the *De Clementia* (1.23: *On Mercy*) confirms this. Claudius had sent him into exile on Corsica at the urging of Messallina (41–49 after Christ), simply on the grounds of intrigues at court. It was not until after Messallina's downfall that the new consort of Claudius, his niece, Agrippina, whose family Seneca had always loyally supported, arranged for the philosopher's return to Rome with highest honors. In the year 41 after Christ, Claudius had personally forestalled a death sentence against Seneca, to be sure, but still Seneca never forgave the emperor for the injustice of his exile. It is from this attitude that the pamphlet is to be understood as stemming, so that neither the evidence of Cassius Dio nor that offered by the manuscripts is to be doubted. It is perhaps worth noting that Cassius Dio (60.35.2) has also preserved a plainly venomous bit of wit of Seneca's elder brother, Gallio, involving the dead Claudius. The sarcastic comments of Nero probably belong to a later time.

It was implicit in the subject matter that the essay was first intended exclusively for the innermost circle of court society. It is even possible that it was first recited anonymously there. This could explain why later authors are silent about it, although there are, of course, other probable reasons for this.

This satire has been preserved in its entirety with the exception of a break in the middle following chapter 7. The first days, or at any rate weeks, after the young Nero assumed power may be taken as the time of composition. The attempt to assign the writing to a later time, perhaps to the years in which Nero was planning and trying to bring off an annulment of Claudius' deification, has not been convincing.[9] The situation which the satire presupposes is this: on October 13, 54 after Christ, Claudius had died, poisoned by a mushroom dish at the instigation of his wife Agrippina. Nero, the son of Agrippina and the adoptive son of Claudius, was greeted by the army and the people with jubilation as their new leader, and, as a matter of fact, the first five years of Nero's reign were a golden time for Rome. The death of the Emperor Claudius and especially the cause of his death were kept secret at first on the order of Agrippina, until Nero had entered the succession. Then the deceased was buried with extravagant pomp and

ceremony and elevated to a god by a decree of the Senate. He may
have had his peculiarities and he may have been too susceptible to the
influence of his different wives and favorites—as Ausonius says, *non
faciendo nocens, sed patiendo* ("He was guilty not because of what
he did, but because of what he allowed.")[10]—but he had fulfilled his
obligations as regent very conscientiously, though without any sense
of moderation or proportion, it is true. And Seneca was without doubt
aware of the positive aspects of Claudius' rule. His satire can only
be understood as the product of a completely personal animosity.

In the *Apocolocyntosis* Seneca did not scoff at any of Claudius' political or statesmanlike measures. Quite to the contrary, he sketches an
extremely venomous and completely devastating caricature of the man
as a person. His malice acquires its overwhelming pungency mainly
from the fact that its author is familiar with the tiniest peculiarities and
inclinations of the person he is attacking and exposes everything with
fierce scorn. Whether he is dealing with bodily weaknesses of Claudius
—the way he dragged his right foot, his confused way of speaking and
his occasional stuttering, his trembling hands, his loose gestures, the
way his head shook, his nervousness in general—or whether Seneca is
talking about Claudius' extreme forgetfulness, his occasional absent-
mindedness, his free and easy ways and his naïveté, his good appetite,
his Gallic origins, or his amusements, such as his partiality for philology,
quotations from the poets, sitting as a judge, and dice-playing—all of
this serves the single purpose in this satire of making the deceased
laughable and contemptible in every conceivable way. This negative
coloring, then, leaves no doubt about the purpose of the pamphlet. To
attribute a moral aim to it and suggest that its author may have been
out to make the idea of imperial deification just plain laughable seems
completely absurd. The theory that the *Apocolocyntosis* represents not
only an assault on Claudius but also an attack against the Empress-
mother Agrippina deserves just as little consideration. Quite to the
contrary, even in unimportant details Seneca keeps strictly to the official version of Claudius' death as it had been laid down by Agrippina
and he does not censure a single one of the atrocities which were per-
petrated after his marriage to her.

On the other hand, it is perfectly clear that on the positive side the
piece was designed to celebrate the new regime of Nero (especially
4). But once again it is going too far to theorize that the pamphlet was
inspired in any way at all by Nero himself. The coloring of the whole
by Seneca's hatred is much too personal for that.

The form which Seneca chose is that of the Menippean satire. The narrative was developed in prose, and obviously in a style which was meant to sound intentionally common and low but which shows a strong refinement throughout, especially in the blending of the individual levels of style. Hercules and the goddess of fever, for example, speak quite differently from Augustus; his way of speaking is for its part shot through with peculiarities that had been true to life for the historical Augustus.

There are poetic passages scattered through the work. These are quotations from the poets used directly or adapted for purposes of parody and especially original passages in hexameters, anapaests, and iambic trimeters. In meter, then, these are probably much less varied than the poetic insertions perhaps were in Varro's Menippeans. But they also show such a very close attention to perfection of form that the writer himself occasionally makes fun of it. These passages of verse are sometimes meant to elaborate in a second style what has been said in prose and sometimes the prose is used to elucidate the verse. The rest consists of purely poetic insertions for purposes of description, although the narrative can be carried forward in the verse as well. Often the parody can be found in the passages of verse as had been characteristic of the tradition since the times of Menippus and Varro. The scenery is also Menippean. Important main themes like ascension, *descensus ad infernos* (descent to the underworld), council of the gods, judgment of the dead can be connected with the Menippean diatribe in Greek along with a profusion of secondary and individual motives.

But Roman models, which were in Seneca's mind and to which he makes explicit reference, may also be detected. For the council of the gods, for instance, there was above all the first book of Lucilius from which the quotation *ferventia rapa vorare* (9.5: "to devour boiling turnips") is probably taken, and for the whole idea of the piece there is Varro whom Seneca quotes at one point (8.1). But in spite of all the models, the *Apocolocyntosis* is a completely original work of Seneca. The topical reference to a specific Roman event of the time, the purpose of destroying a particular man for all time, the personal hatred that pulses through everything, the purely political purpose—all of this was missing in the Greek Menippean. The outlook there was more philosophical and much more general, although apparently even in that context the question of the deification of Alexander had been touched upon incidentally. Generally speaking, however, the Greek Menippean had attacked particular types rather than individual people or even politically prominent personalities, and Varro had had a similar conception of the form.

Finally, in spite of all the personal animosity, there is an additional factor in Seneca which comes through especially forcefully and which was to become of great importance for the subsequent development of the Menippean form. This was the element of parody. This goes so deep that Weinreich could make a very good case even for self-parody on Seneca's part by comparing the figure of Hercules here with its counterpart in the tragedies, especially in the *Hercules Furens* (*Mad Hercules*), for example. It also seems that in matters of detail the dirge (12.3) mocks the *laudatio funebris* (funeral eulogy) for Claudius that has already been mentioned. Undoubtedly the *Apocolocyntosis* gives us a clear idea of the whole genre, in spite of the completely individual arrangement of details; and yet Varro's Menippeans must have left quite a different impression.

The content briefly sketched is as follows: The theme is established with an exact chronology in an introduction (1–2) and the authenticity of the account is vouched for. Already at this point the Menippean character of the piece reveals itself, and parody of the standard introduction to historical treatises and of the assurances of truthfulness given by those writing about marvels is also clearly present.

In an abrupt transition which is characteristic of the style, the next two sections (3–4) bring a scene between Apollo and the Fates. The death of Claudius is decided on and the dawn of a new golden age is announced. And so Claudius dies and heads for Olympus to request admission (5–7).

The gods send Hercules, who has traveled everywhere in the world and knows all languages, out to meet him and ask him where he hails from. He does this with a verse from Homer, and Claudius, who is overjoyed that even in heaven there are philologists who have time left for Homer, answers accordingly. And right up to this strongly mimetic scene Seneca's description is splashed with wit and malice. Claudius wins Hercules over to his side and a meeting of the gods is called to decide whether the emperor should be recognized as a new god or, since his consecration has already taken place, whether his deification should be invalidated. The gathering of the gods is put together as a parody of a meeting of the Senate as Lucilius had already done in his first book. Jupiter, for instance, addresses the gods as *patres conscripti* ("conscript fathers"), and so does Augustus later;

then there is the delivery of *sententiae* (opinions) and the stylized word-ing of the motions. All of this should recall the hard and fast rules and ritual that governed the sessions of the Roman Senate. The con-clusion of the speech Claudius made before the gate of heaven to win over Hercules, the introduction of Claudius by Hercules into the heavenly senate, and the angry reaction of the heaven-dwellers to this have probably all been lost in a lacuna following chapter 7. A gap is also indicated by textual details.

What is really the main part of the satire now follows—the gods' deliberations (8–11). First is heard the unofficial opinion of a deity who expresses himself with much frivolity and funmaking, and others may have preceded him. Now Jupiter finally gets to work and calls the meeting to order so that the dignity of Olympus might be main-tained. In these farcical scenes any antireligious purpose certainly lay far from Seneca's thoughts; the whole thing is just a play of wit for him. Janus speaks against admitting Claudius, Diespiter decides for it, and Hercules in the meantime engages in open canvassing with the promise that "one hand washes the other."

From chapter 10 on the tone changes completely. In a devastating speech filled with completely individual touches, Augustus reveals the crimes of Claudius, and his negative judgment prevails. Mercury has to remove Claudius again (12), and the deceased is taken to the under-world by way of the Forum. Here he listens with great pleasure to his own dirge which is devised as a great parody of a tragic lament in anapaests.

In Orcus, crowds of people whom he had allegedly put to death with unfair verdicts come to meet him (13). Then follows the arraign-ment of the deceased emperor before Aeacus, the judge of the dead, which was meant to be a parody of a scene in the Roman courts (14–15). Aeacus, repaying like with like, listens only to the plaintiff and not to the defendant and then hands down his judgment: Claudius is to dice for all eternity using a dice-box without a solid bottom in it. Throwing dice was a favorite pastime of his when he was alive, and he had even written a pamphlet on the subject.

Then the plot, which has been very carefully developed throughout, is brought to a conclusion *molto allegro*. Caligula appears, claims Claudius as a slave, gives him to Aeacus who passes him on to his freedman Menander to serve as his bailiff. Thus Claudius in death is destined to be the slave of a freedman as he had been in life, and, as Bickel has recognized, this ending is Seneca's most personal revenge.

It was only by sheer chance that this pamphlet was preserved, for it was not dealt with in the schoolroom in antiquity. Moreover, reference to it is very scant indeed. There seem to be several reminiscences in the pseudo-Senecan *Octavia*, while a passage in Ausonius seems to presume a knowledge of the *Apocolocyntosis*.[11] But these are probably all the echoes of the little work that are more or less certain. Whether Julian used it in his *Caesares* is completely questionable.

Then in the ninth century there is a solitary quotation in the *Vita Walae* (*Life of Wala*) of Radbertus, and it is shortly after this that our direct tradition takes up. A miscellaneous codex from St. Gall dated to the tenth or eleventh century has turned out to be by far the best witness for the text.[12] Older, but far less valuable as far as the text is concerned, is the *Valenciennensis 190* from the tenth century (hardly from the ninth century) which was the *Codex Amandi* of Hadrianus Junius. Twelve other manuscripts from the Bibliothèque Nationale in Paris are known, some of them in fragmentary form. Relatively speaking, the best of these is probably the *Codex Parisinus 6630* of the thirteenth century. Finally, there exist four more Vatican manuscripts from the thirteenth through the fifteenth centuries, a hastily written *Marcianus* of the fourteenth century, and a *Guelferbytanus* of Italian provenience from the fifteenth century. Gronovius' *Harlemensis*, the codex of Lipsius, the *Weissenburgensis* of Rhenanus, the codex of Curio which contained several *lumina* (comments), as well as the forerunners from Germany of the hastily written, very extensively interpolated first edition of C. Sylvanus Germanicus (Walter?), published in Rome in 1513, apparently are lost or have not yet been reidentified.

All of these manuscripts go back, probably indirectly, to be sure, to a single carefully written ancient manuscript in capitals—not uncials —which transmitted the *Apocolocyntosis* separately from the corpus of Seneca's philosophical writings and separately from his tragedies. Probably this manuscript was already mutilated in the middle after chapter 7 through a mechanical error, but perhaps this did not happen until a copy was made in the early medieval period.

Early in the Middle Ages, the tradition seems to have divided in such a way that the *Sangallensis* has to be considered the more accurate witness to the text and all the others less so. This dichotomy can be detected, for example, in the way the Greek that is interspersed is handled or from other passages such as the end of 3.1. Undoubtedly there was a mixing of texts in the medieval period that must be taken into account, and this was subsequently intensified in Renaissance times.

The imitations that were the most important by far—and they might even be called congenial—were the *Somnium* (*Dream*) of Justus Lipsius, which he dedicated to Joseph Scaliger during his professorship at Leyden (1579-1590), and the satire of Petrus Cunaeus (Peter van der Kun) with the title *Sardi Venales* (*Sardinians For Sale*), which appeared at Leyden in 1612. Gottlieb Cortius published all three works together in a Leipzig edition in 1720. It is worth mentioning that J.J. Rousseau produced a very inaccurate translation of the *Apocolocyntosis* (Geneva, 1781). The first German translation comes from Ad. Grön-inger (Münster, 1798) and the best and most accurate is that of Otto Weinreich (Berlin, 1923).

In this work of Seneca, Menippean satire appears as a political pamphlet; this feature represents an innovation not to be found in Varro's Menippeans. It is entirely possible that other clever men had already gone in this direction before Seneca, and there is a distinct possibility that the μωρῶν ἐπανάστασις,[13] which was directed against Claudius and probably appeared anonymously, was a Menippean satire. Because of its fantastic form and its criticism which was ostensibly general, but actually topical, this was just the form for expressing opinion that might have appeared to be a suitable medium for the political pamphlet when freedom of speech was curtailed.

We may also with some caution connect the byform of the fictitious will with the Menippean in this function. Through this, the emperor or other personalities in high places could be unmasked with malice and spite. This was a form of abuse that Augustus had still refused to suppress.[14] The best-known pieces of this kind were the *codicilli* ("tablets" = will) of Aulus Fabricius Veiento which were publicly burned in the year 62 and for that reason were eagerly read.[15] But when the ban was lifted they sank into oblivion. But probably such writings are to be connected more closely with the invective literature than with Menippean satire.

Another byform related to the Menippean, though only in part, is the parody. Burlesque drinking rules—as they were listed, for instance, in the *Lex Tappula* mentioned earlier—had developed at an early time out of legal parody. But this kind of thing also lived on in later times. And so the elder Pliny was clearly aware of such *leges conviviales*,[16] and there is also a similar piece from a later period at the end of the *Querolus* (*Grumbler*) which we can still read today.[17] Now in Varro's Menippeans, for example, there is another fragment that closely follows the rules for a Roman will (543) but purposely transforms them into something comical. Parodies which made use of legal formulae were also circulating in imperial times as separate brochures in prose, but since here it was only a case of quite modest writings serving the purpose of amusement, our knowledge of them is both casual and very incomplete. Jerome expresses his concern in passing that the school-boys laugh heartily at the will of the little pig, Grunnius Corocotta, while the *Timaeus* of Cicero remains incomprehensible to them. This will has been preserved for us in a series of manuscripts and is an apparently late and not particularly humorous product in the form in which it has come down to us.[18] We might be bold and take it as a *specimen* (example) of a whole genre.

Again in quite a different way the form of the Menippean satire influenced the romance.

« IX »

Petronius' Novel

LARGE fragments of an extensive novel written in Latin have survived under the name of Petronius Arbiter. These are unique in the corpus of ancient literature so far as it has been preserved for us and are invaluable not only for the history of customs and culture, but also for matters of language, literary history, and art. The fragments describe with the greatest realism the adventures which Encolpius experiences in his travels, and a great variety of episodes are intertwined with the main plot. The date of composition of the work, its author, title, literary form, and other fundamental questions are subjects of lively dispute, so a few prefatory remarks about them might be in order.

First of all, the time of the action is established with certainty. Living conditions, mores, facts, and characters, as well as language, style, and meter, point quite clearly to the Julio-Claudian era, and in particular to the reign of Nero. So, for instance, the decline of easel-painting in favor of wall-painting is deplored, as is the decay of eloquence. The freedman class is to the forefront; these people have succeeded in acquiring substantial wealth and as a result also have leading roles to play in society. In the matter of details, there is mention, for example, of Mamercus Aemilius Scaurus (77.5), who is well known from the collection of the elder Seneca. The tragic actor Apelles (64.4) enjoyed great popularity in the time of Caligula, and the songs of Menecrates (73.3) or the story of the unbreakable glass (51.1) also point to the same time. The lengthy verse interlude (119–24) with its introduction (118) should be a counterpart to Lucan's epic on the civil war, and it leads right into the contemporary debate on the subject. Knowledge of the first three books of the *Pharsalia* is certainly assumed, though Lucan himself is not named. He probably should be thought of, then, as still being alive, and this would point to the period between 60 and 65 after

Christ. Furthermore, there are references to the edict of Claudius *De flatibus* (*On Breaking Wind*), allusions to remarks of Seneca the philosopher, and the like. On the other hand, it is not absolutely certain whether the poem on the *Troiae halosis* (89: The Capture of Troy) is aimed at the corresponding piece by Nero, just as the references to Christianity which some people want to find are not certainly demonstrable.

In this way a firm *terminus post quem* for the time of composition of the work has been determined. As far as a *terminus ante quem* is concerned, after the references in Martial and Juvenal have turned out to be inconclusive, the earliest citations are those by the metrician Terentianus Maurus in the third century after Christ. B.G. Niebuhr wanted to put the novel in this late period, in the reign of Severus Alexander, but his reasoning did not stand up to criticism. Most recently U. Paoli has argued for the idea that the work is late by pointing above all to the fact that *manumissio per mensam* is presupposed at one point (70–71).[1] This was the custom that was originally Greek of freeing slaves by inviting them to the table of the master, and it cannot be shown as existing among the Romans before the third century. But scholars saw right away that the passage did not at all presuppose *manumissio per mensam* and did not even refer to it. Therefore Paoli later formulated his opinion more carefully and according to the new version, the novel originated after the time of Martial since it contained imitations and even misinterpretations of Martial's text.[2] There was nothing very persuasive about this formulation of the argument either.[3] It is simply not possible to assign the work to the period of literary decline, and, what is more, it is still completely free from any trace of an archaizing tendency. And so it is perhaps best not to move the time of composition too far from the time of the fictitious action, and the usual dating which assigns the work to the Neronian period seems the most plausible. The long initial silence of the indirect tradition proves nothing to the contrary, for in ancient times the novel was not considered to be a legitimate literary genre that was worthy of mention. It is a well-known fact that the fables of Phaedrus also remained unknown for centuries for similar reasons of stylistic theory. In addition, Petronius' work, because of a subject matter that was often extremely risqué, was completely unsuitable for school instruction, and this is another reason for expecting only infrequent citations. The Roman elegiac poets—Propertius, for example, or Ovid in his *Amores*—were treated in a very shabby way by the ancient grammarians for this same reason.

Now we come to the question of the author's personality. In both the direct and indirect tradition he is called Petronius or Arbiter or Petronius Arbiter. There can be no doubt at all about the name, though a first name is missing. Now it is by no means absolutely certain, but it is entirely likely that the author of the novel is to be identified with Nero's well-known *elegantiae arbiter* (arbiter of elegance), Titus Petronius (possibly Gaius, but hardly Publius), whom Tacitus considered as deserving a character sketch of his own.[4] The historian portrays him as a master at enjoying life in a very merry and refined way, but also as a man who was quite equal to serious undertakings when he wanted to be, as his proconsulate in Bithynia showed, and who played an important role in Nero's most intimate circle as a master of libertinism. The nickname may have been coined with reference to his cognomen *Arbiter*. Having excited the envy of Tigellinus because of the influence he was exerting on Nero, Petronius was slandered and fell into disfavor, and in the year 66 after Christ he departed life voluntarily. Tacitus graphically describes his last hours as he spent them eating and composing wanton verses, averse as he was to any kind of serious discussion. At the end he sent a list (*codicilli*) of Nero's sexual lapses to the emperor, mentioning by name his male and female partners.

The author of our novel certainly reveals himself to be one of the most versatile artists in the Latin language and a man of the world with a complete inner freedom and a surpassing charm and sense of irony. He is characterized by an ever-ready boldness, a brightness, a flippant, easygoing manner and outlook, an inexhaustible flow of ideas, a thorough understanding of men, and the kind of nonchalance which leaves the impression almost of a naïveté—a characteristic to which Tacitus gives special emphasis in his portrait of Nero's *elegantiae arbiter*. And so far as outlook and disposition are concerned, an identification of the historian's easygoing man of the world with the author of the *Satyricon* is extremely likely. Certainly the *codicilli* mentioned by Tacitus are not to be identified with our novel, for they were a tabulated list of sins which has naturally been lost.

Attempts have been made to draw strange conclusions about the origin of Petronius' work from the silence of Tacitus, Quintilian, and other writers regarding it. So it has been theorized that we are dealing with a youthful work or with a work that made its appearance either posthumously, incomplete, anonymously, or outside of Rome, perhaps in Massilia, or possibly that it is a piece of popular fiction. None of these conjectures has any plausible basis at all; nothing is known about the way in which the work originated.

The manuscript tradition gives the following possibilities as a title: *Petronii Arbitri satiricon* (*The Satiricon of Petronius Arbiter*), *Petronii Arbitri satirarum liber* and *Petronii Arbitri satyri fragmenta* (*The Book of Satires of Petronius Arbiter* and *The Fragments of the Satire of Petronius Arbiter*), and also *Petronii Arbitri Affranii satirici liber* (*The Satire of Petronius Arbiter in the Manner of Afranius*). Buecheler called the work *Saturae* (*Satires*). Others explained the tradition as σατυρικόν (*Satyric* [*Piece*]) or σατυρικῶν with *libri* understood ([*Books*] *of Things Connected with Satyrs*), and this interpretation is probably the correct one. W. Kroll in his article in Pauly-Wissowa (37, 1202–03), on the other hand, emphasizes that a title *Satiricon* was also entirely possible at this time. This could be a hybrid formation in which the Latin word *satura* had blended with the Greek word σατυρικόν to indicate a ribald, sarcastic composition.[5] The reason for mentioning Afranius and the significance of this are not really clear. Perhaps the name is meant to underline the indecency of the work, especially the παιδικὸς ἔρως (love for a boy), as in the Persius tradition the name of Lucilius appears now and then near the title as a generic designation.

The leading character of the *Satyricon* is a young, intelligent, happy-go-lucky fellow named Encolpius who goes through life without any inhibitions. By force of circumstances and often through his own doing, he finds himself again and again in situations which seem grotesque in their apparent insolubility. But again and again he succeeds in making his way through the world at the expense of other people, completely without any moral qualms. Attempts have been made to find in him a self-portrait of Petronius—if this is the case, then the question of the author's identity resolves itself—but the reasons given are insufficient. It is Encolpius, then, who reports his experiences in a most amusing way, and they are experiences which bring him in contact with an unending parade of people from the Italian middle and lower classes. Even the secondary characters are sketched in their actions and speech with extreme liveliness and freshness. Encolpius likes to ally himself with a person who has the same interests he does—first the potent Ascyltos and later the old crafty poet Eumolpus. His escort is the handsome Giton, with whom he carries on a love affair.

The scene of the action is first of all an *urbs Graeca* ("Greek city"),[6] which is called a *colonia* (colony) several times and is situated near the sea. It is possible to imagine the colony as being in Campania, but thus far no one has succeeded in making a positive identification. The arguments for Naples, Cumae, Misenum, Puteoli, or some place else are not conclusive. But perhaps we should not look for any particular city; it may have been Petronius' intention only to create the milieu of a south Italian country town in a general way, just as later in the narrative it is not the historical Croton that is portrayed.

Our fragments begin with a conversation between Encolpius and Agamemnon, one of the fashionable rhetoricians of the time, concerning the reasons for the current decline of eloquence, a theme that is especially familiar to us from Tacitus' treatment of it. Encolpius finally manages to break away and happens into a house of pleasure as he searches for his companion. We learn of the jealousy of Encolpius and Ascyltos over Giton which even leads to a decision on their part to go their separate ways. A whole array of very lively individual scenes are attached to the main framework of the action—the troop of sarcastic *scholastici* (students), the old woman who leads Encolpius unawares into the bordello, the action there, and so on.

Whether the section which follows (12–26.6) has been transmitted in its proper place seems uncertain. It has been suggested, for instance, that it belongs before our first chapter, and such disturbance of the tradition would not be out of the question as far as Petronius is concerned.[7] There are really two scenes here which are closely related. The first is a transaction in the market between Encolpius and Ascyltos on the one hand and a farmer and a woman who is muffled up on the other; it is accompanied by a very spirited give and take—material for a complete mime (12–15). In the chapters which follow (16–26.6) it turns out that the muffled woman is Quartilla, the priestess of Priapus, whom Encolpius and Ascyltos disturbed at the sacrifice to Priapus. The reconciliation is celebrated with a wild orgy.

Next comes the Banquet of Trimalchio (26.7–78) which is the best known episode and the part of the whole work that is developed in the greatest detail. Trimalchio, whose name already points to his arrival from the east, is portrayed as a good-natured, unbelievably tasteless, snobbish upstart who gives a banquet. Besides Encolpius, Ascyltos, Giton, and the rhetorician Agamemnon, his guests are different friends who, like him, are freedmen. Each one of them is sketched as a separate character. Among others, there is the somewhat sentimental Seleucus, the old-fashioned, narrow-minded Ganymedes, the zealous Echion, the passionate Hermeros, as well as Niceros, who is partial to gruesome stories, Plocamus with his educated, artistic talent, and finally Habinnas with his wife Scintilla, who has become wealthy through contracting for stone work. Apart from the extremely amusing action in which one grotesque and comic incident follows closely on the other, the *Cena* (Banquet) is by far the most important source for popular and vulgar Latin as it was spoken by the inhabitants of southern Italy in the time of the Claudian emperors.

Encolpius and Ascyltos dissolve their association after this, according to plan (79–99). Giton unexpectedly joins Ascyltos, while Encolpius, the abandoned lover, indulges in a series of emotional outbursts. He meets the old poet Eumolpus in an art gallery and discusses education and the fine arts with him. Then Eumolpus recites a poem on the fall of Troy for which his listeners want to stone him (89). Encolpius then finds his Giton again, Ascyltos is duped, and Encolpius, Eumolpus, and Giton board a ship and escape. This sequence of scenes is also governed by a brisk change of tempo. The struggle between Encolpius and Eumolpus over Giton is played quickly, as are the brawl that accompanies this (93–95) and the duping of Ascyltos. Balancing these are scenes that serve as pauses in the action—the obscene story of the old lecher Eumolpus, for example, that is inserted (85–87), and also the discussion of art (88) and the description of the picture (89).

When they are at sea it turns out (100–15) that the captain of the ship is Lichas from Tarentum, and he has the wealthy Tryphaena accompanying him, both of whom have been the victims of a mean trick played on them by Encolpius and Giton at some time or other. So they must not be recognized. After an extremely amusing consultation, it is finally decided that Eumolpus will pass them off as his slaves. He has their heads shaved and paints terrible inscriptions on them to mark them as real rogues. But the deception is discovered and a hand-to-hand fight ensues which ends, however, with a general reconciliation.

In the happy carouse that follows Eumolpus tells the story of the widow of Ephesus (110–12), the Song of Songs of woman's fickleness and a short story which has been retold more than once in the modern literatures in the tradition of Petronius. A storm at sea puts an end to the celebration. Encolpius and Giton save themselves and they also find Eumolpus again in the wreckage of the ship. Tryphaena is put in a lifeboat and disappears from the action of the novel, while Lichas dies.

The survivors decide to wander into nearby Croton and to enjoy their life by swindling people (116–41). Eumolpus is to play an enormously rich old man with a slight cough and in this way lead on the legacy hunters. Encolpius and Giton play his slaves. The plan is a great success and all three live there in magnificent comfort. The poem of Eumolpus on the civil war (118–24) provides a long pause in the action. This was seriously intended as a counterpart to Lucan's epic and was written in hexameters that were highly polished and in the classical style. The force of its parody came only from the frame in which it appears. The love story of Encolpius and the beautiful Circe who involves him in various adventures provides brisk action.

This is the general content of the fragments that have been preserved. From what point of view they were excerpted from the complete work is not at all clear. Here and there a recognizable *ratio* (rationale) seems to have been at work, while in other places the impression of a mechanical deterioration of the text is very strong. Our collection of fragments may in the final analysis go back to an extract from the original which was made toward the end of antiquity—perhaps during the time when the Vandals were ruling in north Africa?—and then in the next period suffered further mechanically, as did other works transmitted like this.

Besides the fragments that have been mentioned, several rather short and very short fragments of the work have come down to us mainly from the grammatical tradition, many of which need fresh scrutiny. Then we also have a series of individual poems, though Petronius' authorship for all of them is by no means certain. An accurate interpretation with the purpose of determining the authenticity and the place of the poems in the general framework of the novel is necessary and would be profitable. The problem of the so-called Petronian glosses should be considered as solved.

The original length of the whole work cannot be determined with any certainty, since there are no comparable works of the same literary type. According to the evidence of the *Codex Traguriensis* (see below), the large fragments which have been preserved come from the fifteenth and sixteenth books. Accordingly, the original length of the whole thing would have to be estimated at about twenty books. Moreover, the (extended) quotation of Fulgentius from the twentieth chapter might also suggest a lengthy work. E. Paratore (see below) has taken a contrary stance and has argued for a shorter length for the original— approximately six books. According to this line of reasoning, a good half of the novel would be preserved. This could be possible, but the tradition militates against it and so do several other factors. The parts that have come down to us contain references to things that precede and follow them so that we are forced to the conclusion that in Petronius there are no elements of the plot and no themes that are separate and disconnected.

If the references or the thematic foreshadowings which are not completed because of the fragmentary state of preservation are looked at systematically, then the supposition of a very considerable size for the original seems well founded. Immediately before the parts that have come down to us a number of episodes have been lost— the adventure with Quartilla, the story of the gold pieces being sewn in the coat, the loss of the coat, and others as well. Moreover, the description of Encolpius' love affair with Tryphaena, the story of the adultery with Lichas and the ridicule of him, the role of Giton in this, and other episodes no longer exist. Similarly the reader must already be familiar with the *vestis divina* ("divine robe") and the *sistrum* ("rattle") that are mentioned during the shipwreck scene (114.5). And the references to an earthquake, a voyage, an indictment, a conviction, a sojourn with gladiators, a presumed murder (out of jealousy?), and many other things suggest a rich and exciting sequence of events for the original plot. In addition, there are different people mentioned by name who played a part at some point or other in the work. And above all we can no longer know how Petronius introduced the leitmotiv of the novel, the *gravis ira Priapi* (133.3, 139.2: "the dread anger of Priapus"), which pursues Encolpius, like a reincarnated Odysseus, over the earth. The suggestion of Cichorius that Encolpius at some point, perhaps at the beginning of the novel and possibly in Massilia, disguised himself as the god Priapus and carried out a trick in this role is attractive but not completely free from doubt.[8] On the other hand, the rescue of Tryphaena from the shipwreck is a sure indication that she was meant to appear again in a later part of the work. Perhaps Ascyltos too appeared again, and at the end an appeasing of the angry Priapus might certainly be expected.

Just as a great array of episodes and events may be made out, so there can be no doubt that the scenery also changed often. Even the pieces that have been preserved take place in two different locations. The voyage mentiond at 81.3 makes it possible to imagine at least one other earlier city. It is conceivable that a part of the action took place in Massilia. Fragment 4 suggests this, while fragment 1 is not conclusive. These scenes would in this case have stood most logically at the beginning of the novel. It is clearly not possible to show that Encolpius was later also driven off course to Egypt. Petronius' purpose in creating this variety of settings was probably not to make each new city a typical representative of a new vice, as Reitzenstein suggested.

The reconstruction of the plot along the lines that have been briefly indicated here is a worthwhile exercise. But in spite of this our loss is irreparable, for in Petronius the "how" is more important by far than the "what." Still, the incidents that have been pointed out here suggest a significant range for the original work, especially if we take into account the great breadth of presentation which in all its liveliness and its wealth of ideas characterizes the work. Indeed, the plot as we have glanced at it is very rich in pauses, in occasional short stories, declamations, discourses and discussions of rather general content, poems, and so on. The whole *Cena Trimalchionis* (Banquet of Trimalchio) would really be superfluous as far as the main action is concerned.

The question of the original length of this literary piece would best be answered if it could be successfully and convincingly assigned to a particular genre of literature. But as far as things go—or, for that matter, went—it stands all by itself among the literary monuments from antiquity that have come down to us. Every direct and convincing parallel that could provide information about the literary genre is lost, so that we have to look to the ancients first for their opinion. Ancient aesthetic tradition on the one hand makes mention of Petronius in connection with the Latin satirists.[9] This involves their common pleasure in insult and ridicule, not literary form. The grouping of Petronius with Martial that is found in Marius Mercator[10] points to the obscenity of the two of them and therefore to an aspect of content. From the literary-historical point of view, then, the mention by Macrobius remains the most important reference we have. Here Petronius is named with Apuleius after new comedy as being literary fiction (*comoediae ... vel argumenta fictis casibus amatorum referta, quibus vel multum se Arbiter exercuit vel Apuleium nonnumquam lusisse miramur* = "comedies . . . or plots filled with fictional escapades of lovers in which Arbiter indulged quite a lot and with which even Apuleius amused himself from time to time, much to our wonder").[11] Now it cannot be denied that some relationship exists between Petronius' books and the *Metamorphoses* of Apuleius as far as literary form is concerned. Both pursue the same purpose of instructing the reader and at the same time amusing him; both describe—and, what is more, they do it in the first person—adventures which show a preference for the pungent; both create the illusion of extreme realism. And the connection in literary form can also be shown in particulars, as in the great emphasis on direct speech, the sprinkling in of short stories, the consideration of popular superstition, and many other similar things.

Accordingly, Petronius' work would seem to be somehow connected with the tradition of the literary romance. But with what type is Petronius connected and how is the connection to be shown in matters of detail? Only a tiny and random sample from ancient romance literature has been preserved or is otherwise known. We can put together, for example, a tolerable picture of the novel of love and emotion and of several forms of the historical romance. There are also those involving biography, fantasy, and travel. But we know that there were other forms besides, and very likely these already existed in the time of Petronius, for the Hellenistic romance is not a product of the so-called Second Sophistic.

E. Rohde, to the contrary, denied any connection between Petronius and the Hellenistic romance and expressed the belief that the work was to be explained purely from Latin literature.[12] Certainly the title, no matter what form we may imagine it to have taken, leaves the impression of a connection with Roman satire, and Lydus, too, points to this.[13] The influence of the Varronian Menippeans seems to be evident in the insertion of carefully composed pieces of poetry of many different kinds into the underlying prose narrative. And it is not just coincidence that later—in Fulgentius, for instance, who knew Petronius well—the personified *Satira* who appears there is closely related to *Petulantia* (Wantonness). But it is quite impossible to derive Petronius' work from Menippean satire exclusively. The novel looks like a long continuous narrative; it is without any philosophical or moral purpose. And there are more basic differences of the same kind. In form, then, Petronius' work can and probably must be connected with Menippean satire, although even in the Hellenistic romance the narrative could probably now and then change to verse even when it was not in direct speech. We see this, for example, in the Alexander romance, in the *Historia Apollonii* (*History of Apollonius*), and a predecessor of Chariton perhaps did this. But otherwise Petronius' connection with the Greek novel is probably much closer than his connection with the Menippean tradition.

In a well-known article, R. Heinze developed the view that Petronius' books represented a single lengthy parody of the romantic love novel of Hellenistic times.[14] Here the pair of lovers are Encolpius and

Giton, each of them in himself a real rogue, who experience adventures, though they are adventures quite different from those in the Greek love romance. Here they involve eccentric litterateurs, priestesses of Priapus, beautiful women who are for sale, people like Trimalchio, and a similar crowd. In Petronius, coarse, spur-of-the-moment sensuality replaces true, ideal love, and lofty concepts of fidelity are of little value. Giton belongs at one time to this person at another to that person, and his lover Encolpius has his own experiences. Moreover, it is not the powerful god Eros, but Priapus who holds sway over everything. It seems to be a correct conclusion of Heinze that with all this Petronius intended and created a parody of the love romance. The latter was meant to be taken seriously and, according to our notions of it, was extremely high-flown, while parody, ridicule, and raillery extending even to details are the mainspring of Petronius' work. Again and again what is ideal is undermined and made laughable by a realism that is both drastic and down-to-earth. But it will not do to explain Petronius' novel from this source alone. It is certainly very probable that in Nero's time there already existed a realistic-comic adventure romance and a satiric romance containing parody. And it is quite likely that even before Petronius' time a hybridization of the types had taken place. Heinze's conclusions might be expanded in this direction. When it is viewed as a whole, then, Petronius' work is fed from several sources, and the problem of finding a literary prototype cannot be solved with a simple "either-or" answer.

Examination of individual works confirms this impression of a complexity of form as far as both expression and composition are concerned. For example, it is quite certain that Petronius was familiar with the pungent and in part coarsely realistic novel writing of the Greeks as the form perhaps appeared in the Milesian tales of Aristides. Sisenna had brought this to Rome, and it was well known how far Petronius let himself be influenced by him. The Milesian tales were undoubtedly a collection of short stories, and in the story Eumolpus tells about his relations with a boy (85–87), Petronius may be giving an idea of the make-up of the individual tale. Secondly, it has been possible to show the probable influence of the Hellenistic miracle tale on Petronius' novel. But Petronius adapted this too for his own purposes, for the real concerns of the miracle tale—the religious intention and the description of the purification of the hero—are completely missing from Petronius. The motifs in his novel are at best part of the satiric purposes. Thirdly, the influence of the mime is clearly present in matters of theme and individual portraits and was already felt by antiquity. But the mime too should not for this reason be considered the main source of the novel. And besides, other preponderantly popular literature has also left its clear impression on Petronius—the diatribe, the Cynic symposium literature, and, last but not least, the full complement of pungent anonymous writings that were in circulation.

And so the question of which literary form Petronius' work is to be associated with is not completely answered. It seems to follow, however, that it is not to be taken as coming from any one particular literary form, but that Petronius undertook a mixing of forms for purposes of parody and satire. New discoveries, which might perhaps be anticipated, will probably only confirm the fact that through Petronius, the great individualist, the available literary forms underwent quite basic changes both as a result of the Roman's intention to strengthen his power of expression and to enrich his repertory, as well as from the correct realization that in this kind of fiction everything depends on what the author makes of his material. And here is where Petronius' incomparable freedom and individuality come into play. Whether he, as Stubbe (see below) comments, ". . . undertook the crossing of types with the purpose of raising a popular and non-literary genus to the level of literary art by adding elements from a type recognized as being literary," may remain open here. This formulation probably simplifies the true situation to some extent, but does point the right way. In attempting to cope with the question of literary models, Petronius' extreme independence should not be forgotten.

At first it was the tone, the carelessly comic charm of the work and the realistic presentation of manners and morals, that brought admiration for Petronius, especially among the French Epicureans of the seventeenth century. It was not until much later that an attempt was made to study his style and language more closely. The conversations of the freedmen at the *Cena* were the focal point here. Then followed H. Stubbe's splendid interpretations of the long passages of poetry, including Petronius' poetic program.[15] Stylistic consideration of the rest of the long fragments is not yet complete and examination of those that have come down separately has still hardly begun. The general result that has emerged is that Petronius must be considered one of the "finest and most confident artists in the Latin language" (Löfstedt) who strove to the utmost to give each event and each mood its appropriate form (Haffter).

By a very rough analysis two levels of language may be detected in the prose parts—that belonging to the educated and that of the un-educated.[16] Then again within these two categories there are numerous gradations and shadings, but the basis is the educated speech of silver Latin with all of its nuances and refinements. Encolpius himself, who is the narrator, makes particular use of it, and it can be heard besides in the conversations he reports and from the mouths of Ascyltos, Agamemnon, Eumolpus, Giton, Lichas, Tryphaena, the proud maid (126.1–7) who even displays clause rhythm as she speaks, and from others as well. This language is capable of the greatest flexibility and can be adapted to the situation at the moment. And so there exists an important stylistic difference between the love lament with its false pathos (81), the serious discussion of the decay of eloquence with its explicit dependence on Cicero (1–5), a switch from indirect to direct speech (e.g., 99.2–3), a polite request (e.g., 20.1), the angry word (90.3–4), or an insulting speech which the partner on his side immediately outdoes (e.g., 9.6–10.2). Not only in these contexts, but also throughout his novel, Petronius is fully aware of how to use language to characterize his different personalities in widely varying situations.

The parts of the work that are in popular Latin stand on a different level from this. Here it is the language of the freedmen at the *Cena* that comes into question, for Quartilla, the priestess of Priapus, whom Petronius has speak in a pleasant conversational tone at one point (17) and then in a thoroughly informal way when she is in a good mood later (24–25), uses correct language on the whole. But the conversations between freedmen are a rich and quite priceless source of common speech for us—really a *unicum* (one of a kind) in all of Latin literature before the dominance of vulgar Latin in the late centuries. For as far as we can see, no other Latin author, with perhaps the exception of Novius, dared to use this level of language for delineating the character of individuals and a particular milieu. Here forms and constructions are encountered in rich profusion which, as collateral evidence like the graffiti at Pompeii or the curse tablets show, reflect with complete realism—though certainly in a stylized selectivity—the vulgar speech of everyday life and lead directly to the romance languages. Accordingly, the problems presented by vulgar Latin were thoroughly and accurately investigated from the philological point of view.

Then an attempt was made to interpret the language of the freedman class from the cultural and literary-historical side as well. But the effort to find a practical illustration here of contemporary lessons about barbarisms in language with satiric point seems to have found just about as little acceptance as the idea that Petronius characterized his speakers as original *Graeculi* (Greeklings) with the intention of presenting them to the Romans along with their native shortcomings. But what Petronius offers us is a bit of small-town life in an account that is laced with humor, charm, and perspicuity; his perspective is that of the tasteful, refined, ironic city-dweller. As he did this, he knew how to put together not only what was typical of the milieu but also the individual characteristics of the people themselves by using their manners and especially their speech. Gustav Meyer has best described how the individual personality comes through in this situation:

> The speakers are not really differentiated from one another in a formal way at all. Rather, their personalities are delineated primarily through the content and the overall structure of their speeches. *How* they put forward their thoughts, *how* they explain and narrate (a slower or a faster tempo, short sentences, anacoluthon, completely different ways of beginning sentences, a sudden divergence of thought, and so on)— watching for this kind of thing is more productive than considering formalities.[17]

And so interpretation should begin not with the word and word-form and not with the separate types of vulgar expression, but actually with the sentence and the tone of the whole speech.

With this in mind, the second invective of Hermeros (58.2–14) might be contrasted with the account of the werewolf which Niceros narrates (61.6–62.14). Words, forms, and turns of expression from vulgar speech are found in both, and yet the two passages leave completely different impressions. And the reason is that the mixing of the vulgar elements and the tempo of the speaking are quite different in the one passage from what they are in the other. This in turn serves to delineate two completely different personalities to such a degree that each of them even has his own favorite turns of phrase. Hermeros, for example, wants to play a special trump, so he summarizes using the words *ad summam* (58.8; earlier in 57.3, 57.9: "in summary"). His standard word for money is not *nummus* ("five cents") but *dupondium* (58.4, 58.5, 58.13: "a nickel"), and when he curses he follows a specific pattern (58.2, 58.5, 58.7). Or else he has his own set phrases with which Ascyltos gets just what he deserves (58.2, 58.3). It is also possible to point to his preference for the word *bellus* from vulgar speech (58.12, 58.13; earlier in 57.3), for the exclamation *mehercules,* and so on.

At the same time, Hermeros' preference for coining words on occasion is worth noting, as is his partiality for invective phrases of two words like *crucis offla* and *corvorum cibaria* (58.2: "gallows bird," "crowfodder"), for offhand and gratuitous insults in a subordinate clause (58.10; cf. 57.3, 57.10), and for the frequent insertion of self-cursing (58.3, 58.5, 58.12; cf. 57.2, 57.6). The introductions to his sentences are very monotonous (58.2; cf. 57.2, 57.7, 57.8, 57.9); if the thought breaks off, he always has an adage ready (58.3, 58.12; cf. 57.3, 57.5, 57.8); he is fond of extravagant comparisons. The whole thing is a specimen of affected speech without any logical development. Petronius wants to present a completely uneducated man here as he blusters along, and his purpose is to amuse his reader.

The speech of Niceros (61.6–62.14) is also rich in vulgar elements, but the choice, distribution, and mixing are completely different. He too has fixed and favorite turns of speech, so that clothes for him are always only *vestimenta* (62.5, 62.8, 62.12); *venire* means "go" as well as "come" (62.2, 62.4, 62.9, 62.12, 62.13); he loves the circumlocution with *coepi* and even *coeperam* (62.4, 62.7, 62.11: "I begin," "I began"); he likes particles and treasures a superfluity of pronouns (62.2, 62.4, 62.5, 62.6, 62.8 [four times], 62.9). On the other hand, there are very few shorthand expressions in what he says and no anacoluthons at all. All of the foregoing is meant to indicate the direction only, and a broad and fruitful field is still open here for a more penetrating interpretation of style.

Passages of verse are put together differently again and are quite unlike one another. Hexameters, trimeters, distichs (among them a very strange, vulgar form in 34.10 comprising two hexameters and a pentameter), senarii, limping iambics, anacreontics, hendecasyllables, and sotadeans have been preserved. It is entirely possible that Varro's Menippeans had an influence on this profusion of meters. Stubbe gives the best introduction in his book which has already been mentioned.

Citations from Petronius and references to him are few and far between in ancient literature. Nevertheless, knowledge of his work—and certainly in more complete form than we have it now—can be traced from the third century on. But even then the echoes are weak. Without doubt Fulgentius read Petronius toward the end of antiquity and a passage (3.2) was at one point cited by an Ostrogoth scholar. But even in the glossaries the work receives little attention. By comparison there seems to have been greater interest at the end of antiquity in the poetic parts. Apparently only a single manuscript of excerpts survived into the Middle Ages, and this was damaged mechanically in the bargain. But even its influence was slight, for in medieval times Petronius belonged among the rarities of literature.

A knowledge of the novel can be shown for the period from the ninth century on. There are several abridgements of Petronius in anthologies that go back to the eleventh or twelfth century,[18] while in the twelfth century John of Salisbury read it and in the thirteenth century, Vincent of Beauvais. But in no case is there any evidence of a more comprehensive knowledge than that conveyed to us by the extant manuscripts containing the excerpts. We have several copies of these which come from the tenth through the fifteenth centuries, and they divide into three classes: the short excerpts, the more extensive excerpts, and the excerpts together with the *Cena*. To the first group belongs a series of manuscripts among which is the oldest Petronius manuscript that has been preserved—the *Codex Bernensis B* from the tenth or eleventh century. This group corresponds to the older vulgate (O).

The second class is represented by the *Leidensis L*, the very accurate copy which Joseph Scaliger had produced, perhaps from a manuscript of Cuiacius which is now lost. It has considerably more to offer at times than the older vulgate, especially in the prose parts of the work. The poem that appears at 82.5 has been transmitted out of place. This same tradition influenced the editions of Tornaesius and Pithou (see below).

The third group is represented by the *Traguriensis* (now *Parisinus 7989*) which was found about 1650 by Marinus Statilius at Trau in Dalmatia. This is the only manuscript that contains the *Cena Trimalchionis* along with the other fragments of the first class mentioned above. This manuscript was perhaps written for Poggio Bracciolini in the year 1423, apparently after the text of the *Cena* appeared in England.[19] The *Cena* was first published in 1664 (simultaneously in Padua at Frambotti and in Paris by Jac. Mentel). The older editions of Petronius, however, are not for this reason dispensable as far as the text critic is concerned, since they contain in part traces of an independent tradition. From among these special mention should be made of the editions of Jo. Tornaesius (Leiden, 1575), Cl. Binetus (Poitiers, 1579; with the epigrams), J. Dousa (Leiden, 1585), and P. Pithou (Paris, 1587). M. Hadrianides produced the first complete edition (Amsterdam, 1669). Of the later editions the great collection of P. Burmann might be mentioned *honoris causa* (first Utrecht, 1709; then Amsterdam, 1743 with valuable remarks by N. Heinsius). The additions which F. Nodot (Rotterdam, 1692; Paris, 1693) published, allegedly on the basis of the discovery of a manuscript, are forgeries, as Leibniz and Bentley recognized immediately, and the same is true of the complete Petronius of Lallemandus (Paris, 1800) which was only a half-serious effort.

The great authoritative edition of Franz Buecheler which appeared in 1862 represented the most important achievement for Petronian studies. It serves as the basis for all later editions and even today is still indispensable, although it certainly is in urgent need of revision. Among the smaller editions only those of Buecheler-Heraeus (6 ed., Berlin, 1922), A. Ernout (Paris, 1922, 1931; with their own collations; 3 ed., 1950), and E.T. Sage and B. Gilleland (2 ed., New York, 1969) might be recommended here. The edition of E. Paratore (Florence, 1933) makes larger claims with its introduction and very extensive commentary which is primarily aesthetic. For the *Cena* L. Friedlaender's edition with commentary and translation (2 ed., Leipzig, 1906) is to be included here, although in a number of important respects it has been superseded. Also worth mentioning are the special editions of W. Heraeus (2 ed., Heidelberg, 1923) and W.B. Sedgwick (2 ed., Oxford, 1950). For the poetic insertions reference might be made to H. Stubbe's studies in his book mentioned earlier.[20] The *Lexicon Petronianum* of J. Segebade and E. Lommatsch (Leipzig, 1898), moreover, is an indispensable tool. On the history of the discovery of Petronius and the bibliography on it. A. Rini is very informative.[21] A. Collignon is also well worth reading.[22] Among translations into German that of W. Heinse (first at Rome, 1773) was epoch-making. That of Ludwig Gurlitt (Berlin, 1924) is philologically more accurate and in many parts is downright congenial. That of Carl Hoffman (Heimeran, Munich, 1937) matches this one. W. Kroll's Petronius article in Pauly-Wissowa (37, 1201–14) deserves special mention.[23]

Petronius' novel shows a certain connection with Menippean satire in a formal way only. If the Alexander romance is left aside, the prosimetric feature recurs in the *Historia Apollonii regis Tyri* (*The History of Apollonius, King of Tyre*), a work of pure fiction that in many respects is dependent on the *Metamorphoses* of Apuleius. Still later the Menippean had a further influence on the style and form of Martianus Capella's *Marriage of Mercury with Philology*, as well as on the *Mitologiae* (*Tales from Mythology*) of Fulgentius. Both authors are clearly aware of the connection of their works with Menippean satire, though in the final analysis, of course, these represented something completely different. Then at the very end of antiquity there is the *Consolatio philosophiae* (*The Consolation of Philosophy*) of Boethius from the year 523/4 which also still makes use of elements of the Menippean form.

After this survey of Menippean satire, the subsequent history of poetic satire should be considered. And this becomes clearly discernible again with the poems of Persius in the time of Nero.

« X »

Aules Persius Flaccus

AULES Persius Flaccus was born on December 4, 34 after Christ at Volaterrae (modern Volterra) in the northwest part of Etruria. He was the son of respected and very wealthy parents of equestrian rank. The family, which clearly made much of the Etruscan tradition in its history, was related directly and by marriage to the Roman aristocracy. When he was about six years old, Persius lost his father, and soon after this his mother, Fulvia Sisennia, was remarried to a Roman knight whose name was Fusius. But she lost him too a few years later.

Persius received his first instruction in his hometown until he was about twelve years old and then he was sent to Rome where two leading men were selected as his teachers—the eminent grammarian, Remmius Palaemon, who is also known to have been Quintilian's teacher and whose very human habits were certainly the subject of lively and outspoken controversy, and the rhetorician, Verginius Flavus, whom Quintilian also quotes several times in his handbook of rhetoric as an authority in his field. Persius' first efforts at poetry fall in this early period. While still a boy he attempted a *praetexta*, that is a Roman tragedy, the title of which is indeed lost (perhaps *Vescia* or *Decius*). Besides this he had written a poem in one book, perhaps a travel book, and finally a few verses on the elder Arria. All of these youthful pieces were destroyed at the poet's death by his mother on the advice of Lucius Annaeus Cornutus.

Cornutus was a native of north Africa and perhaps a freedman of Annaeus Mela, the father of the poet Lucan. Persius came to know him at the age of sixteen, and Cornutus exerted a profound influence on the course of the young poet's life. In their daily association he filled the youth with an enthusiasm for the Stoic reform of life, and Persius himself, deeply moved by the intense experience, has briefly described it (5.41–51). A short work written by Cornutus in Greek

on the allegorical meaning of the old myths of the gods has been preserved and provides just a faint glimmer of this important personality.
A circle of students and friends with the same interests gathered
around the philosopher, who apparently represented a considerable intellectual power in Rome, for about the year 65 he had to go into exile
at the order of Nero.

In this exclusive circle of discriminating men devoted to matters
of the intellect, friendships were struck without any regard for rank
or origin. Here Persius became acquainted with the young poet Lucan
who died early, but he also came to know Claudius Agaturrinus—the
conjecture Agathinus seems doubtful—a doctor from Sparta, and
Petronius Aristocrates from Magnesia, both of whom were mature
men who undertook to live a practical life according to the Stoic ideal.
Ties ran from Cornutus to the circle of Caesius Bassus, poet and
theorist, who at that time would have been almost sixty years old and
who took care of Persius as a fatherly friend. There the young poet
may also have become acquainted with Calpurnius Statura who is
otherwise unknown. He did not get to know Seneca until later, but
no close connection resulted mainly because Persius could not reconcile
himself to Seneca's manner.

His formative years show Persius occupied with the subjects he
preferred—rhetoric, philosophy, and poetry. There is no indication in
the sources that he prepared himself in any way for a government position or one of the other recognized occupations in Rome. As far as
material things went, he was completely independent and lived for his
self-education alone. This view is confirmed by the information that
at his death he had a library of no fewer than 700 volumes. He left
these to his friend and teacher, Cornutus, along with a bequest which
the latter naturally refused.

Undoubtedly Persius also associated freely with the aristocracy in
Rome, as was only natural because of his family background, but even
here only men with a distinctly intellectual profile are named. For ten
years, probably between 52 and 62 after Christ, he was a frequent visitor
at the house of Thrasea Paetus, the husband of the younger Arria who
was related to Persius. Paetus was the author of a eulogy on Cato and
a leader of the Stoic-republican opposition against Nero. Persius is
also said to have become attached to the historian Servilius Nonianus,
who died in 59 after Christ, as to a father. Our poet addressed his
second satire to a friend of this house, Plotius Macrinus. Persius clearly
fostered these human relationships with great devotion, and in the

same way, his *pietas* (dutifulness) toward his family, that is, his mother, sister, and aunt, is also praised in the vita. Besides this we hear about his pleasant appearance, his great gentleness, his almost girlish shyness, and his blameless reputation.

He probably spent most of his life in Rome, but there is mention of occasional trips, of stays on his estates, as at Luna[1] and in a villa at the eighth milestone of the Appian Way where he died from a stomach complaint on November 24, 62, in his twenty-eighth year.

Cornutus was given the job of settling the poet's literary estate. He had Persius' youthful attempts at poetry destroyed and what remained was the small volume of satires which has been preserved for us, and which his reading of Lucilius is said to have spurred him to write. But even this small book was not complete, for Cornutus removed a few verses from the end in order to provide the poems with a definite conclusion, and he undertook several slight alterations within the book as well. It remains uncertain whether these changes include the famous passage (1.121) where Cornutus is said to have replaced the original version, *auriculas asini Mida rex habet* ("King Midas has the ears of a jackass."), with the more harmless wording *auriculas asini quis non habet* ("Who does not have the ears of a jackass?"), so that Nero would not take it to heart. In any case, it is not probable that Persius here or elsewhere in his satires intended to give expression to feelings of antipathy toward Nero, though they certainly may have existed.

Whether the little book contains indications of incompleteness that can still be identified today is a matter of dispute. Self-quotations might be counted among these,[2] while well-known scholars point to the author's doublets in our Persius text.[3] In the same way attempts have been made to apply the hypothesis of incompleteness to such difficult lines as Satire 6.37–41. Further investigations are necessary on this point. The edition of the six satires that Cornutus had revised was then published by Caesius Bassus, certainly before Nero's death in 68, probably before Lucan and Petronius died, and before Cornutus was sent into exile. They perhaps appeared as early as 63 after Christ.

Attached to the six satires of Persius which comprise 650 hexameters is a series of fourteen verses in limping iambics. In the great majority of the manuscripts these appear as a prologue, while in some they are an epilogue. Here Persius presents himself not without a certain irony and along with learned allusions to literature as a simple half-farmer in the realm of poetry. Just as hunger teaches certain birds human speech, he says, so it is the primary motivation for so many poets and poetesses. It should not be doubted that these verses are genuine. But it is less certain whether the little poem is a unit or whether it is put together from two fragments (lines 1–7 and 8–14), whether it is complete or truncated, whether it is a separate composition or whether it stands in some relationship to the satire collection and, if so, what the connection is. The most likely suggestion is that the series of verses is to be taken as a prologue to the satires which is not mutilated at the end, since the last line seems to parallel and echo the first.[4] W. Kroll explains the lines more cautiously as being rough copy of Persius which Cornutus took as an appropriate introduction to the book.

The first satire presents Persius' justification of his satiric poetry on the basis of Lucilius, Horace, and old comedy with its frankness. In other words, he refers to the specific technical character of Roman satire that had been generally recognized since Horace's time. Modern poetry, which, weakened and corrupted by dilettantes, had degenerated to a mere jangle of words, is rejected, though it is less a matter of the decadence of literature than it is the vanity of the writers and their nullity that have caused this. In contrast to this, Persius' satire aims at being a form of confession and so something genuine. The poet will speak the truth with bite, for he considers human folly as being a subject for laughter, and from the blending of his enthusiasm for the subject with his earnest attention to art, something meaningful for the future should emerge. The poet wants only serious and competent people as his audience, completely certain as he is of his enduring fame. From among his contemporaries two readers or even none at all will satisfy him, he insists in a variation of a very old formula and one taken up again by the Stoics especially.

The first satire presents the poet immediately as a resolute moralist of Stoic fiber with highly capricious ideals of poetry and style. The poem offers in passing very lively glimpses into the literary life of the Neronian period. In this respect it comes closest in character to Horatian satire and even closer to that of Juvenal.

The remaining satires are much more sharply separated from life with its fresh and pulsating activity. The basis throughout is an experience derived from formal education, that is, the Stoic moral philosophy with its popular stamp. These five satires reveal far more than the first one does of the poet's nature that is turned away from life and from the world, and they show that he lacks the plasticity that could prove itself by establishing something solid and separate. The poet is doctrinaire; he is seldom an observer. Horace's ease and agility and his humor are completely lacking in Persius.

Right away in his second satire Persius deals with a theme that was a favorite of the Stoic diatribe. It is one that recurs often in Seneca, for example, and it was treated very extensively by Juvenal later:[5] the immorality, contradictions, and folly of human wishes as they appear especially in prayers and in the conceptions of the gods that underlie these.

The third satire begins with the lively picture of a late-sleeper who cannot make up his mind to get out of bed. This is used by Persius to introduce his discussion of the human weakness—especially of the educated man—of fully recognizing what is right but doing just the opposite because it is so pleasant. This divergence between knowing and doing had become an important problem, especially for the Late Stoa, in contrast to the Socratic-Platonic teaching that right action follows naturally and spontaneously from correct knowledge. Woven into the satire is an appeal that people not live their lives without a fixed plan but allow themselves to be put on the right track by Stoic ethics, even if the philistines laugh at this. Actually, then, this is a προτρεπτικὸς πρὸς φιλοσοφίαν (persuasion to philosophy). The sick man who behaves contrary to his doctor's orders necessarily dies, and human impulse and emotion are also sicknesses. The unity of this difficult satire is a matter for debate.

The fourth satire is brief and is put together much more clearly; it deals with knowing oneself. Beginning with a charming scene in which Socrates admonishes Alcibiades, Persius comes to the consideration of the general unwillingness of men "to get down into themselves." Instead of doing this, they would rather criticize others' faults. It ends with the imperative that men struggle through to self-knowledge, personal conviction, and purity without depending on people's opinions.

Next to the first satire, the fifth is the most suitable one for introducing the reader to Persius' poetry. It begins with a dedication to Cornutus which is the most personal statement we have from Persius. This is followed by descriptions of the different wishes and aspirations of men with a contrast drawn between these people and Cornutus who has a firm and philosophic manner of living. The rather lengthy conclusion brings a discussion of man's freedom and of curbing one's desires, once again from the Stoic point of view.

The sixth satire begins in a similarly personal way with its address to Persius' older friend, Caesius Bassus, but the poet soon turns to the general question of the right attitude to wealth and the correct use of possessions. There is a debate as to whether the editor shortened this poem or whether it is complete as it stands. The chronological sequence of the individual poems cannot be established with certainty, for there is a lack both of external testimony and clear references to dated events within the satires, as fits their general nature.

Persius belongs among the most difficult writers of pagan Roman literature, and certainly reading him can give the modern reader no real satisfaction and pleasure. Theodor Mommsen even called him "an ideal example of an arrogant and spiritless young man wrapped up in poetry."[6] Generally speaking, it is possible to find a relaxation of the power of composition among the writers of so-called silver Latin as compared with the classical writers, and there is also a conscious turning away from the media of composition used earlier. On the other hand, individuality is developed with great care and remarkable ability. This goes for Persius, too, and in his case there is the added consideration that, as a satirist who wanted to create free conversation in the image of the popular lecture and in very close dependence on Horace, he was dominated by his determination either to conceal his plan of composition in the particular case or to give it up completely. Certainly in the fourth satire he succeeded in working out a clear, tripartite structure. But right next to this he puts a creation like the third satire which organizationally is very obscure and to which scholars like G. Hendrickson have taken exception, and with good reason.[7]

Deficiencies in composition appear everywhere in matters of detail: abrupt transitions, unclear assignment of speakers in the dialogue sections, and more of the like. How far ability or purpose or both are responsible in Persius' case for the obscure organization and the inclination to ramble remains to be decided. On the other hand, Persius' satires do also present many a happy individual scene and many a successful picture. Ancient artistic theory makes Sophron and his influence responsible for that,[8] and, besides everything else, the mime undoubtedly exerted an occasional influence on Persius' presentation.

The difficulties with Persius' language in the narrower sense can, however, be completely overcome. The poems are, of course, full of colloquialisms, as the satiric style demands, as well as abbreviated expressions, vulgar phrases and words, expressions currently in vogue, metaphors from popular speech, and much more. On the other hand, there are quite a number of archaisms which should perhaps serve as a reminder that Lucilius was one of his models. Like these, the often vague hints at data from the ancient workaday world or at specific conditions of education, all of which are lost to us today, cannot be taken as representing real difficulties.

On the other hand, the style of Persius is extremely difficult and intentionally so. It is reported that *scriptitavit et raro et tarde* ("He wrote infrequently and slowly."),[9] and still today we can easily feel the pretentious obscurity of expression, the phrase that he wants to convey appearing in an affected form, the persistent, rationally anchored, often hypersophisticated aversion to the natural way of expressing something, the passion for putting the simple in new and unusual terms and preferably expressing it in as obscure a manner possible. Persius turns to a pampered public who take delight in advice in riddles, and I have no doubt that definite theories of style guided him in this. To indicate the direction, the ancients themselves used to mention him in the same breath with Lycophron,[10] and Persius apparently considered the obscurity and sparseness of expression as itself being the language of masculine bitterness which alone is suitable for the Stoic censor.

The tendency toward pointed brevity and startling originality is characteristic of Persius' style and reveals itself especially in his skill at creating new *iuncturae* (rhetorical combinations) and here in turn most clearly in his treatment of epithets and metaphors.[11] Kugler has stressed the fact, and rightly so, that Persius has basically tried to enliven his metaphorical expression in a new and thrilling way by "concretization." With this he stands in the rhetorical tradition which the elder Seneca makes especially clear to us with numerous examples. And so the poet frequently appears as a declaimer who again and again challenges the understanding of his listener and keeps him constantly in suspense with his puzzling, affected, and paradoxical way of putting things—completely different in style from a *homo antiquus* (a man of the old stamp). For the poet, this results in his not only wanting to twist incidental phrases again and again for the startling effect, but also in his frequently using several metaphors at the same time. Here the result is pictures that overlap with each other and are in conflict, and the unity of expression, thought, and picture is disrupted. A twisting of the ordinary turn of phrase *venit tibi in mentem* ([whatever] occurs to you) to *venit tibi in penem* (*Sat.* 4.48: "[whatever] occurs to your penis") is original and successful, but a crossing of pictures that are very different from one another as it is found in other passages militates against good taste.[12] Persius' poems are just as far removed from Horace's grace as they are from Juvenal's dazzling vehemence. And there is no depth of conception or concretization of the imagination that can hide the great defects in the formal structure on which their originator worked so diligently.

Persius' versification also shows a high level of artistic skill and an obvious reaching for style. This can be illustrated briefly in a few examples. His model is the satiric verse of Horace. In Persius' poetry too each hexameter is divided by caesura—Jahn's conjecture at *Satires* 5.19 is for this reason not probable—and Persius shows a decided preference for the male or penthemimeral caesura, going beyond Horace in this respect. The verses which are put together in this way are usually divided by a secondary caesura as well, for the most part after the fourth long syllable or before the fifth longum, and less often also by one after the fourth trochee. The caesura in the third foot is missing in only thirty-four verses, and here the appropriate places are bridged by a heavy word that begins in the fourth longum at least and comes to an end only in the fifth foot of the verse. In five cases the word begins with a long first syllable immediately after the penthemimeral. The verses divided by trithemimeral and hephthemimeral caesuras are far fewer in number, and this concurs with the practice of the contemporary epic poets. There are only four certain examples of the feminine caesura after the third trochee, and each of these verses also has a secondary caesura. According to ancient theory the feminine caesura was considered to be weak, and this is clearly the case with Persius. In the same way the satirist seems to have considered the *versus spondiacus* (spondaic line) as feeble. There is only a single example, and this is in a verse of a contemporary poet whom Persius quotes as decadent (*Sat.* 1.95).

The poet was fully aware of the rules for the close of the narrative and elegiac hexameter which were set up by the classic poets, refined by Ovid, and very strictly observed by Lucan, among others. But as a satirist Persius adhered to the norm of the Horatian hexameter. And so he did not hesitate to end his line with words of four or even five syllables which no longer were proper names. On the other hand, real monosyllables—among which I am not even counting close word combinations such as *hic est, si quid, de me, in re,* and so on—were acceptable at the end of the line for him, just as they were for Horace, and this was true when they followed immediately after both monosyllabic and polysyllabic words. Finally, Horace's satiric verse provides the precedent for Persius' ending a hexameter with a word which joins this line very closely with the next one—a relative pronoun, for example (*Sat.* 1.81), or a conjunction (*Sat.* 3.109). This is important for the delivery of the verse, for the end of the line is meant to strike the ear differently from epic verse where the verse ending is stressed by a pause. In this too, then, there is an *imitatio sermonis* (imitation of conversation). All of these characteristics of the satiric hexameter appear again in much the same way later in Juvenal which is an indication that all of this was taught by rules in antiquity. As with his meter, Persius' prosody is very precise and faultless. The only hiatus that has been transmitted, for example, may be explained away (*Sat.* 3.66). Elisions are also managed carefully.

Persius himself indicates the literary place of his satire by referring to Lucilius whose influence on him was relatively insignificant and to Horace whom Persius imitates everywhere. But in content and way of thinking Persius is perhaps even more in the sequence of Phoenix-Musonius-Epictetus. He no longer sees in satire the topical "battle writing," but a recognized literary form. His further reference to the old Attic comedy seems to be more a matter of convention than anything else, for he avoided taking a position on topical, especially political, questions of life in Rome to an even greater extent than Horace had. And he also kept completely away from making personal attacks on his contemporaries. In the time of Nero it was hardly possible to do otherwise. The anonymous lampoon had become the safety-valve of satire, with preference given to that in epigrammatic form. With very few exceptions personal themes are completely absent from Persius' satires. The range of his subject matter is on the whole much narrower than that of his predecessors. In a certain sense it is even narrower than that of Juvenal who, because of his powerful attacks on Roman life, became one of the most important sources of all for the history of Roman culture and customs. Instead of this, Persius' satire aims at the universal, closely connected as it is with the Stoic diatribe. It is the folly of man in the general sense that is its concern. On the other hand, the personal point of view of the poet remains firmly fixed. It is that of the Stoic, but there is still a job to be done of showing to what particular tendency of the Stoic school Persius chiefly adhered. Of course, we must be careful not to try to find in Persius an independent philosophical nature. But it was precisely the simplicity of his moral beliefs about life working chiefly on the unphilosophical reader that made him ideally suited to become the progenitor of moralizing poetic satire. Through him too its basically serious tone was fixed for his successors in the genre.

The certainty and strictness of his moral principles, his sincerity of purpose, his constancy and firmness in his battle against vice, superficiality, and inconsistency, the earnest forcefulness of his judgment, and certainly the intricate, difficult, and unique way in which he expressed himself have produced admirers of Persius at widely different times. Right after its appearance the little volume of satires was received with a veritable storm of enthusiasm, and Lucan seems to have been one of its most outspoken eulogists. From the generation immediately following comes the high praise of Quintilian[13] and Martial.[14] Juvenal, Rome's last great satirist, also read Persius carefully.

Besides this intense interest in the satires of Persius on the part of the reading public, the linguistic care and control that they attracted is to be noted. The eminent grammarian Marcus Valerius Probus probably put together a scholarly edition of the text in the Flavian era which was in full accord with the state of philological knowledge at that time. The text was in all likelihood provided with critical marks according to the Hellenistic pattern to help with oral exegesis. Moreover, the main part of the first-rate life of Persius that has been preserved seems to have had Probus as its author.[15] But it is not likely that Probus himself also produced and published a critical and exegetical commentary of this abstruse poet. Certainly he would have offered oral explication of Persius, and, as I see it, his successors used his explanations and his notes for further interpretation of the text.

It is almost certain, moreover, that Persius' little book was also read and discussed in the schools in the second and third centuries after Christ—by the learned Helenius Acron, for example[16]—and it was probably in this period that the matrix of the old commentaries first took shape. It is possible that the allusion of Jerome involves this corpus.[17] This commentary was then surely abbreviated and lengthened over and over again as a school textbook, so that what we have in the so-called older Persius scholia represents the results of work with the author extending over a number of centuries. In these, then, along with the remains of first-rate scholarship and conscientious and accurate philological research, there is also a certain amount of sheer drivel. With the exception of several additions, this final editing probably appeared about 400 after Christ. But, as has already been mentioned, Persius was read and worked on well before this without any interruption, and there can be no doubt that a whole series of old variant readings goes back to that early period.

It can be shown that Persius was read in many parts of the Latin-speaking world at the end of antiquity. He was even known in the Greek-speaking East. And so it follows that the number of Persius manuscripts must have been very great. Many of these old texts were undoubtedly also provided with explanations of words (glosses). Since in the long run, however, all of these manuscripts probably went back to the authoritative edition of Probus, their text was well established. For this reason, the authenticity of the extra verse in the fifth satire, which Kugler defends, is quite unlikely.[18]

On the other hand, there must have been considerable differences in the wording of the text. We can see this in the ancient citations and in the differences among our manuscripts. As far as the individual wording is concerned, there are essentially two main forms of the text. The oldest textual evidence, then, that has been preserved is in fragmentary condition and comes from the end of the fourth or beginning of the fifth century. This is the leaf of a manuscript from Bobbio (*Vaticanus Latinus 5750*) which shows Persius already linked with Juvenal in the tradition. At about the same time, in the year 402, Flavius Julius Tryfonianus Sabinus put together an edition of the text that was patently the work of a dilettante—*sine antigrapho* ("without a copy"). This is the so-called Sabinus recension which today is for the most part equated with a. It makes use of older variant material without great independence. As far as the designation of the Sabinus recension is concerned, it should be observed that the corresponding subscription in manuscripts A and B was added later.

The very many Persius manuscripts of the Middle Ages and Renaissance—which by the way should be examined more closely—probably in the last analysis go back to several manuscripts of late antiquity. And so they provide us with a gratifyingly large section from the tradition belonging to antiquity as it neared its end. Unless appearances are deceiving, then, only a little latitude is left for criticism based on conjecture as far as Persius' satires are concerned. The tradition is sound.

The first completely preserved manuscripts, then, come from the

early medieval period, that is, from the ninth century. It is clear that
Persius was already being read again in the schools at this time, especially in France, southern Germany, and Switzerland. The satirist
was copied, excerpted, and annotated anew for schoolroom purposes.
These are the so-called Cornutus scholia which have nothing at all to
do with Cornutus himself. Their oldest form, as Wessner recognized,
was in the *Commentum Leidense* from the ninth century. From the
tenth century, too, there is a trite commentary that has been preserved.
In the eleventh century Persius now appears among the *poetae aurei*
(golden poets), and the mass of manuscript material shows a con-
tinual increase. It should be mentioned that men like Dante, Petrarch,
and Boccaccio belonged among the devotees of Persius. The high Renaissance next brought a further flood of manuscripts, so that the total
number of Persius manuscripts today reaches into the hundreds. It
might be pointed out that for practical purposes an eclectic method is
advisable for the text critic. In the individual case the genuine tradition
is most safely established when the evidence of P (*Montepessulanus
125*), α (=A, *Montepessulanus 212* and B, *Vaticanus tabularii basilicae
H 36*), and Ramorino's *recensio emendata* (see below) is in agreement.
But even this basis for judgment is hardly infallible. For instance, at
Satire 1.97 the reading *vegrandi* is preserved only in the indirect tradition, and Satire 1.111 also presents difficulties. There is more of this
kind of thing.

Among the published editions of Persius the text with commentary
of the candid and conscientious Isaac Casaubon (first published, Paris,
1605) occupies a place of honor. It has been said of it that here the
sauce is better than the fish. The great edition of Otto Jahn represents
a further landmark (Leipzig, 1843) with its prolegomena and critical
edition of the scholia. Jahn undertook for the first time to master the
tradition with its superfluity of manuscripts and bring order to it with
good results. A revision on very broad principles is something that is
needed. All of the modern editions are based on this one. The small
version of Fr. Buecheler comes directly from this one (Berlin, 1886,
1893) and so does that of Leo (Berlin, 1910; anastatic reprint, 1932).
The manuscript basis for these is certainly too thin and is not even
quoted correctly all the time.

Otherwise the modern editions that might be mentioned, most of
them with commentary, are: G. Nèmethy (Budapest, 1903; with an
index of words), S. Consoli (3 ed., Rome, 1913), F. Ramorino (2 ed.,
Turin, 1920), A. Cartault (Paris, 1920). Especially noteworthy are the

editions of J. van Wageningen (Groningen, 1911) and Fr. Villeneuve (first published, Paris, 1918). The English edition of J. Conington and H. Nettleship (3 ed., Oxford, 1893) deserves to be recommended. There is also much that is useful in the older commentary of C. F. Heinrich (Leipzig, 1844).

German translations that might be cited are those of F. Passow (Leipzig, 1809), W. E. Weber (Bonn, 1834), F. Hauthal (Leipzig, 1837), W. Teuffel (Stuttgart, 1857), and that of W. Binder (Berlin, 1915). Herder also translated Satires 1, 3, and 5.[19]

« XI »

Satire in the Time of Domitian

THROUGH Persius Roman satire in poetic form had received new impetus. The writers of the Neronian period were openly in competition with the Augustan period as they tried to enliven a whole series of the older poetic forms. Domitian for his part started from these efforts of Nero. Quintilian provides evidence that satiric poetry was fostered in his time too with promising results.[1] Of course only a few random references have survived which provide any more precise information on the subject.

We learn from Statius that Publius Manilius Vopiscus not only worked with lyric and epic, but that he also attempted satires and poetic epistles.[2] If Valla's Probus is to be believed,[3] then a certain Silius should also be mentioned as a satiric poet of the time. Perhaps he is to be identified with Silius Proculus, the younger Pliny's friend.[4] An attempt has been made to find another satirist in the person of Julius Rufus on the basis of a statement of Martial,[5] and quite a few of the many poets of these decades whose names have come down to us in great numbers may also have written satires without our having any indication of it.

Turnus is mentioned by the tradition as being the best-known name from that period and as one that was well known to Greek literary tradition as well.[6] The Juvenal scholiast, probably drawing on a historical source, reports that Turnus was ambitious and rose from very modest circumstances to great distinction at the court of Titus and Domitian,[7] and Martial already refers to him as a recognized poet having a place next to his brother, the tragic poet Scaevus Memor.[8] At a later time, too, he is mentioned with great respect and he is even referred to in the same breath as Juvenal.[9] Only two hexameters by him have been preserved through the Juvenal scholia.[10]

Then there is the poetess Sulpicia whom Martial put next to Sappho, while in another poem he praised her happy marriage with Calenus.[11]

There are several other pieces of evidence from which comes the information that she wrote erotic *nugae* (trifles) and probably thought of herself as a dilettante. She should probably not be included in the catalogue of satiric poets, even though a poem seventy lines long has come down under her name which Buecheler and others have called a *satura*. This is most easily accessible in Leo's edition of Persius and Juvenal.[12] Neither the tradition nor the style and meter warrant interpreting these verses as a satire. In fact, the introductory lines seem to contradict this idea. In the poem the poetess puts a question to Calliope —whether Rome's glory would come to an end—and it reaches a climax in the complaint about the emperor's recent expulsion of the philosophers from Rome. The muse comforts the poetess and promises the downfall of the tyrant.

The manuscript of this poem was found in the year 1493 at Bobbio along with that of Rutilius Namatianus but, like the latter, it has in the meantime been lost. And so the edition of Merula published at Venice in 1498 (revised, Strassburg, 1509) and the edition of Ausonius put together by Th. Ugoletus at Parma in 1499 (revised, Venice, 1501, but of less value) must be relied on. The poem probably does not come from the time of Domitian at all. The many serious awkward turns of language and prosody, which cannot all be explained as errors in transmission, would militate against this idea.[13] But at the same time it does not seem to be a medieval product, in spite of what Boot and Buecheler say. Mistakes in readings in the old editions seem to suggest an apparently ancient–early-medieval connection for the Bobbio manuscript in particular. The suggestion of E. Baehrens who assigns the poem to a time shortly after Ausonius is very plausible. A thorough and systematic rehandling of the question would certainly be desirable.

Though Roman satire from the period between Persius and Juvenal is for all intents and purposes lost, still there can be no doubt that it was a popular and much-practiced genre of poetry in those decades. It is possible to assume with confidence that at this time satiric style underwent a thoroughgoing rhetorical refinement in a direct line from the old classical writers. Contemporary criticism, especially that which took the form of polemic against living personages, had already disappeared at that time, as was subsequently the case in Juvenal. This was a result of the strict limitations put on freedom of speech as well as the resulting ignorance of and indifference toward things political of which Tacitus complains so bitterly. Besides different prose forms, the verse form used most often for topical criticism now was chiefly the satiric epigram,[14] generally anonymous, as had been the case earlier under Tiberius and Nero. The situation was already such that if the satirist wanted to criticize the times and mention the wrongdoers specifically, he could only do so by referring to the past. The single fragment of Turnus that has been preserved points in this direction. Certainly the satirist who was projecting his satire into the past could also say a great deal that was applicable to the present, as the satires of Juvenal show. It is only with him that Roman satire becomes clearly visible again.

« XII »

Decimus Junius Juvenalis

THE sources that are at our disposal for a biography of Juvenal are sparse and of unequal value. A series of manuscripts do provide brief biographical sketches of the poet, but they differ from one another on important points, so that their relationship to each other and their reliability in details need more accurate investigation. In all of them good information is hopelessly mixed together with material that is of dubious value and just plain wrong. Indeed, attempts have been made to put together a kind of original life in broad outline from them, but the results have been very different. A comparison between Ribbeck's vita in his edition[1] and that recognized by Paul Wessner[2] will perhaps illustrate the problem. Whichever choice we may make, the original vita does not even bring a knowledge of the facts that can be depended on and it does not at all go back to Suetonius or even to Probus, although the schema of Suetonius' biographical sketch was familiar to its author. Probably it did not exist until the last years of the fourth century, more than 250 years after the poet's death. Most of the information in it would have been drawn from the older store of scholia where in many cases the lack of real information was already glossed over by legend and philological conjecture. And so extreme caution is necessary when it comes to interpreting this material.

Besides this, there are several comments about Juvenal in the ancient writers and finally there are the satires of the poet himself. But in spite of the fact that these poems give a clear idea of the poet's inclinations and feelings, his point of view, and the whole method that he uses, the information they have to offer about the external circumstances of his life is insignificant. For Juvenal, quite unlike Lucilius and Horace, has conscientiously avoided speaking about himself, and a great deal that at first sounds personal has turned out to be fiction—the names of the people, for instance, to whom the individual satires are directed. Never-

theless, there are a few references in the poems that can be used to put
together a chronological outline.

The name of the poet is well established: Decimus Junius Juvenalis.
Even the ancients were no longer able to provide the name and rank
of his father with certainty. The lives are uncertain as to whether
Juvenal was the son or foster-son of a well-to-do freedman. According
to a version that cannot be verified, he himself is supposed to have
been a freedman.[3] The seemingly accurate statements of a very late
manuscript about his mother Septumuleia, a sister of the same name,
and also his brother-in-law Fuscinus should be put down as invention
pure and simple.[4] Even the poet's birthdate has not been preserved, but
we should look for it between 50 and 70 after Christ on the basis of
reasonable inferences. It probably fell in Nero's reign. The vita of
a manuscript from humanist times, which also provides detailed information about the poet that is otherwise not verifiable, puts his birth
in 55 after Christ.[5] This estimate, however, is probably too early.

The information that his place of birth was the Volscian town of
Aquinum is gathered from a reference in the satires (3.319). It may
be true, but it does not have to be. An inscription from Aquinum now
lost, but certainly not a forgery,[6] which contained a dedication to Ceres,[7]
provides information to the effect that a certain Junius Juvenalis occupied a military post in the *cohors I Delmatarum* (First Dalmatian
Cohort) as well as two high positions in municipal government. But
since the praenomen is missing, it remains uncertain whether the inscription refers to our poet. In any event, it can probably be taken as
valid evidence that his father's or stepfather's family was connected
with Aquinum and that it was socially respected there.

From a passing mention of a paternal estate in one of the satires
(6.57), some scholars have tried to infer a certain wealth for the family;
but today the passage is explained differently. The fact that Juvenal enjoyed a thorough education in grammar and rhetoric is a better argument in favor of the family's being wealthy. It is even possible that
Quintilian was among his teachers. Until about the middle of his life
the poet is said to have occupied himself with declamation, more for
his own enjoyment than as training for a specific occupation. The fact
is believable, but the motivation is unnecessary. If this is right, then
Juvenal lived an independent life in moderate and probably even
comfortable circumstances. The question of whether the eleventh satire
is evidence that the poet even had an estate, perhaps at Tibur, must re-

main open, but in the twelfth satire too he appears as landowner.[8] Vitas
V and VI of Jahn even convey the information that in the course of
time he rose to equestrian rank, but this seems very doubtful on other
grounds.

There are two poems of Martial from about the years 91 and 92
after Christ which show his close relationship with Juvenal.[9] An attempt has been made to find in the first epigram a reference to the fact
that Juvenal now and then appeared as a lawyer. In the second poem
Martial calls his friend *facundus* ("eloquent") which can be taken as
referring to the poet's occupation with declamation. Through these
poems we get a real and reliable date for his life: the reign of Domitian.
This experience was very important for the poet, and these are also the
times that he denounces in his satires with a hatred and loathing that
never flag. And the *Suda* dated him to this period with good reason.
This is also the time when Martial, Statius, and Quintilian were active
as writers.

A charming letter of Martial written in verse to his friend takes
us a step further.[10] It was composed after Domitian's death, about
98 or 100, and in it Martial presents Juvenal as a man who has put on
the burdensome toga and must waste his day in the big city perform-
ing the thankless duties of a client. Martial does not refer to any poetic
activity of his friend here either. But the allusions in the poem to
Juvenal's pursuits, his residence in Rome, and his social position fit
well with the impression the satires leave. For these show the greatest
familiarity with goings-on in Rome and also with the literary life of
Domitian's time. They tell again and again of Juvenal's disillusion with
the degeneracy of the Roman nobility and reveal an understanding of
the position of the clients which may very likely be based on the poet's
personal experiences. Tradition has it that Juvenal did not come before
the public with his satiric poetry until he was well into manhood; that
is, after he had passed forty, and this seems plausible. As he himself
says, he moved in literary circles in Rome earlier, but his personal attempts at poetry from an earlier period no longer exist. It has been
surmised, of course, that one or another of his satires was written
while Domitian was still alive, and some scholars have supposed that
here and there in the satires there is a sprinkling of poetry from earlier
periods of the poet's activity. But none of this can be proved. To the
contrary, it seems most likely that Juvenal did not begin his satiric
writing until after the death of Domitian in 96, that is after the re-
establishment of freedom and probably not until after Trajan's acces-

sion in 98. In all likelihood publication of the satires was not begun at all before the year 100 after Christ. The first book presupposes the death of Domitian at several points and contains a clear reference to the year 100 (*Sat.* 1.49). In the second book there is an allusion to the time between 114 and 116 (*Sat.* 6.407–12), while at the beginning of the third book there is a reference to Hadrian's accession in 118. Finally, in the fifth book the year 127 is referred to.[11] This book was probably completed before 131 after Christ. The division of the satires into five books may be taken as original. Moreover, it is very likely that they were published in this sequence.

Although Juvenal's satires deal mainly with the horror-filled time of Domitian, the poet's period of production falls in the reigns of Trajan and Hadrian, that is, in a time when Tacitus, the younger Pliny, and Suetonius were active. His success is said to have been immediate and striking. The poet seems to have stayed mainly in Rome, but he also saw the world. And so in Satire 15 he shows his knowledge of Egypt, and it is also possible that he was in Britain once.

As far as his experiences are concerned, the lives are unanimous in reporting a period of exile for the poet. The accounts of the circumstances surrounding this are, however, contradictory and are surely in part contrived. If the lives are taken as a starting point, then for the time of his exile there is a choice between the reigns of Claudius Nero, Domitian, Trajan, and Hadrian, when Juvenal was already said to be eighty years old. As far as the place of exile is concerned, the accounts are divided between Egypt and Britain. The length of his exile is sometimes described as quite short and sometimes as being for the rest of his life. Then the poet is said either to have returned to Rome or to have died abroad "from grief and worry," as it is reported in words that recall what Suetonius says in his biography of Terence. Jahn's Vita IV even contains the remark that the poet expanded his satires while he was in exile and revised them considerably. This observation was an important element in hypotheses formulated in the last century about the origin, history, and state of preservation of the satires. Finally the reason for the exile was alleged to be the emperor's anger at a passage in the seventh satire (7.90–92), accompanied in part by very complicated and implausible surmises. And so the account of Juvenal's exile seems overgrown by a deceptive and tangled undergrowth of completely contradictory details that are in part definitely false. If Juvenal was ever in exile, then it was either before the year 83 (perhaps 81 or 82), and then only for a short time, or in the later years of Hadrian's reign. But perhaps the whole story of the exile is to be considered a fairy tale which was certainly already believed about the middle of the fifth century[12] and was making its way at that time into the Greek handbooks like those of Malalas and the *Suda*.

In the same way later antiquity had no certain information about the place, year, and cause of the poet's death, as well as the immediate circumstances surrounding it. In any case, the accounts differ on these points and are irreconcilable. It is certain, however, that Juvenal reached a ripe old age and lived to see the second half of Hadrian's reign and perhaps even the accession of Antoninus Pius in 138.[13]

Sixteen hexameter satires of Juvenal have been preserved, divided into five books. The last one is truncated, the victim of the unkind tradition. But its authenticity which was already questioned in antiquity is beyond any doubt. Only O. Ribbeck, using internal arguments, has denied not only the sixteenth satire—about this one he is certainly suspicious—but also satires 10, 12, 13, 14, and 15 as belonging to Juvenal.[14] He would have their author be a declaimer from the generation after Juvenal. Ribbeck with his feeling for language and his brilliant insight has certainly taken exception to a large number of passages with good reason. But the defects, insofar as this scholar has not simply gone wrong, can be eliminated in other ways as well and his radical conclusions no longer seem convincing. Quite to the contrary, there are serious arguments of a stylistic kind that oppose them, and so many differences in the later poems can be explained from their epistolary nature and from the greater emphasis that is placed on the popular philosophical basis for life. They have even been called moral essays in poetic form. And so the whole collection is to be taken into account when any attempt is made to put together a picture of Juvenal's poetic personality.

Book 1: In the first satire Juvenal reveals his poetic program. He represents himself as a satirist in the tradition of Lucilius and Horace, but does not yet refer to Persius as a classic, though he does know him well. Driven by anger and moral indignation, he will pillory and scourge human wickedness, the high point of which he is presently living through in Rome. This seems to him to be an undertaking with more currency than the activity of the poets who have taken a more objective course. He is certainly not going to mention the names of living people.

The poem immediately puts before the reader's eyes Juvenal's skill as an observer as well as his expertise at rendering graphically the individual scene and finding the well-aimed expression. And it also shows the poet himself in his role of an emotionalist passing judgment. Here, as in what follows, minor problems can be removed, at least in part, through the use of philological criticism.

In the second satire the poet in a series of lively pictures scourges the vice of homosexual passion among men, especially those who try to hide their perversion behind the mask of the rugged philosophical moralist.

The third satire contains a description, in a composition with a frame, of the trials and tribulations of living in Rome put into the mouth of a friend. It stands out as being one of the best of Juvenal's satires and is well suited as an introduction to his poetry.

The main part of the fourth satire is a description of the deliberations of Domitian's privy council over a precious fish. It shows an independence of form, and probably the ancient reader heard a parody here of an epic poem of Statius, the *De bello Germanico* (*On the War in Germany*). The first part of the poem (1–33) is only very loosely connected with the main part.

The theme of the fifth satire is a client's dinner party at the house of his proud patron with all of its attendant formalities for that person who is so humble. This satire too shows a graphic power of description and unusually strong feelings of indignation.

Book 2: Satire 6 is the greatest female character study coming from antiquity, and it is this that really settles Juvenal's reputation as a satiric poet. In a loose and not always clear arrangement a host of individual scenes are presented in which the weaknesses and the vices of the women of Rome are revealed. The poetic value of the piece vies with the cultural. It might be mentioned for the text critic that in 1899 a surprising addition was made to this poem consisting of 36 lines found by Winstedt (*Sat.* 6.365.01–034; 6.373A–373B). But Buecheler, among others, immediately recognized the passage as being undoubtedly an ancient forgery,[15] while other important scholars came to the opposite conclusion.

Book 3: In the seventh satire, the arrangement of which also presents certain difficulties, Juvenal speaks about the misery of those engaged in intellectual pursuits in Rome, while in Satire 8 he deals coherently with a favorite theme and one which recurs often in the satires—the debasement of the Roman nobility. The ninth satire is a talk with an aged homosexual. It is very vivid and is shot through with a striking irony that is seldom found in Juvenal.

Book 4: The tenth satire resembles a declamation in poetic form on the folly of human wishes. It is much more clearly—almost schematically—organized than all the satires which precede it, and it comes much more strongly than they do under the influence of popular philosophy. In spite of this, it also contains many scenes of truly Juvenalian color and forcefulness: Sejanus' downfall (56–77), Hannibal in Italy (147–67), Messallina's foolish marriage (331–38), and more. There are also genuinely Juvenalian turns of phrase that are resoundingly terse: *panem et circenses* (81: "bread and circuses"), *mens sana in corpore sano* (356: "a healthy mind in a healthy body"), and so on, as well as other evidences of the genius of the great satirist.

In the main part of the eleventh satire there is a description (with several glances back toward old Latium) of a country meal to which the poet invites a friend. As in the fourth satire, this is preceded by a section which seems only tenuously connected with the main subject (1–55). The twelfth satire is probably the weakest and contains a description of a celebration which the poet gives out of joy at the rescue of a friend from a storm at sea. Connected with this is a strong invective against legacy hunters in Rome.

Book 5: Satire 13 is a letter of consolation addressed to a friend whom another friend has cheated of a *depositum* ("deposit"), while Satire 14 speaks vividly about the bad example which fathers set for their sons with special emphasis on greed. At the end the straightforward common claims of *natura* (nature) and *sapientia* (wisdom) are contrasted. In the fifteenth satire Juvenal recounts a case of cannibalism in Egypt, while the sixteenth deals in a very lively way with the advantages enjoyed by the military class as exemplified by the metropolitan guard.

The subject matter that Juvenal wants to present is the activities of men (*Sat.* 1.85–86), and in comparison with his predecessors, this represents a conscious restriction of content. Themes like personal attack, Horace's letters on literature, portrayal of the poet's personal life, description of nature, and others—all of this is missing in Juvenal. Whether he is talking about the gods or the ant, about mythology and history or the drowsy peace and quiet of hill-towns, all of this in Juvenal is applied strictly and unequivocally to men. But he deals with only a certain section of what is really involved in humanity: the depravity and wickedness of human activity. In this he is not convinced that human faults can be remedied or that they can be changed for the better or even understood and forgiven. Rather, it is his feeling that man from the beginning and by nature was constituted as a wicked thing and the high point has now been reached which cannot be surpassed. The fate of man, then, is degeneration, and it is inescapable. And so in Juvenal the feeling of being placed by fate at the end point of a hopeless era is given expression just as it is in Tacitus.

Juvenal takes his examples for the most part from the Roman world. A cosmopolitan outlook, as is quite common in Hellenistic philosophy, is not part of his thinking. And certainly he puts the shadowy side of the Roman world vividly before our eyes in an unparalleled array of very graphic scenes that are priceless for the information that they offer about cultural and moral history. It is the time of Domitian in particular to which he refers again and again, and he has been criticized from time to time for these attacks on an era that was past. But if he sees a human destiny in wickedness, should he be blamed for choosing the most hair-raising examples of this wherever he finds them? And could he not make his criticism even sharper by such recourse? His judgment claims a timeless validity.

He confronts monstrous depravity, which he identifies everywhere, bravely and boldly and as an individual. He is not the man to take refuge in the realms of mythology as so many other poets of the time did. He identifies anger and indignation as the driving forces of his satiric poetry, and these are genuine and strong. It is not fair either to Juvenal's attitude or to his poetic achievement to brush him off as a declaimer, for as such he would not be part of his subject, and what he had to say would have only a virtuoso value. Juvenal's poetry aims at being a personal creed, and the poet is always directly concerned with his subject. Actually, he could be criticized for an excess of inner commitment rather than the opposite. The subject matter, as a matter of fact, takes him prisoner, and he hardly ever has the power to separate himself from it and to raise himself above it. This is the powerful source of his descriptive strength, but it is also probably the main reason that Horace's joy in understanding, especially understanding the weaknesses of his fellow man, is missing in him, as is the ironic laughter which finds its high point in the amiable self-irony of the earlier satirist.

From this outlook of his Juvenal gathers the power to praise and condemn without compromise, the right to make everything either black or white. Attempts have been made to deny him this right also, since it has been asserted that he lacked any ideal that had to be based on philosophical principles. Certainly, while the influence of popular moral philosophy, especially that with a Stoic direction, on Juvenal's satires may be indisputable, a philosopher the poet most certainly was not, and he himself rejected a commitment to philosophy.[16] But a guiding principle is by no means missing from his judgments on this account. His opinion is firmly and clearly determined by his wide practical experience and his respect for the old Roman traditions; he clings firmly to these. And since the life of his time ran directly contrary to these ideals, because he also recognized the impossibility of bringing the old values into play again generally, and because, moreover, all of this appeared to him to be natural necessity arising from the human plan, he had to pass unilateral judgment, and frequently with a sharpness and accentuation which from the modern point of view does not always completely suit the subject. This, however, is no *declamatio* (declamation), but, in spite of all the strangeness in the individual instance, the indignation is always genuine and sincere. Here is where the essential point of this brittle poetic personality with its fundamental pessimism lies. Of course, personal disillusionment and bitterness may have had a part to play in shaping his conception of life, but this determines the degree of his censure, not its subject matter and direction.

On these premises Juvenal's poetry represents the epitome of serious satire. Not without reason did Joseph Scaliger characterize it as *satirae tragicae* ("tragic satires"). Burlesque and even sentimental features appear from time to time, but Horace's laughter is missing on the whole, and it is replaced by an unparalleled bitterness and gloom. Even in terribleness Juvenal sees grandeur. His tone, as Fr. Schiller correctly pointed out, is that of the emotionalist throughout.

Since he pillories social conditions more than individual men, Juvenal always begins from the concrete. With a sharp eye for the event, he is in the habit of choosing an example and elaborating it in an unusual and graphic way and with the greatest realism. And since Juvenal above all intends to present vice stripped naked, his reader had better not be prudish. Now if the poet sees depravity as basic to human nature, it is easy to understand why in his poetry a single picture takes on the function and meaning of the example that is generally applicable. And this *is* an important characteristic of his creative method. Whenever Juvenal presents an example, usually an ulterior motive accompanies it and, what is more, he now and then even expresses it openly:

"Look! This is the general thing! This is the norm and improvement is completely impossible!" There can be no doubt that the poet is outspokenly subjective in this respect. The scholar must be especially careful to take this into account when, as he is in the process of exploiting Juvenal's satires for moral and cultural history, he runs up against the description of conditions given by writers like the younger Pliny, which is quite the opposite of Juvenal's.

On the other hand, reflection and contemplation have no part to play in Juvenal. He would rather bolster his opinion not with reasons, but with direct persuasive power, the evidence of his pictures which he reinforces from time to time even by using contrasting examples such as those from the good old times in Rome. As has already been mentioned, the individual case is usually raised to the level of the norm and for this reason the individual picture itself is in turn raised to the monumental. The picture is meant to be the direct expression of the poet's thought and opinion with all their emotion and fervor. In Juvenal there is, generally speaking, no overlapping of pictures and thought as is perhaps characteristic of Persius. But there is an intensification of thought through an extremely concentrated buildup of successive pictures in a step-by-step process. Judgment as a rule results automatically from this without further deliberation and then it almost seems as if Juvenal just records it. This is a strong source of his psychagogic power. But he is also able to formulate his opinion with the terseness that is found elsewhere only in the aphoristic sketches of Seneca or Lucan. There is hardly another Latin writer who is as rich in familiar quotations as Juvenal is.

Genuine moral conviction for the most part without extended reflection and contemplation, representation of human vice with an unmatched candor, and a pessimistic conception of life as a wrestling-ground for extravagant wickedness are basic characteristics of Juvenal's great power of expression. At the same time he has the ability to describe the brightest array of events vividly, singlemindedly, and crassly, to raise them to the level of the typical, and to sum up unforgettably the meaning of the general and particular together in the briefest and most completely successful expression. All of this together constitutes the reasons for Juvenal's acquiring far greater importance than even Horace as a model in the history of occidental satire.

In all of this he also shows a masterful control of the medium of production—in language and style, meter and prosody, though his tech-

nique of composition still raises many questions. As far as his language
and style are concerned, there is a large number of useful studies. Josué
de Decker's *Juvenalis declamans* (Ghent, 1913) might still be mentioned as the best general work. People have become used to characteriz-
ing Juvenal's artistry as "rhetorical." And rightly so, only the pejorative
connotation that has been attached to the word since the time of German idealism must be removed from it. Rather it must be kept in mind
that from about the time of Ovid there was really no form of education
and verbal art other than the rhetorical. And so what was special could
be set off against this background. At the same time, it is just possible
that the rhetorical with its preference for the surprising juxtaposition of
contrasting pictures and thoughts is also the appropriate mode of expression for times and men who, like Juvenal, felt so painfully and right to
the bottom of their souls the contrast between the ideal situation and the
reality they knew.

Apparently Juvenal's satires were read very little for more than 250
years after the poet's death. Moreover, they did not at first stand under
the protection of the philologists. And so there is every indication that
the worst damage to the text occurred in these years—lacunas, the adding of lines, and thorough corruption of individual words. The first
period ended in the last third of the fourth century after Christ, for it
can be taken as certain that at this time a philologist from the school of
Servius, whose name may have been Nicaeus, put together in Rome
an accurate critical edition of the satirist with a detailed commentary.
This is the basis for our whole direct tradition, and the old commentary has been preserved in good part.[17] Immediately after this, about the
end of the fourth or the beginning of the fifth century, the rise of an
unusually strong interest in our poet can be observed. From this time
until well into the sixth century Juvenal was a favorite author of the
reading public in Italy, Gaul, Spain, and Africa; he was even read in
the Greek-speaking East. At the same time, the poet belonged with the
classical writers read in the schools at the time; this was especially true
in the West, but was also the case in the East. The basis of the text was
a vulgate which was built on the critical edition of the fourth century,
but which renounced the use of critical accessories and in individual
instances frequently changed the reading arbitrarily to make it easier
or to improve it. Even the text of this interpolated secondary edition
can be accurately reconstructed by combining manuscripts. It corresponds to our recension Ω. The old grammarians were already able in

many cases to reject further accretions to the text that occurred in late antiquity.

Three Juvenal fragments from this early period still exist today: the page from Bobbio dating from the fourth or fifth century (*Vaticanus Latinus 5750*) which shows Juvenal associated with Persius in the tradition, the Ambrosian fragment from the fifth or sixth century, and the page from Antinoë from the same time which shows that Juvenal was read in the Greek-speaking world of Egypt and was taught in the schools there.

In the so-called Dark Ages even Juvenal's satires disappeared from the hands of the reading public. But in spite of everything, several manuscripts must have survived from late antiquity. These were then rediscovered, first probably in France, by the scholars of the Carolingian period at the end of the eighth century and immediately copied. A knowledge of Juvenal can be shown just a few years later in the area around Lake Constance also, and already in the ninth century he definitely belonged to the writers recognized as classical. The text was treated with caution by the scholars of the early medieval period, and all of the damage which happened at that time is, strictly speaking, superficial. Moreover, the collation of different texts was begun early and carried out generally, so that the contours of the separate text-classes and groups disappeared. Furthermore Juvenal was excerpted early for school use and he was glossed and annotated anew with the help of material from late antiquity. And so, for example, the bipartite tradition of our superficial scholia of the Ω class, which are most incorrectly named after Cornutus, can be traced back to the activity of the school at Auxerre in the second half of the ninth century. Heiricus and Remigius were among those working here at this time. But besides this there were still other medieval commentaries on Juvenal of a trivial kind.

Then our oldest manuscripts of Juvenal that have been preserved complete come from the ninth century, both representatives of the purer form of the text Π—the most complete representative is *Montepessulanus 125* (P)—and also those of the vulgate recension Ω, in most cases, certainly, containing an admixture of other readings.

Juvenal enjoyed very great attention through the medieval period as an *ethicus* (moralist), and from the eleventh century on he also appears among the *poetae aurei* (golden poets). Accordingly, the number of manuscripts from the medieval period is extraordinarily large. The humanistic period brought a further plethora, so that the number of manuscripts that exist today, if the fragments are included, runs to well over 500. By following the tradition back over its intermediate phases, the text of the fourth-century archetype can be established with considerable certainty right down to its details. The tradition of the single manuscript is firmly established.[18]

Then begins the much more difficult task of getting from this reliable base to the genuine text of the poet himself. The struggle over points of departure as far as method is concerned is in full swing. Ribbeck's separation of a genuine from a spurious Juvenal is probably just as generally rejected today as the ultraconservative approach of Buecheler and Friedlaender who wanted to find no interpolations in our Juvenal text at all, except for a verse in the sixth satire (6.126). The hypothesis of a double editing of the satires by the poet himself which was first argued by Teuffel and later was taken up very convincingly by Leo[19] is debatable. The supposition that the really serious disruptions of the text are mainly the work of ancient interpolators seems much more convincing than all of this.[20]

Some fifty printings of Juvenal are known from the time between 1470 and 1500. Many of them have the value of being codices. The great edition of H. C. Henninius, first published at Utrecht in 1685, contains a summary of the most important earlier commentaries. The first half of the last century brought a number of noteworthy contributions to our understanding of Juvenal in matters of content and literary criticism. Among those that might be mentioned are the edition of G. A. Ruperti, who was a conscientious scholar, but irresolute when it came to decisions (Leipzig, 1801 and 1819), that of the erudite expert, E. W. Weber (Weimar, 1825), the posthumous edition of the unprejudiced and impulsive C. F. Heinrich (Bonn, 1839), as well as the collection of N. L. Achaintre (Paris, 1810).

Juvenal criticism was put on a new basis that is essentially the current one by the masterly edition of Otto Jahn which appeared in 1851 (Berlin) and contained the old scholia and an index of words. Jahn recognized the basic bipartite division of our Juvenal tradition as well as the relatively greater reliability of the branch of the tradition represented by P as opposed to the vulgate. And, going beyond the results of Heinrich and Hermann, he was the first to use this knowledge consistently for his *recensio*. But in his edition he also demonstrated great skill in his superior handling of higher criticism; in one case, for example (*Sat.* 7.192), his views very recently enjoyed astounding confirmation from the page found at Antinoë. The verse, which is rejected by Jahn, is there marked with a double critical obelus. The pocket editions of Buecheler (Berlin, 1886 and 1893) and Leo (4 ed., Berlin, 1910; repr. 1932) derive directly from Jahn's large edition. The small text edition of C. F. Hermann (Leipzig, 1854, etc.), moreover, has independent critical value. But the most important critical achievement after Jahn is A. E. Housman's Juvenal (2 ed., Cambridge, 1931). In an edition which shows his industry, N. Vianello seeks to make new manuscript material available, but his statements are not absolutely reliable (Turin, 1934).

As far as commentaries go, that of L. Friedlaender (Leipzig, 1895) will be consulted first. In addition to this the older commentaries of A. Weidner (2 ed., Leipzig, 1889) and especially that of J. E. B. Mayor (London, 1888, 1893, selected) are indispensable. The selected editions of H. L. Wilson (Boston, 1903) and J. D. Duff (Cambridge, 1898 [rev. 1970]) are also useful. For more detailed study special editions of individual satires may be consulted. There is, for example, the edition of Satire 1 by S. Consoli (Rome, 1911) and of Satire 7 by J. A. Hild (Paris, 1890), and so on. The best German translation is probably that done by the doctor, Ed. Casp. Jac. von Siebold (Leipzig, 1858). A satisfactory overall appreciation of Juvenal does not yet exist, although in recent years a number of Italian scholars have applied themselves to this; some of them have worked from an historical point of view and others from a patently aesthetic point of view.[21]

Juvenal's satires stand at a terminus. Satiric characteristics can be found in authors belonging to the succeeding generations, especially Apuleius, Tertullian, and the Christian polemical writings which follow them. The anonymous satiric epigram may have flourished, especially under the military emperors. But satire as an artistic form apparently did not have a definite second blossoming until the fourth or fifth century when, in spite of the fact that Rome's real power was broken, the intellectual power of the metropolis took a significant upswing once again. The satire of that time is to be differentiated from the invectives of Claudian and similar writings, which are strongly bound to the satirists in style and theme, but which belong to a different genre. Late antiquity did not always draw the boundary lines sharply by any means. And so the *versus satirographi* ("verses of a satirist"), for example, of which Sidonius Apollinaris speaks,[22] were named from the spirit of polemic criticism, not from the literary form, and we would be just as hesitant about calling Ausonius' *De herediolo*

(*On the Poet's Patrimony*) a satire as the compiler does. On the other hand, it is clear that Tetradius, the friend and student of Ausonius, wrote real satires in the fourth century,[23] and Rutilius, who himself knew the Roman satirists very well, in the year 416 placed his friend Lucillus beside Turnus and Juvenal as a satirist.[24] Finally, it is probable that one or two satires appeared in the circle of Sidonius who frequently mentions satire and even quotes the older satirists from time to time. Sidonius hints to his friends Lampridius and Secundinus at plans in this direction, but as a careful man he wanted to have nothing to do with satire himself.[25] Nothing more from these writings has come down to us today. But their mere presence shows that Roman satire had maintained its vitality right to the very end of antiquity.

Notes

Chapter I. Satire: A Roman Literary Genre

1. *The Anatomy of Satire*, Princeton, New Jersey, 1962.
2. *Origines* 8.7.7.
3. *Institutio oratoria* 10.1.93.
4. *Satires* 1.4; 2.1; *Epistles* 2.2.58–60.
5. Cf. U. Knoche, "Horaz, der Klassiker der römischen Satire," *Neue Jahrbücher für Wissenschaft und Jugendbildung* 12 (1936), 500–515.
6. *Institutio oratoria* 10.1.95; cf. Probus on Vergil, *Eclogues* 6.31; Aulus Gellius, *Noctes Atticae* 2.18; Cicero, *Academica* 1.8, etc.
7. *Institutio oratoria* 10.1.93.
8. *Satires* 1.10.31–48, and especially line 66.
9. Lydus, *De magistratibus populi Romani* 1.41.
10. U. von Wilamowitz-Möllendorff, *Griechische Verskunst*, Berlin, 1921, p. 42, note 1.

Chapter II. Origin and Name of the *Satura*

1. Cf. the perceptive treatment by W. Kroll in Pauly-Wissowa, 2 Reihe, 3, 192–200, and also the encyclopedias and bibliographies mentioned there. The ancient testimony dealing with these problems is most conveniently gathered together in Friedrich Marx, *C. Lucilii carminum reliquiae*, Leipzig, 1904, 1, CXX–CXXV. [The best account of the meaning of *satura* in English is to be found in C. A. Van Rooy, *Studies in Classical Satire and Related Literary Theory*, Leiden, 1966, pp. 1ff.]
2. *Institutio oratoria* 10.1.93.
3. *Grammatici Latini*, ed. Keil, 1, p. 485, line 30.
4. *Ab urbe condita* 7.2.
5. Cf. Valerius Maximus 2.4.4; Plutarch, *Moralia* 289 C–D. Comparable and yet quite different is Horace, *Epistles* 2.1.139–70.
6. *De grammaticis* 1.
7. *Georgics* 2.197; cf. *Schol. Bern.* ad loc.
8. "Zur Geschichte der römischen Satire," *Philologus* 78 (1923), 230–80.
9. Vergil, *Aeneid* 7.801, and, in imitation of this, Silius Italicus, *Punica* 8.380.
10. *Corpus Inscript. Latin.* 9, 6415a.
11. "Satire und Satura," *Studi e materiali di storia delle religioni* 9 (1933), 129–56.
12. *Epochen der römischen Geschichte*, Frankfurt a.M., 1935, 2, pp. 245ff.

13. Lucretius, *De rerum natura* 5.1379–1408; Tibullus, *Elegies* 2.1.51–56; cf. Persius, *Satires* 1.30.

14. *Satires* 2.1.1.

15. *Satires* 2.6.17.

16. *Augustus* 87.2.

17. Cf. G. A. Gerhard, "Satura und Satyroi," *Philologus* 75 (1919), 247–73.

18. *Grammatici Latini*, ed. Keil, 1, p. 485.

19. *Acron. et Porphyr. comment. in Quint. Horat. Flacc.*, ed. Havthal, p. 3. Instead of Ceres, Venus too appears as a variation.

20. Cf. Isidorus, *Origines* 5.16; 8.7.8; in short form, *Schol. Pers.*, p. VIII.

21. *Lucilius und Kallimachos*, Frankfurt a.M., 1949, p. 195.

22. *Origines* 5.16; 20.2.8.

23. *De verborum significatu*, ed. Lindsay, p. 416 (from Verrius).

24. B. L. Ullman, "Satura and Satire," *Classical Philology* 8 (1913), 172–94.

25. Lucilius, *Satires*, ed. Marx, 48.

26. *De verb. signif.*, ed. Lindsay, p. 306.

27. Cf. E. Fraenkel, Pauly-Wissowa, sup. 6, 640, 32.

28. *Satires* 1.86.

29. *Satires*, 1.10.66.

30. Karl Büchner, review of U. Knoche, *Die Römische Satire*, *Gnomon* 22 (1950), 242.

Chapter III. The Satires of Quintus Ennius

1. E.g., O. Skutsch's Ennius article in Pauly-Wissowa 10, 2589–2628, and especially Friedrich Leo's chapter on Ennius in his *Geschichte der römischen Literatur*, Berlin, 1913, pp. 150ff. the fragments are cited after the edition of J. Vahlen: *Ennianae poesis reliquiae*[3], Leipzig, 1928. The highly original and useful work of E. H. Warmington should also be mentioned: *Remains of Old Latin*[2], London, 1961, vol. 1. [As far as work in English is concerned, besides Warmington's edition and the accounts in the literary histories, there are chapters on Ennius' satires in J. W. Duff, *Roman Satire: Its Outlook on Social Life*, Berkeley, 1936, pp. 38ff. and in C. A. Van Rooy, *Studies in Classical Satire and Related Literary Theory*, Leiden, 1966, pp. 31ff.]

2. Ennius, *Annales* 376.

3. *Punica* 12.393.

4. Aulus Gellius, *Noctes Atticae* 17.17.1.

5. *De grammaticis* 1.2.

6. *Punica* 12.390–402.

7. *De consulatu Stilichonis* 3. *praef.*, esp. line 12.

8. *Cato maior* 10.

9. Ennius, *Annales* 377.

10. *De oratore* 2.276.

11. Aulus Gellius, *Noctes Atticae* 12.4.5.

12. Cf. Cicero, *De oratore* 2.276.

13. *Cato maior* 14.

14. *De grammaticis* 1.

15. *Annales* 213–17.

16. See esp. E. Laughton, "The Prose of Ennius," pp. 35-49, and E. Fraenkel, "Additional Note on the Prose of Ennius," pp. 50-56, both in *Eranos* 49 (1951).

17. On Horace, *Satires* 1.10.46.

18. On Terence, *Phormio* 339.

19. *Institutio oratoria* 9.2.36.

20. *Noctes Atticae* 2.29.1.

21. Aesop 379; Babrius 88; Avianus 21.

22. *Römische Satiren*, Zurich, 1949, pp. 7ff.

23. *M. Terenti Varronis De lingua Latina*, Leipzig, 1833, pp. 133f. (note on *L.L.* 7.35).

24. *Histories* 1.141.

25. *Fables*, 1 *praef.*

26. Quintilian, *Institutio oratoria* 5.11.19.

27. *Satires*, ed. Marx, 980-89.

28. *Epistles* 1.1.73; 1.7.29-33.

29. *Satires* 2.6.79-117.

30. Callimachus, ed. Pfeiffer, fr. 194.

31. Callimachus, ed. Pfeiffer, fr. 192.

32. E.g., Plutarch, *Moralia* 500 C-D.

33. *Lucullus* 51.

34. Dionysius Chalcus in Athenaeus, *Deipnosophistae* 15.669 E.

35. *Satires* 6-7; 14-19; probably also 12-13, etc.

36. *Satires* 57-58; 8-9; or 2; cf. 70.

37. *Noctes Atticae* 4.73.

38. *Noctes Atticae* 6.9.

39. *Odes* 4.8.

40. *Lucilius und Kallimachos*, Frankfurt a.M., 1949.

41. Horace, *Satires* 1.10.66; K. Büchner, rev. of U. Knoche, *Die römische Satire*, *Gnomon* 22 (1950), 242.

42. *Satires* 2.4.

43. The comments of S. Mariotti, "Titoli di opere enniane," *Maia* 5 (1952), 271-76, on this point are well worth reading.

44. *Satires* 1.10.66.

45. *Institutio oratoria* 10.1.93.

Chapter IV. Gaius Lucilius

1. Diomedes, *Grammatici Latini*, ed. Keil, 1, p. 485; Porphyrion on Horace, *Satires* 1.10.46.

2. *Letters to Atticus* 13.6.4.

3. *Satires*, ed. Marx, 1307.

4. *Corpus Inscript. Latin.* 5, *supplem. Italic.* 898; Dessau 8761.

5. Horace, *Satires* 1.4.1-7; 1.10.16; cf. Diomedes, *Grammatici Latini*, ed. Keil, 1, p. 485, lines 30-32.

6. Horace, *Satires* 1.10.48; 2.1.62-68.

7. The authoritative collection of fragments which completely overshadows all earlier efforts is that of Friedrich Marx (*C. Lucilii carminum reliquiae*, Leipzig, 1904/5; reviewed by F. Leo, *Göttingische Gelehrte Anzeigen* 168 [1906],

837–61). The fragments are cited in the present chapter according to the numbering of Marx's edition. This scholar's *Studia Luciliana* (Bonn, 1882) had appeared earlier. The edition of Marx was supplemented very extensively by the *Untersuchungen zu Lucilius* (Berlin, 1908) and *Römische Studien* (Leipzig-Berlin, 1922) of Conrad Cichorius. The Munich dissertation of W. Schmitt (*Satirenfragmente des Lucilius aus Libri XXVI–XXX*, Munich, 1914) is devoted to the fragments of books 26 through 30. The large edition of N. Terzaghi (*C. Lucilii saturarum reliquiae*, Florence, 1933) and his book on Lucilius (*Lucilio*, Turin, 1934) brought further important advances in scholarship, as did the quite original edition of E. H. Warmington (*Remains of Old Latin*, Vol. 3, *Lucilius, The Twelve Tables*, London, 1961 = *Loeb Classical Library* 329). Also useful and at the same time well up on the scholarship is the collection by E. Diehl in the *Poetarum Romanorum veterum reliquiae* (Berlin, 1935), as is the Italian translation of E. Bolisani (*Lucilio e i suoi frammenti*, Padua, 1932). Fr. Leo in his *Geschichte der römischen Literatur* (Berlin, 1913, pp. 405–29), E. Kappelmacher in Pauly-Wissowa (26, 1617–37), as well as the usual handbooks provide an overall view.

[In English, besides the accounts of Lucilius in the literary histories and the edition with translation of Warmington mentioned above, there is a chapter in Duff, *Roman Satire: Its Outlook on Social Life*, Berkeley, 1936, pp. 43ff. and in Van Rooy, *Studies in Classical Satire and Related Literary Theory*, Leiden, 1966, pp. 51ff. G. C. Fiske's classic study, *Lucilius and Horace*, Madison, 1920 (*Univ. of Wisconsin Studies in Language and Literature* 7), should also be mentioned.]

    8. Juvenal, *Satires* 1.20 and the scholia ad loc.; cf. Ausonius, *Epistulae* 15.9 (ed. Peiper, p. 237).

    9. Horace, *Satires* 2.1.71–74 and the scholia ad loc.

    10. *Satires* 2.1.34.

    11. Scholia on Horace, *Satires* 2.1.29; Velleius Paterculus 2.29.2.

    12. *De oratore* 2.284.

    13. *Satires* 2.1.74–75.

    14. Tiro in Aulus Gellius, *Noctes Atticae* 6.3.28 = Lucilius, *Satires* 1169.

    15. Cicero, *Academica* 2.102.

    16. Cf. Cicero, *De oratore* 1.72.

    17. *Satires* 1.10.54.

    18. E.g., 597–608.

    19. Velleius Paterculus 2.9.4.

    20. *Satires* 2.1.69.

    21. Lucilius, *Satires* 694, 695; from Book 27.

    22. *Rhetorica ad Herennium* 2.19; cf. 1.24.

    23. *Satires* 1.4.9–13.

    24. *De lingua Latina* 5.17.

    25. *De grammaticis* 2.

    26. Aulus Gellius, *Noctes Atticae* 2.24.4.

    27. Quintilian, *Institutio oratoria* 10.1.93; Tacitus, *Dialogus de oratoribus* 23.

    28. E.g., 1228–34 and 1326–38.

    29. Porphyrion on Horace, *Odes* 1.22.10.

    30. *Life of Persius* 10; Porphyrion on Horace, *Satires* 1.10.53.

31. *Satires* 2.1.
32. *Satires* 2.1 and 1.10.
33. Cf. 1008, 1009, 1028.
34. *Satires* 2.1.57–60.
35. Horace, *Satires* 2.1.68–70; cf. Persius, *Satires* 1.114–15 with the scholia.
36. 1027; cf. Horace, *Satires* 1.4.63–143.
37. *Satires* 2.1.
38. *Satires* 1.6.
39. *Satires* 2.1.30–34.
40. Cf. esp. Ennius, *Annales* 60–65.
41. *Satires* 1.5.
42. Scholia on Persius, *Satires* 3.1.
43. Aulus Gellius, *Noctes Atticae* 18.8.
44. Porphyrion on Horace, *Odes* 1.22.10.
45. Cicero, *Brutus* 160.
46. *Satires* 2.8.
47. *Satires* 2.1.30–34.
48. E.g., 394–95, 594, 688–89, 1138–42, 1280.
49. Horace, *Satires* 2.1.69–70; Persius, *Satires* 1.114; cf. Lucilius 1259, 1260.
50. E.g., 484–89.
51. *Satires* 2.5.
52. *Satires* 1.4.6–8; 1.10.3–5; 2.1.75.
53. *Satires* 1.10.64–67.
54. Varro, *De lingua Latina* 10.70.

Chapter V. Varro's Menippeans

1. Quintilian, *Institutio oratoria* 10.1.95.
2. Dahlmann's Varro article in Pauly-Wissowa (sup. 6, 1172–1277), which goes well beyond the handbooks, gives a comprehensive account of the events of Varro's life and of the character of this intense, erudite, and unusually productive man. Dahlmann also describes his literary achievement and his extreme importance for the history of culture, an importance that extends right down to our times. The present account will be limited to Varro's Menippean satires, and in the paragraphs which follow the fragments will be cited after the pocket edition of Buecheler-Heraeus (*Petronii saturae*[6], Berlin, 1922, pp. 177–250) and not after the older yet still important collection of A. Riese (*M. Terenti Varronis saturarum menippearum reliquiae*, Leipzig, 1865). A full bibliography which includes work on specialized topics by Vahlen, Ribbeck, Buecheler, Norden, and others is to be found in the article of Dahlmann mentioned above.

[There is very little in English on Varro's Menippeans. Besides chapters in Duff's *Roman Satire* (pp. 241ff.) and Van Rooy's *Studies in Classical Satire* (pp. 55ff.), three articles might be mentioned: E. Courtney, "Parody and Literary Allusion in Menippean Satire," *Philologus* 102 (1962), 86–100; B. Marti, "The Prototypes of Seneca's Tragedies," *Classical Philology* 42 (1947), 1–16; B. P. McCarthy, "The Form of Varro's Menippean Satires," *Univ. of Missouri Studies* 11, 3 (1936), 95–107.

In this chapter the titles of Varro's Menippeans have all been translated into English. The original Latin or Greek may be found by checking the fragment numbers in Buecheler-Heraeus. Where there is no other reference in the German text at the first occurrence of a title, its fragment numbers will be provided in italics.]

3. *Noctes Atticae* 2.18.7.

4. Probus on Vergil, *Eclogues* 6.31.

5. *Academica* 1.8.

6. C. Cichorius, *Römische Studien*, Leipzig-Berlin, 1922, pp. 207ff.

7. *Charakterköpfe*, Leipzig, 1910, 2, pp. 1ff.

8. *Vitae philosophorum* 6.8.

9. 281, 314, 469, 542, etc.

10. Cicero, *Academica* 1.8.

11. E.g., 559, 560.

12. Cf. also 318, 175, etc.

13. 513: *crede mihi* = "believe you me"; 318, 319, etc.

14. E.g., 535, 536: *non vides?* = "don't you see?"

15. Cf. 542, *mea Philophthonia* = "My love of envy."

16. *Griechische Verskunst*, Berlin, 1921, p. 265, note 1.

17. 195, 197, 376, 537, 553.

18. See C. Cichorius, *Römische Studien*, p. 223.

19. Cf. 167, 548, etc.

20. 488: en patriam! = "look at my country!"

21. 304–21, esp. 316–19.

22. Esp. *The Festival of Minerva* 447–48, and *The Funeral of Menippus* 542, and elsewhere.

23. 94–100, 79–81, 109–10, etc.

24. Esp. *The Lyre-Listening Ass* (348–69).

25. Phoenix of Colophon, in *Collectanea Alexandrina*, ed. J. U. Powell, Oxford, 1924, fr. 6, lines 18–21 (p. 236). And also Varro, fr. 6, 36, 110, 366, etc.

26. 294–302; especially drastically in fr. 301, 302. Cf. also *The Lyre-Listening Ass* 361.

27. Cf. 181, 240, 537.

28. 115; cf. 285, 406.

29. 456; on this see C. Cichorius, *Römische Studien*, pp. 197ff.

30. Cicero, *Academica* 1.8.

31. 559, 561, 573, etc.

32. E. Norden, "Die varronische Satura Prometheus," *Neue Jahrbücher für Philologie und Pädagogik* sup. 19 (1893), 430; to the contrary, U. von Willamowitz-Möllendorff, "Lesefrüchte," *Hermes* 34 (1899), 226–27.

33. 60, 167, 175?, 256, 460–84, 505, 562.

34. 40, 59, 142, 189, 233, 254, 302, 522, etc.

35. 123, 269–87, 423–36, etc.

36. 213, 218, 355; fragment 8 is spurious.

37. R. Hirzel, *Der Dialog*, Leipzig, 1895, 1, p. 442.

38. E.g., 550: *adulescentiaris* = "you are behaving like an adolescent."

39. 64, 259, 312, 496, etc.

40. 33, 61, 100, 384, 420, etc.

41. 89, 127, 257, 301, 406, 518, etc.

42. E.g., 209, 211, 323, 503, 539, 564, 571; from the theater: 302, etc.

43. E.g., 42, 50, 289.

44. E.g., 217, 263, 454, 475.

45. E. Norden, *Die antike Kunstprosa*, Leipzig, 1898, 1, pp. 194ff. E.g., fragments 44, 236, 264; or descriptive passages like 375 as well as 432, which according to the correct judgment of Norden are reminiscent of the style of an Aristides or a Sisenna.

46. E.g., 390, 463.

47. *Noctes Atticae* 13.11.

48. "Die Composition und Litteraturgattung der horazischen Epistula ad Pisones," *Hermes* 40 (1905), 481–528.

49. Augustine, *De civitate Dei* 6.5.

50. Aulus Gellius, *Noctes Atticae* 6.16 = fr. 403.

51. Cf. 415 and 416.

52. Cf. 80, 122, 362, for example.

53. 80, 83, 295, 296, 412, 483, 484, 560, 575, etc.

Chapter VI. Satire at the End of the Republic

1. Horace, *Satires* 1.10.46.

2. *De grammaticis* 5.

3. *Res rusticae* 3.2.17.

4. Suetonius, *De grammaticis* 15.

5. Cicero, *Epistulae ad familiares* 12.16.

Chapter VII. Horace's Satires and Epistles

1. *Satires* 2.1.22 and 1.8.11.

2. *Satires* 1.4.71–74; also 1.10.74.

3. *Satires* 1.4.92 = 1.2.27.

4. *Satires* 1.10.50 = 1.4.11; 1.10.65 = 1.4.90.

5. Cassius Dio 48.54.

6. Cf. A. Cartault, "Les satires d'Horace," *Journal des savants* 10 (1912), 308–16; 357–66; 490–503.

7. Appian, *Bellum civile* 5.549.

8. Esp. *Satires* 2.1.28–29.

9. E.g., *Satires* 2.6, and next to this most eloquently in *Epistles* 1.16.

10. *Epistles* 1.4.1; 2.2.60.

11. *Satires*, ed. Marx, 1039.

12. On Horace, *Satires* 1.1.1 and *Epistles* 1.1.1.

13. Fr. Klingner, *Q. Horati Flacci opera*², Leipzig, 1959, p. 2, line 25.

14. On this poem see the dissertation of R. Heinze, *De Horatio Bionis imitatore*, Bonn, 1889.

15. Vitruvius, *De architectura* 9. *praef.* 16; Velleius Paterculus 2.36.

16. *Satires* 1.4.45–48; 56–62; 2.6.17; *Epistles* 2.1.250–59; cf. Callimachus, *The Oxyrhynchus Papyri* 7, 1910, 31.

17. 1.4; 1.10; 2.1; 2.6, and others.

18. Cf. Quintilian, *Institutio oratoria* 5.11.20: poema! = poem.

19. *Vitae philosophorum* 4.46–57.

20. Above, note 14.

21. Perhaps *Epistles* 1.7.98.

22. Cf. Fr. Klingner, *Q. Horati Flacci opera²*, Leipzig, 1959, pp. 314–38.

23. Cf. *Satires* 2.3.

24. Cf. R. Hirzel, *Der Dialog*, Leipzig, 1895, 2, p. 5.

25. Cf. J. Martin, *Symposion*, Paderborn, 1931 .

26. On Horace, *Satires* 1.1.1 and *Epistles* 1.1.1.

27. *Epistles* 2.1.250–59; cf. 2.1.4.

28. Cf. E. P. Morris, "The Form of the Epistle in Horace," *Yale Classical Studies* 2 (1931), 79–114.

29. E.g., *Epistles* 1.11, 1.16, and others.

30. R. Heinze, "Horazens Buch der Briefe," *Neue Jahrbücher für das klassische Altertum* 43 (1919), 305–15; E. Courbaud, *Horace, sa vie et sa pensée à l'époque des épîtres*, Paris, 1914.

31. Esp. *Epistles* 1.19.

32. "Die Composition und Literaturgattung der horazischen Epistula ad Pisones," *Hermes* 40 (1905), 481–528 .

33. *Neoptolemos und Horaz, Abhandlungen der Preussischen Academie* 14, Berlin, 1918.

34. *Horazens Epistel über die Dichtkunst*, Leipzig, 1932 (*Philologus* sup. 24, 3).

35. *Horazens Brief an die Pisonen, Bericht über die Verhändlungen der Sächsischen Akademie* 88, Leipzig, 1937.

36. *Der Begriff des* πρέπον *in der Ethik des Panaitios*, 1934.

37. *Studien zur Ars poetica des Horaz*, Würzburg, 1939.

38. E.g., *Satires* 1.3.131–32; 1.6.126; *Epistles* 1.16.52.

39. E.g., *Satires* 1.4.35; 1.8.39; 1.10.86.

40. "Über die Recensio der Horazhandschriften I, II," *Hermes* 70 (1935), 249–68; 361–403, and in the introduction to his larger text edition (Leipzig, 1959).

41. E.g., *Satires* 2.4.44; 2.8.88; *Epistles* 1.16.43.

42. E.g., *Satires* 1.4.87; 1.6.102; 1.8.41; 2.3.303; 2.7.15; *Epistles* 1.17.31; 1.18.37; *Ars poetica* 101; 197.

43. *Dialogus* 20.

44. Juvenal, *Satires* 7.225–27.

45. Cf. F. Leo, Review of O. Keller and A. Holder, *Q. Horati Flacci opera* I, *Göttingische Gelehrte Anzeigen* 166 (1904), 849–56.

46. On Horace, *Satires* 1.3.21.

47. E.g., *Satires* 2.2.50; *Epistles* 1.3.10; 2.2.54.

48. E.g., *Satires* 2.3.208 and 255.

49. *Adversus Rufinum* 1.16.

50. E.g., *Satires* 2.3.126; *Epistles* 1.1.30; 1.7.69.

51. *Scholia in Horatium* λ, φ, ψ, Amsterdam, 1935.

52. Cf. R. Newald, "Nachleben der Antike," *Jahresbericht über die Fortschritte der klassischen Altertumswissenschaft* sup. 250 (1935), 1–144, passim.

53. Most recently, K. Büchner, "Horaz, 1929–1936," *Jahresbericht* sup. 267 (1939).

54. *Satiren*[10], vol. 2; *Briefe*[10], vol. 3; Berlin, 1959/60.

55. *Q. Horati Flacci opera*², Jena, 1899 and 1925; short version 1878.

56. Berlin, 1933; cf. also *Jahresbericht* sup. 250 (1935), 1–144.

57. Paul Stechel, *Wielands Übersetzungen*, Berlin, 1913, 4, pp. 15–697. This was a revision of the translation by H. Conrad, Munich, 1911.

58. [There is much scholarship in English on Horace, as is clear from the bibliographical supplements below. Just a few of the editions, translations, and general studies will be mentioned here. E. C. Wickham's edition of Horace's complete works in the *Oxford Classical Texts* series (Oxford, 1912, revised by H. W. Garrod) is still important and useful, while his older edition with commentary (London, 1891–96) is still the best in English. A. Palmer's text of the satires with notes (*The Satires of Horace*, London, 1883) has by now gone through a number of printings, as has A. S. Wilkins' pocket edition of the epistles (*The Epistles of Horace*, London, 1885). Both have the merit of being inexpensive and easily accessible, but they are old and must be used with caution. For the first book of the epistles there is the more recent edition with commentary by O.A.W. Dilke (2 ed., London, 1961).

As far as translations of the satires and epistles are concerned, two might be mentioned. That of H. Fairclough in the *Loeb Classical Library* (*Horace: Satires, Epistles, and Ars Poetica*, London, 1926) has worn well. For those who prefer something more recent there is the much "smarter" rendering of S. P. Bovie (*The Satires and Epistles of Horace*, Chicago, 1959).

Two general works on Horace also deserve mention. E. Fraenkel's study (*Horace*, Oxford, 1957) is still indispensable for anyone approaching Horace for the first time. K. Reckford's more recent book (*Horace*, New York, 1969) should also be consulted. On the satires themselves there is the work of N. Rudd (*The Satires of Horace*, Cambridge, 1966) in which the writer attempts an overview while giving equal time to each of the satires. It is a pity there is nothing like this for the epistles. The closest we can come is a series of essays by M. J. McGann (*Studies in Horace's First Book of Epistles*, Brussels, 1969 [*Collection Latomus* 100]), especially the brief final chapter, and a study by C. O. Brink (*Horace on Poetry, Prolegomena to the Literary Epistles*, Cambridge, 1963). On the *Ars poetica* there is now Brink's *Horace on Poetry II, the Ars poetica*, Cambridge, 1971.]

Chapter VIII. Seneca's Apocolocyntosis

1. *Epistles* 1.3; 2.2.

2. The first really critical edition of this writing accompanied by an introduction and commentary was put together by Franz Buecheler in the year 1863, and it is still the basic edition today (*Symbola Philologorum Bonnensium*, Leipzig, 1864–1867; in addition, Buecheler, *Kleine Schriften*, Leipzig, 1915, 1,439ff.). Buecheler republished this in his pocket edition of Petronius (first in Berlin, 1871; now 6 ed., revised by W. Heraeus, Berlin, 1922), where the critical apparatus is indeed too abbreviated. Allan Perley Ball (*The Satire of Seneca on the Apotheosis of Claudius*, New York, 1902) presents the text in a very conservative form with an extensive introduction, full bibliography, and useful notes. Essential also is Otto Weinreich's conscientious and far-sighted interpretation of the satire (Ber-

lin, 1923; with translation), as are the Budé edition of R. Waltz (3 ed., Paris, 1966; with French translation) and that of von Wagenvoort (Amsterdam, 1936; with translation into Dutch). The edition of Rossbach in Lietzmann's *Kleine Texte* series (Bonn, 1926) might also be recommended. From the large number of worthwhile specialized studies that exist only a very few may be mentioned here: R. Helm, *Lucian und Menipp*, Leipzig, 1906; K. Münscher, *Senecas Werke*, Leipzig, 1922, pp. 49ff.; R. Heinze, "Zu Senecas Apocolocyntosis," *Hermes* 61 (1926), 49–78.

[The *Apocolocyntosis* has not received a great deal of attention from the English-speaking world. There are two editions with commentary: that of A. P. Ball mentioned above (New York, 1902; with translation) and that of W. B. Sedgwick (2 ed., Oxford, 1950) with the Banquet of Trimalchio from Petronius' *Satyricon* and some inscriptions from Pompeii. There are two very interesting and at the same time very different translations. Robert Graves has included a version of Seneca's satire in his *Claudius the God* (New York, 1935, 566–82; also many other editions and printings), while more recently J. P. Sullivan has produced one in article form ("Seneca, the Deification of Claudius the Clod," *Arion* 5, 1966, 378–99). W. H. D. Rouse's translation in the Petronius volume of the *Loeb Classical Library* series is also worth consulting (2 ed., London, 1969). There is no substantial general study of the *Apocolocyntosis* in English. J. M. K. Martin's article, "Seneca the Satirist," is a good, though brief introduction (*Greece and Rome* 14 [1945], 64–71). Otherwise, all that can be recommended is the chapter in J. W. Duff's *Roman Satire* (pp. 91–96).]

3. "Deification" [This word is used by Cassius Dio.]

4. E.g., Apuleius, *Metamorphoses* 1.15 .

5. Tacitus, *Annales* 13.2–3.

6. Cassius Dio 61.10.

7. Ibid.

8. Tacitus, *Annales* 12.8 .

9. Suetonius, *Claudius* 45; E. Bickel, "Der Schluss der Apokolokyntosis," *Philologus* 77 (1921), 219–27.

10. Ausonius, *Caesares* 5.

11. *Epistulae* 23.

12. No. 569, pp. 243–51.

13. *Elevation of Fools*, in Suetonius, *Claudius* 38.3.

14. Suetonius, *Augustus* 56.

15. Tacitus, *Annales* 14.50.

16. Laws of conviviality; Pliny, *Natural History* 14.140.

17. Buecheler-Heraeus, *Petronii saturae*[6], p. 267.

18. Buecheler-Heraeus, *Petronii saturae*[6], pp. 268–69.

Chapter IX. Petronius' Novel

1. "L'età del Satyricon," *Studi italiani di filologia classica* 14 (1937), 3–46.

2. U. Paoli, "Ancora sull'età del Satyricon," *Rivista di filologia e d'istruzione classica* 16 (1938), 13–39.

3. R. Helm, "Römische Satiriker 1936–40 (ausser Horaz)," *Jahresbericht über die Fortschritte der klassischen Altertumswissenschaft* 282 (1943), 5–11.

4. *Annales* 16.18.

5. Cf. G. A. Gerhard, "Satura und Satyroi," *Philologus* 75 (1919), 247–73.

6. 81.3, where a textual emendation is to be rejected.

7. Cf. 82.5.

8. C. Cichorius, *Römische Studien*, Leipzig-Berlin, 1922, pp. 438ff.

9. Lydus, *De magistratibus populi Romani* 1.41.

10. *Liber subnotationum in verba Juliani* 4.1; 5.1 (*Patrologia Latina* ed. Migne, 48, cols. 127, 133).

11. Macrobius, *Commentarii in somnium Scipionis* 1.2.8.

12. *Der griechische Roman*[4], Leipzig, 1960.

13. *De magistratibus populi Romani* 1.41.

14. "Petron und der griechische Roman," *Hermes* 34 (1899), 494–519.

15. 132.15: *Die Verseinlagen im Petron*, Leipzig, 1933.

16. A. Marbach, *Wortbildung, Wortwahl und Wortbedeutung als Mittel der Charakterbezeichnung bei Petron*, Giessen, 1931, diss.

17. G. Meyer, Review of A. H. Salonius, *Die Griechen und das Griechische in Petrons Cena Trimalchionis*, *Gnomon* 5 (1929), 149.

18. These are probably from Northern France; cf. B. L. Ullman, "Petronius in the Mediaeval Florilegia," *Classical Philology* 25 (1930), 11–21, and "The Text of Petronius in the Sixteenth Century," *Class. Phil.* 25 (1930), 128–54.

19. Facsimile of the *Cena* by S. Gaselee, *A Collotype Reproduction . . .* , Cambridge, 1915.

20. See note 15.

21. *Petronius in Italy*, New York, 1937.

22. *Étude sur Pétrone*, Paris, 1892.

23. [Petronius has attracted considerable attention from scholars writing in English, as the bibliographical supplements below show. As far as annotated texts go, there are two that stand out as being useful, and both have been mentioned above—that of W. B. Sedgwick (2 ed., Oxford, 1950) and the more recent edition by E. T. Sage and B. Gilleland (2 ed., New York, 1969). There have been a number of translations of the *Satyricon* into English, and three can be recommended as being reliable and attractive. M. Heseltine's version in the *Loeb Classical Library* series (2 ed., London, 1969) is an old friend updated. The translations of J. P. Sullivan in the *Penguin Classics* (Harmondsworth, 1965) and W. Arrowsmith in the *Mentor Classics* (New York, 1959; also hardbound, Ann Arbor, 1959) are both lively and have the advantage of being in paperback.

Several general studies of Petronius have appeared. Two of these are devoted mainly to identifying the writer and establishing a chronology: G. Bagnani, *Arbiter of Elegance, A Study of the Life and Works of C. Petronius*, Toronto, 1954 (*Phoenix*, sup. 2) and K. F. C. Rose, *The Date and Author of the Satyricon*, Leiden, 1971 (*Mnemosyne*, sup. 16). As Knoche points out below (p. 184), Bagnani's book contains both good and bad. Well worth reading by way of introduction is J. P. Sullivan's study which provides a good overall view of the *Satyricon* and its problems: *The Satyricon of Petronius, A Literary Study* (Bloomington, 1968). Two other books should be mentioned: H. D. Rankin, *Petronius the Artist, Essays on the Satyricon and Its Author* (The Hague, 1971) and P. G. Walsh, *The Roman Novel, The Satyricon of Petronius and the Metamorphoses of Apuleius*

(Cambridge, 1970). It is impossible to mention all the articles that have been written, but two stand out as being representative of recent trends in Petronian scholarship: E. Courtney, "Parody and Literary Allusion in Menippean Satire," *Philologus* 106 (1962), 86–100, and F. Zeitlin, "Petronius as Paradox, Anarchy and Artistic Integrity," *Transactions of the American Philological Association* 102 (1971), 631–84.]

Chapter X. Aules Persius Flaccus

1. Persius, *Satires* 6.6; probably at the end of 61 after Christ.

2. E.g., 3.77–78 resembles 5.189–91.

3. E.g., 1.36–37 and 1.38–39.

4. G. A. Gerhard, "Der Prolog des Persius," *Philologus* 72 (1913), 484–91.

5. Esp. Satire 10.

6. *Römische Geschichte* 1, p. 233 [Eng. transl., W. P. Dickson, New York, 1894 (repr. 1957), 1, p. 301].

7. G. L. Hendrickson, "The Third Satire of Persius," *Classical Philology* 23 (1928), 332–42. W. Kugler, *Des Persius Wille zu sprachlicher Gestaltung in seiner Wirkung auf Ausdruck und Komposition* (Würzburg, 1940, diss.), goes further, following the precedent of N. Terzaghi in *Scritti per il XIX centenario della nascita di Persio*, Volterra, 1936, pp. 85ff.

8. Lydus, *De magistratibus populi Romani* 1.41.

9. Life of Persius, in *A. Persi Flacci et D. Iuni Iuvenalis saturae*, ed. by W. V. Clausen, Oxford, 1959, p. 33 (*Oxford Classical Text*).

10. Lydus, *De magistratibus populi Romani* 1.41.

11. Cf. *Satires* 5.14.

12. E.g., *Satires* 1.32–35.

13. *Institutio oratoria* 10.1.94.

14. *Epigrams* 4.29.7–8.

15. Life of Persius, in F. Leo's edition, Berlin, 1910, pp. 64–66; also in Clausen's edition (see above, note 9), pp. 31–34.

16. Scholia on *Satires* 2.56.

17. *Adversus Rufinum* 1.16.

18. *Satires* 5.53a = *Anthologia Latina* 950.8.3.

19. The best general study of Persius to my knowledge is Fr. Villeneuve's *Essai sur Perse* (Paris, 1918). Also well worth reading are W. S. Teuffel, *Studien und Charakteristiken zur griechischen und römischen Literaturgeschichte*, pp. 520–34 (2 ed., Leipzig, 1889); D. Nisard, *Études de moeurs et de critique sur les poètes latins de la décadence*, 1, pp. 199–257 (5 ed., Paris, 1888); G. F. Hering, *Persius, Geschichte seines Nachlebens und seiner Übersetzungen in der deutschen Literatur* (Berlin, 1935), and the Pauly-Wissowa article of W. Kroll (sup. 7, 972–79).

[Some work has been done in English. By now W. Clausen's text has superseded all others (Oxford, 1956), although it is without commentary. There are extensive comments of Knoche on this in the supplement on pp. 187–88. This now appears with a shorter apparatus criticus in an *Oxford Classical Text* combined with Clausen's Juvenal (Oxford, 1959). There is need for an up-to-date edition with English commentary, since what is perhaps the best—that of Conington-

Nettleship mentioned above (3 ed., Oxford, 1893)—is by now long out of date. This also contains a translation.

There are two translations of Persius' satires that should be mentioned. G. Ramsay's in the *Loeb Classical Library* series (London, 1918; with Juvenal) is still serviceable. More literary is that of W. S. Merwin (Bloomington, 1961).

There is only one general work on Persius in English: C. Dessen, *Iunctura callidus acri, A Study of Persius' Satires* (Urbana, 1968). There are also a few articles that are well worth reading. J. M. K. Martin's "Persius—Poet of the Stoics," *Greece and Rome* 8 (1939), 172–82, is a well-written appreciation of the poet and provides a good introduction. G. L. Hendrickson's articles on the first and third satires in *Classical Philology* 23 (1928), 97–112; 332–42, are still helpful. K. Reckford's "Studies in Persius," *Hermes* 90 (1962), 476–504, deserves careful reading. Finally, mention should be made of J. C. Bramble's study of Persius' purposes and methods: *Persius and the Programmatic Satire* (Cambridge, 1974).]

Chapter XI. Satire in the Time of Domitian

1. *Institutio oratoria* 10.1.94.
2. *Silvae* 1.3.103.
3. On Juvenal, *Satires* 1.20.
4. Pliny, *Epistles* 3.15.
5. *Epigrams* 10.99.
6. Lydus, *De magistratibus populi Romani* 1.41; cf. Leo's edition of Persius and Juvenal, Berlin, 1910, pp. 286–87.
7. On Juvenal, *Satires* 1.20.
8. Martial, *Epigrams* 7.97.7–8; 11.10.
9. Rutilius Namatianus 1.603–04; Sidonius Apollinaris, *Carmina* 9.266; Lydus, *De magistratibus populi Romani* 1.41.
10. On Juvenal, *Satires* 1.71.
11. *Epigrams* 10.35; 10.38.
12. Berlin, 1910, p. 281.
13. In spite of G. Thiele, "Die Poesie unter Domitian," *Hermes* 51 (1916), 233–40.
14. Suetonius, *Domitian* 23.2.

Chapter XII. Decimus Junius Juvenalis

1. Leipzig, 1859, p. XII.
2. *Scholia in Juvenalem vetustiora*, Leipzig, 1931, p. 1.
3. Vita IV in O. Jahn's edition, Berlin, 1851, p. 388.
4. L. Friedlaender's edition, Leipzig, 1895, p. 15.
5. Ibid.
6. *Corpus Inscript. Latin.* 10, 5382; *Dessau* 1, 2926.
7. Cf. *Satires* 3.320 where she is mentioned.
8. Cf. *Satires* 16.39–40.
9. *Epigrams* 7.24; 7.91.
10. *Epigrams* 12.18.

11. Probably *Satires* 13.16–17; certainly *Satires* 15.27.

12. Sidonius Apollinaris, *Carmina* 9.271–73.

13. Vita IV in O. Jahn's edition, Berlin, 1851.

14. O. Ribbeck, *Der echte und der unechte Juvenal*, Berlin, 1865, and already earlier in his edition, Leipzig, 1859.

15. Cf. U. Knoche, "Ein Wort zur Echtheitskritik," *Philologus* 93 (1938), 196–217.

16. E.g., *Satires* 13.120–25.

17. P. Wessner, *Scholia in Juvenalem vetustiora*, Leipzig, 1931.

18. U. Knoche, *Handschriftliche Grundlagen des Juvenaltextes*, Leipzig, 1940.

19. "Doppelfassungen bei Iuvenal," *Hermes* 44 (1909), 600–17.

20. Esp. G. Jachmann, "Studien zu Juvenal," *Nachrichten von der Gesellschaft der Wissenschaften zu Göttingen* 7 (1943), 187–266 .

21. E. Aguglia, *Spiriti e forma della satira di Giovenale*, Castrogiovanni, 1921; Piccoli Genovese, *Giovenale*, Florence, 1933; Enrica Malcovati, *Giovenale*, Cremona, 1935; P. Ercole, *Studi Giovenaliani*, Milan, 1935; E. V. Marmorale, *Giovenale*, Naples, 1938, and others.

[There is much good material in English on Juvenal. J. E. B. Mayor's edition already mentioned has a commentary that is very full. He omits satires 2, 6, and 9. The standard and most accessible text with commentary is that of J. D. Duff, also mentioned above (Cambridge, 1898; revised 1970). Duff omits satires 2 and 9, parts of 6, and scattered verses from the other satires. Although it does not have a commentary, W. Clausen's excellent *Oxford Classical Text* should be mentioned (Oxford, 1959). This volume also contains his text of Persius.

Juvenal has been translated a number of times into English, not always with great success. G. G. Ramsay's version in the *Loeb Classical Library* series (London, 1918) is a little out of date but still readable. More modern and at the same time more lively are those of R. Humphries (Bloomington, 1958) and P. Green (Harmondsworth, 1967).

It is impossible to do justice in such a short space to all the monographs and especially the articles that have appeared in English on various aspects of Juvenal's life and poems. Hopefully, the interested reader will turn to the bibliographies at the end of the book for a more complete picture. G. Highet's *Juvenal The Satirist* (Oxford, 1954) is discussed below (pp. 189–90); it must be used with caution. Perhaps the best introduction to an appreciation of Juvenal is H. A. Mason's long essay "Is Juvenal a Classic?" in *Critical Essays on Roman Literature, Satire*, ed. J. P. Sullivan (London, 1963, 93–176; reprinted from *Arion* 1). Other books that should be mentioned are I. G. Scott's *The Grand Style in the Satires of Juvenal* (Northampton, Mass., 1927) and W. S. Anderson's *Anger in Juvenal and Seneca* (Berkeley, 1964). Articles by Anderson, E. J. Kenney, and D. Wiesen, that are listed in the bibliographies, cover a number of important topics.

In recent years there have been many first-rate analyses of the individual satires, so that by now nearly every poem is the subject of at least one essay. W. S. Anderson has worked on book 1: *Yale Classical Studies* 15 (1957), 31–90. For Satire 1 there are also articles by W. C. Helmbold, *University of California Publications in Classical Philology* 14 (1951), 47–59; E. J. Kenney, *Proceedings of the Cambridge Philological Society* 8 (1962), 29–40; and J. R. C. Martyn, *Antichthon* 4

(1970), 53–61. Satire 3: E. C. Witke, *Hermes* 90 (1962), 244–46; A. L. Motto and J. R. Clark, *Transactions of the American Philological Association* 96 (1965), 267–76; E. C. Colton, *Traditio* 22 (1966), 403–19; and S. C. Fredericks, *Phoenix* 27 (1973), 62–67. Satire 4: W. C. Helmbold and E. N. O'Neil, *American Journal of Philology* 77 (1956), 68–73. Satire 6: W. S. Anderson, *Classical Philology* 51 (1956), 73–94. Satire 7: W. C. Helmbold and E. N. O'Neil, *Class. Phil.* 54 (1959), 101–08; and D. Wiesen, *Hermes* 101 (1973), 464–83. Satire 8: S. C. Fredericks, *Trans. Am. Phil. Ass.* 102 (1971), 111–32. Satire 10: D. E. Eichholz, *Greece and Rome* 3 (1956), 61–69. Satire 11: A. S. McDevitt, *Greece and Rome* 15 (1968), 173–79. Satire 13: S. C. Fredericks, *Arethusa* 4 (1971), 219–31; L. Edmunds, *Rheinisches Museum* 115 (1972), 59–73; and M. Morford, *Am. Journ. Phil.* 94 (1973), 26–36. Satire 14: E. N. O'Neil, *Class. Phil.* 55 (1960), 251–52; and J. P. Stein, *Class. Phil.* 65 (1970), 34–36. Satire 15: S. C. Fredericks, *Illinois Classical Studies* 1, 1974, in press.]

22. *Epistulae* 4.18.6.

23. Ausonius, *Epistulae* 11.

24. Rutilius Namatianus 1.603–04.

25. Sidonius Apollinaris, Carmina 12.22: *ne quisquam satiram vel hos vocaret* ("so that no one will call *these* verses satire").

Supplement to
the Second Edition

THIS book originated under difficult circumstances and it did not have too happy a fate after that. In spite of this, it met with a good reception from Karl Büchner, for example (*Gnomon* 22, 1950, 239–43), and it is now to appear again in a second edition. The text itself remains unchanged, though I would have preferred to rewrite a number of sections and also to answer many questions like those which K. Büchner asks in his review (*Gnomon* 22, 1950, 240) and others which have in the meantime occurred to me—without my always finding an adequate answer. But the publisher wanted it to be this way and a case can be made for it. The book has been loosely arranged as a series of lectures, with the intention, naturally, of transmitting a certain amount of material. But, above all, the reader should be introduced to the scholarly problems posed by the many-faceted subject matter, so that, sparked by what he finds here, he might reach conclusions of his own. And so the book will not and should not lead to a terminus where the reader could then stop. Quite to the contrary, the writer is today "enroute" along with his reader, just as he was earlier.

And so a few economical and carefully culled supplements such as those which follow can perhaps help us on. No attempt has been made to be complete in this, and I must make a broad plea for indulgence if by no means every name and every title is mentioned which the reader might expect. We have done away with the designation "handbook," to be sure, but the book should not for that reason be taken merely as a survey of scholarship.

Chapters I and II.
Satire, a Roman Literary Genre; *Origin and Name of the* Satura.

Surveys of scholarship: To become familiar with what scholarship has discovered about Roman satire in recent years, a person will probably go first to the more general critical surveys such as those of Harald

Fuchs (*Museum Helveticum* 4, 1947, 147–98), Karl Büchner (*Lateinische Literatur und Sprache in der Forschung seit 1937*, Berne, 1951 [*Wissenschaftliche Forschungsberichte, Geisteswissenschaftliche Reihe*, ed. Karl Hönn, 6]), and the one put together by E. Diehl, H. Fuchs, and E. Koestermann in the fifth edition of Eduard Norden's *Die römische Literatur* (Leipzig, 1954 [6 ed., 1961]). The loosely organized collection which Maurice Platnauer edited (*Fifty Years of Classical Scholarship*, Oxford, 1954 [2 ed. 1968]) will be consulted with real profit.

For more detailed investigations the *Année Philologique* in particular is available, meticulously edited by J. Marouzeau and Madame J. Ernst, and in addition to this there are the lists in *The Year's Work in Classical Studies* [1906–47]. I do not have access to the bibliography of classical philology begun by the USSR.

Histories of Latin literature: Then there is a whole series of accounts of the history of Latin literature that are new or that have appeared in new editions. In German that of E. Norden (*Die römische Literatur*[6], Leipzig, 1961) stands out. The harvest provided by the scholarly world of Italy that is so active is especially abundant in this area. The work of Ettore Bignone, reviewed by K. Büchner (*Gnomon* 24, 1952, 84–88), might be mentioned first. Then there are the literary histories of E. Paratore, A. Rostagni, A. G. Amatucci, G. Funaioli, each with a completely individual profile. The collective review of K. Büchner (*Gnomon* 27, 1955, 331–46) might be briefly mentioned in passing. There are also the studies of Francesco Della Corte (with a lengthy bibliography), Ussani, and Marchesi. The literary history of J. Wight Duff (*A Literary History of Rome from the Origins to the Close of the Golden Age*[3], London, 1953; *A Literary History of Rome in the Silver Age*[3], London, 1964) will also not be overlooked for the good taste and critical judgment that the author shows. There is also H. J. Rose's *Handbook of Latin Literature* (3 ed., London, 1954) as well as the useful *Dictionary of Latin Literature* (New York, 1956) by James Mantinband which serves as a source for quick information. Frederik Poulsen's discussion is far-reaching and important (*Römische Kulturbilder*, transl. H. Kobylinski, Copenhagen, 1949), as is that of H. Wagenvoort (*Studies in Roman Literature, Culture and Religion*, Leiden, 1956).

Histories: Also useful are the great historical works, especially that of Gaetano De Sanctis whose important volume 4.2 appeared in 1953 and is reviewed by Joseph Vogt (*Gnomon* 28, 1956, 468–69). The Roman history of J. Vogt which appeared in a newly revised edition in 1951 might also be strongly recommended.

Institutions and customs: A knowledge of these is, of course, extremely important for understanding the Roman satirists. These are treated in works that are at least partly very comprehensive; authors include U. Paoli, M. A. Levi, Léon Homo, J. Carcopino, G. Gianelli, R. Paribeni, F. Poulsen, and F. Altheim whose thoughts and suggestions I always find very stimulating even where I in essence reject them or become almost angry at them.

Other studies: Individual *articles and lectures* that are rather general in content as well as collections of these should not be noted further here. On the other hand, there is a work that deserves particular praise: *Römische Satiren*, which has an introduction by Otto Weinreich and is for the most part newly translated by him (Zurich, 1949). W. Süss reviewed it in *Gnomon* 23, 1951, 288–89; I reviewed it in *Deutsche Literatur-Zeitung* 74, 1953, 205–208.

Finally, mention might be made of the treatment of several themes which cut right across the broad field of Roman satire. For all questions involving the *history of transmission* Giorgio Pasquali's *Storia della tradizione e critica del testo*[2] (Florence, 1952) is at the same time basic and the place to start. Three Tübingen dissertations are devoted to *questions of form and theme*: A. Maisack, *Das dialogische Element in der römischen Satire* (1949; in addition, J. Andrieu, *Le dialogue antique*, Paris, 1954); D. Schmid, *Der Erbschleicher in der antiken Satire* (1951); H. Grupp, *Studien zum antiken Reisegedicht* (1953). The book of J. W. H. Atkins, *Literary Criticism in Antiquity*[2], vol. 2 (London, 1952), covers another important subject of satire.

Chapter III. *The Satires of Quintus Ennius*

To begin with, mention might be made of the survey of research on Ennius in *Anzieger für die Altertumswissenschaft* 5, 1952, 195–212 [by S. Timpanaro, Jr.; transl. F. Bornmann] and of the new collection of the fragments with Italian translation by Raffaele Argenio (Rome, 1951). The bold and sensational book by Mario Puelma Piwonka, *Lucilius und Kallimachos, zur Geschichte einer Gattung der hellenistisch-römischen Poesie* (Frankfurt a. M., 1949), is of quite general importance for the whole field of Roman satire and especially for the understanding of its earlier writers. For all its brilliance the work has not escaped firm and well-founded criticism (cf. K. Büchner, *Gnomon* 22, 1950, 242).

As far as the *Satura* of Ennius in particular goes, Puelma includes all of the so-called *Varia* together under the *genus saturae* (genre satire) with the exception of the *Scipio* and possibly the epigrams. If this is the case, then Ennius cannot be considered the creator of Roman literary satire any longer, for in this *satura* corpus of his, says Puelma, much use would have been made of prose as well as verse. But this interpretation conflicts with the testimony of Horace (*Sat.* 1.10.66) which K. Büchner has explained logically and accurately (*Gnomon* 22, 1950, 242–43). In my opinion, then, Puelma's interpretation will not hold up. I think, to the contrary, that Ennius' so-called *Varia* should be separated from his "medley," that is, the *satura*. Puelma's attempt, then, to connect the *saturae* of Ennius in their origins with Hellenistic popular philosophy, and perhaps with the iambics of a Phoenix of Colophon in particular, could only be convincing if in fact pieces like the *Epicharmus* or the *Euhemerus* belonged to the *genus saturae*, which is just not the case. It should not be denied that thoughts and themes of Hellenistic popular philosophy also surfaced in the *satura* of Ennius in the narrower sense of that title. Imitation in form may also have been evident here and there, and this would fit the whole method of the Hellenist Ennius very well. But when Horace (*Sat.* 1.10.66) designates the old satirist as *Graecis intacti carminis auctor* ("the originator of poetry untouched by the Greeks"), this cannot be rejected without the most convincing proofs. In any case, Puelma's book has raised very vexing questions. But my mention of this clever, imaginative, and thoroughly stimulating work should not degenerate to a review at this point.

A brief article written by Scevola Mariotti, who is well informed about the old Latin poets, is worth reading ("Titoli di opere Enniane," *Maia* 5, 1952, 271–76); the writer deals in particular with the title *Satura(e)*. I cannot suppress different doubts that I have, however, and I confess that I am still unable today, for example, to believe in a dramatic *satura*.

Chapter IV. *Gaius Lucilius*

Puelma tries to revise the picture of Lucilius far more thoroughly than he does that of Ennius (see immediately above on Chapter III). Generally speaking, it is not a matter of his dealing with detail which in Lucilius' case in particular demands investigation so urgently and will continue to demand it. But he is interested above all in the figure of the poet. Puelma formulates his point of view in the preface:

> Of primary importance for the methods of our inquiry was the conviction that we cannot approach the inner nature of an artistic literary

genre like Lucilian satire from outside by accumulating separate 'objective' literary-historical parallels. Quite to the contrary, this seems to me to be possible only if we try to put ourselves into the perspective of the artist himself and try to comprehend the genre fostered by him as a whole from his feelings about life and from his artistic purposes as they reveal themselves in the form and text of his work. According to ideas coming from modern aesthetics, our purpose presents itself primarily as defining the nature of an idea of genre from the 'world' of the poet in the sense of a way of looking at and experiencing the phenomena with which he has come to terms as a man and an artist. Therefore, consideration of the linguistic and human ideals as well as the poetic ideal of the writer of *sermones* has served as a basis of the investigation. The results may even show how from this 'world' of the *sermo*-poet and the style and forms that were peculiar to it a new approach to the literary-historical origins of the Lucilian genre of satire may be developed along with a new outlook on Alexandrian poetry.

Proud sentences spoken by a thoughtful scholar full of bright ideas, who also does not avoid bold conjectures. And what is the result? In opposition to Ennius, the *imitator* (imitator) and *sectator* (adherent) of the diatribe which was generally understood, says Puelma, Lucilius is supposed to have put together his new creation through an imitation of Callimachus consciously undertaken and consistently carried through —especially his iambics. Lucilius, who thereby becomes the originator of an avowed formal claim on the part of Roman satire to being art, would actually be the first neoteric poet, according to Puelma's formulation which he puts forward with a definite, deliberate, and categorical challenge. I cannot go into detail here about how doubtful this seems to me. In any case, Horace, who certainly knew a lot more about Lucilius than we do today, reproached him for his lack of artistic concern while giving him full recognition for his energy and genius— his *ingenium*. Insofar as we can test this (e.g., fr. 1326–38), Horace is completely correct in his judgment. Besides, it may be taken as certain that in the second century B.C. each Roman of rank writing poetry is a dilettante, and this is the case with Lucilius, too. He does not at all feel that he is a poet by vocation, but this is his hobby. I think that he should be put into the same category as men like Mummius or Catulus or Gaius Caesar Strabo whom a self-confident poet like Accius brushed off so fiercely as being a dilettante (Valerius Maximus 3.7.11). That Lucilius furthermore was an extremely well-read man and was recognized as such—we need only think of the dedication of Clitomachus —is undisputed. Undoubtedly he also read Callimachus carefully. But his personal make-up carried him much further, and Wilamowitz long ago correctly recognized this. It is precisely on the basis of these assumptions that he should be given credit for feeling the difference between literary forms clearly and consciously—especially, for example, the fact that iambic poetry and the *satura* are basically quite different things, as Horace later demonstrated by what he did.

The problem, then, of Ennius-Lucilius-Phoenix-Callimachus is rightly posed, but it does not seem to me to be by any means solved by Puelma. Moreover, it might be emphasized that in spite of the monumental work of Marx and Cichorius on Lucilius, there is still a lot of spadework to be done by scholars whose unselfishness again and again deserves the highest praise. The study of fragment 9 by D. Henss (*Philologus* 98, 1954, 159–61) falls into this category. On the whole range of problems there are the very sound comments of K. Büchner (*Gnomon* 22, 1950, 242–43 and *Lateinische Literatur und Sprache*, Berne, 1951, 22–33).

Chapter V. *Varro's Menippeans*

Varro's Menippeans have been made accessible, probably for the first time, to a larger German reading public by Otto Weinreich (*Römische Satiren*, pp. 35–50), especially through his reconstruction of *The Furies*. The article of Luigi Alfonsi ("Intorno alle Menippee di Varrone," *Rivista di filologia e d'istruzione classica* 30, 1952, 1–37) takes us a step further in another passage; here there is an excellent treatment of the *Endymions* and the very interesting fragment 379.

F. Della Corte put together a new edition of the collected fragments (*Varronis Menippearum fragmenta*, Genoa, 1953). For more than twenty years now F. Della Corte has shown a particular expertise as far as Varro is concerned. His work, *La poesia di Varrone Reatino ricostituita* (Turin, 1938), among others, deserves special mention here and above all his comprehensive monograph on Varro, *Varrone, il terzo gran lume Romano* (Genoa, 1954). The title probably recalls a remark of Petrarch to the effect that Varro stands between Cicero, the Republican, and Vergil, the Augustan, as the intermediary. This book is reviewed by the best scholar of the material, H. Dahlmann (*Gnomon* 27, 1955, 176–81). F. Della Corte discusses individual passages under the obscure title "*Suspiciones*" in the memorial volume for A. Beltrami (*Miscellanea philologica*, Genoa, 1954, 69–81).

Karl-Erik Henriksson deals in a sensible and thoughtful way with Greek titles of the individual satires and includes a painstaking bibliography (*Griechische Büchertitel in der römischen Literatur*, Helsinki, 1956, pp. 24–30). Puelma's views on Varro's Menippeans (*Lucilius und Kallimachos*, pp. 172–80) are not to be separated from his general theory.

Chapter VII. *Horace's Satires and Epistles*

Using a judicious selection of material, G. Radke surveys the extensive *scholarship on Horace* in recent years (*Gymnasium* 61, 1954, 231–48).

Monographs: The book of Walter Wili (*Horaz und die augusteische Kultur*, Basel, 1948) is probably the most important Horace monograph of the intervening years. It was not yet possible to consider this in the text of the earlier edition, but since then it has been an indispensable handbook for every interpreter of Horace. The general study of Hildebrecht Hommel, moreover, which is much more modest and more of a handbook will also be used (*Horaz, der Mensch und das Werk*, Heidelberg, 1950). Walter Wimmel wrote an appreciative review of it (*Gnomon* 24, 1952, 112–14). It is unfortunate that Hans Drexler's monograph, *Horaz, Lebenswirklichkeit und ethische Theorie* (Göttingen, 1953), a work that awaits rebuttal, exists in microfilm only. Its purpose is to clear away one Horace myth. Only the review of Karl Bayer might be mentioned here (*Gnomon* 26, 1954, 204–205). The book of Alfred Noyes is written in English (*Horace, A Portrait*, New York, 1947). And not only the expert should read Karl Hönn's *Das Rom des Horaz* (Vienna, 1951).

It is impossible to list here individual studies which advance our understanding of Horace as a satiric poet. The study of Victor Pöschl on Horace ("Horaz," in *L'influence grecque sur la poésie latine de Catulle à Ovide*, [Fondation Hardt II], Geneva, 1956, 93–130) does a good job of taking us into the mainstream of the discussion on this point. At the same time important scholars of different nationalities are also mentioned there. Of course, the satires serve neither as a point of departure nor as a focal point of Pöschl's study, but important ideas that come from him contribute to the understanding of these poems.

Critical editions: Several have been published: A. Rostagni's *Horatii opera ad Johannis Bond exemplum notis ill.* (Turin, 1948), as well as those of Ernestus Curotto (Turin, 1951) and F. Villeneuve (Paris, 1951; with a translation into French). And above all there is now Friedrich Klingner's text of Horace which has appeared in a second edition (Leipzig, 1950). While the first edition was a masterly work with some blemishes—what on Ovid, for instance, would not have felt deserving of criticism—the second edition by comparison represents a great advance. The main features involving judgment about the tradition and principles of establishing a text have naturally remained the same. But all-in-all it is apparent that text, testimonia, and critical apparatus have undergone a fundamental revision. It is not just that the typographical errors of the first edition have been eliminated with rare acuteness (e.g., *Sat.* 1.4.13; 1.4.50; 1.5.30; 1.7.35; 2.3.165; *Epist.* 1.1.104; 1.17.7; 2.2.114 app., etc.), but a look through the testimonia reveals an improvement throughout. It is no secret that in many details the critic should and must pass judgment more boldly than the editor does. And so, for example, I would take the pattern of August Meineke at *Epist.* 1.18.91 as more correct; I would remove the verse at *Sat.* 1.2.13 from the text as being a repetition of *Ars poet.* 421; the same should be done with *Sat.* 1.5.92; 1.6.28; *Epist.* 1.1.56; 1.1.61; 2.1.101, and, last but not least, with *Epist.* 1.19.48-49. Probably also at *Sat.* 1.4.52 the reading *numqui* should be given the preference or at *Ars poet.* 178 the reading *morabimur*. Moreover, in the critical apparatus a word on instances like *Epist.* 1.16.52 would have been very welcome. But how important are such trivia in view of the fact that we have here before us what is actually the best critical pocket edition of Horace that exists!

Wider circles of readers will consult the bilingual Heimeran edition (Munich) which Hans Faerber produced in a fifth edition in 1949; the satires and epistles last appeared in 1953–1954 with a good bibliographical summary. K. Bayer has a good review of this charming and tasteful book in *Gnomon* (26, 1954, 130–31). The bilingual edition of Rudolph Helm should also not be overlooked (Kroener, Stuttgart, 1954). The part translation of Claus Springsfeld (Nördlingen, Bavaria, 1951) is an oddity.

Manuscript tradition: The Hamburg dissertation of Werner Peters, which unfortunately is unpublished, goes to the heart of the Horace recension (*Die Stellung der Handschriftenklasse Q in der Horaztradition*, 1954). Among other things, the question of whether there were not more than just two manuscripts of Horace that came down to the medieval period from antiquity is investigated. The problem of the *Blandinius Vetustissimus* is advanced considerably, and the pseudo-Asconian scholia are evaluated for the history of the manuscript tradition of Horace. A new edition of this mass of commentary should cap this preliminary study.

Günther Jachmann does an impressive job with *interpolations* in Horace ("Zur Frage der Verswiederholung in der augusteischen

Dichtung," in *Studi in onore di Ugo Enrico Paoli*, Florence, 1955, 393–421). To mention a study that is much respected but diametrically opposed, Franz Dornseiff champions obviously contrary principles in his little book, *Verschmähtes zu Vergil, Horaz und Properz* (Leipzig, 1951).

The Satires: As far as the satires are concerned, many ideas of Karl Ernst Laage (*Der Friedensgedanke in der augusteischen Dichtung*, Kiel, 1956, diss.) further our understanding of the subject matter. M. J. McGann broaches questions of structure (*Some Structural Devices in the Satires and Epistles of Horace*, Oxford, 1954, diss.). Nils Ola Nilsson treats metrics in detail (*Metrische Stildifferenzen in den Satiren des Horaz*, Uppsala, 1952, diss.; rev. by H. Drexler, *Gnomon* 25, 1953, 333–35). On individual satires: Satire 1.1: Hans Herter, *Rheinisches Museum* 94, 1951, 1–42. Satire 1.4: N. Rudd, *American Journal of Philology* 76, 1955, 165–75 and *Classical Quarterly* 5, 1955, 142–56. Satire 1.5: H. A. Musurillo, S. J., *Classical World* 48, 1955, 159–62 and W. S. Anderson, *Classical World* 49, 1955, 57–59. Satire 1.9: W. S. Anderson, *American Journal of Philology* 77, 1956, 148–66. Satire 1.10 (on the spurious verses at the beginning): G. D'Anna, *Maia* 7, 1955, 26–42. Satire 2.7.95: M. J. McGann, *Classical Review* 6, 1956, 97–99.

The Epistles: The Freiburg dissertation of Erika Garn deals with the first book of the epistles (*Ordenelemente im ersten Epistelbuch des Horaz*, 1954). On Horace's literary letters Ernst Howald's *Das Wesen der lateinischen Dichtung* (Erlenbach-Zurich, 1948; rev. Erich Burck, *Gnomon* 25, 1953, 389–96) is to be consulted. Friedrich Klingner's essay on Horace's letter to Augustus (*Horazens Brief an Augustus*, Munich, 1950; rev. E. Bignone, *Gnomon* 24, 1952, 89–91) is extremely important. P. Giufrida discusses a detail ("Horat. Epist. II. 1. 118–38, elogio o parodia?" in *Festschrift für Funaioli*, Rome, 1955, 98–119). On the letter to Florus: M. J. McGann, *Rheinisches Museum* 97, 1954, 343–58. H. Dahlmann opens new ways for understanding the so-called *Ars poetica* (*Varros Schrift De Poematis und die hellenistisch-römische Poetik*, Wiesbaden, 1953). Also welcome is the bibliography by A. R. Benham ("Horace and his *Ars poetica* in English," *Classical World* 49, 1955, 1–5).

Chapter VIII. *Seneca's Apocolocyntosis*

Whether the satire mocking the dead emperor Claudius which has been preserved for us is the *Apocolocyntosis* which Cassius Dio quotes (60.35.3: Xiphilinos), whether Seneca is to be considered as its author, whether from the title—Metamorphosis to a pumpkin?—it follows that there is a truncation of our text, whether there is a one-time joke in the title in which only the small circle of gossiping, sharpsighted nobility with whom Seneca associated could take pleasure—these and other questions besides are still answered today each in different ways. K.-E. Henriksson (*Griechische Büchertitel in der römischen Literatur*, pp. 69–73) presents an ideally clear introduction to the problems with an exhaustive survey of the bibliography. My addendum here hardly provides anything more, and our attention should be directed to the high points only. Gilbert Bagnani, who suggests (*Arbiter of Elegance*, Toronto, 1954, pp. 27–46) that it was not Seneca, but rather Petronius who authored the satire that has been preserved, fails completely to take into account Seneca's range and its possibilities. He is by no means only the Stoic philosopher. I see no possibility of doubting his authorship here, especially since the points are arranged throughout in Seneca's usual, well-known way and there is plenty of self-satire. I am therefore also unable to go along with the view of Léon Herrmann (*Phèdre et ses fables*, Leiden, 1950; rev. A. Labhardt, *Gnomon* 24, 1952, 91–95).

Corrado Gallo published a general monograph on the satire with a select bibliography (*L'Apocolocintosi di Seneca, saggio critico*, Arona, 1948). Mention might also be made of the edition of A. Ronconi (Milan, 1947) and especially of the certainly very important new edition of Carlo Russo (*L. Annaei Senecae Divi Claudii Apocolocyntosis*, Florence, 1948). The thoughts that Russo put forward in *Parola del passato* (7, 1952, 48–53) have been used to good advantage in the second edition (1955). Besides the text, the edition contains a very good introduction (with information on the literature), a learned commentary, and useful indices. It is worthy of the *Bibliotèca di Studi Superiori* in every respect. B. Axelson reviewed it briefly (*Gnomon* 24, 1952, 236–37). Of course, if anyone is interested in certain details—for example, the interpolations in the *editio princeps*, such as that in chapter 3 after the word *Britannos*—he will not find sufficient information in Russo and will have to consult the old edition of A. P. Ball (New York, 1902), if Buecheler's large edition is not available.

Chapter IX. *Petronius' Novel*

Survey of scholarship: The efforts of the scholarly world to deal with Petronius and the many difficulties he presents are clearly described in the very important survey of scholarship (between 1941 and 1955) by Robert Muth (*Anzeiger für die Altertumswissenschaft* 9, 1956, 1–

22). This work is indispensable and definitely deserves a place here at the beginning.

Identity of the writer: The arguments about the identity of the writer of our novel, its date, literary form, content, and literary level have by no means subsided, and fortunately so. Salvatore Spoto has expressed himself again on the identity of the author (*L'identificazione di Petronio*, Catania, 1948; I did not have access to this). It is noteworthy that Enzo V. Marmorale has abandoned his old position. In a comprehensive and very learned study he argues for the late dating and places our novel in the time of Commodus or even of Heliogabalus (*La questione Petroniana*, Bari, 1948). The book is thoroughly rewarding even for the reader who rejects the results. W. Süss reviewed it with great expertise and with obvious relish (*Gnomon* 23, 1951, 312–17), and following him I might recommend rejection of the late date. The book of Gilbert Bagnani goes still further in another respect (*Arbiter of Elegance, A Study of the Life and Works of C. Petronius*, Toronto, 1954; rev. W. Süss, *Gnomon* 27, 1955, 136–37). With wit and imagination Bagnani rightly argues for identifying the author with the Petronius of Tacitus. But then he lapses into fanciful speculation and finally identifies this Petronius as the writer also of the Senecan satire on the dead Claudius which has been preserved. *Credat Judaeus Apella*! ("Apella the Jew may believe!").

Title: Most recently Karl-Erik Henriksson has made worthwhile contributions to determining and explaining the title (*Griechische Büchertitel*, pp. 74–77). He decides correctly for *Satyricon* (*libri*), not *Saturae*. For the form of the title he points to the *Milesiaca* of Aristides, which were certainly well known in Rome. And so right away the title provides veiled information about the literary form that was intended. Dissolute tales of a gay and wanton type are anticipated, such as would be typical of satyrs. At the same time Petronius' public could comprehend an ambiguity, *satiricon* (*libri*), in which, as in Roman satire, the truth is said with a smile. Both apply to our novel and this explanation seems to me to be convincing. Ambiguity in a title has its parallels— in the *Catalepton*, for example.

Critical editions: That of Alfred Ernout has appeared in a third edition (Paris, 1950); Helmut Schmeck, a leading expert on the subject, reviewed it (*Gnomon* 25, 1953, 100–103). As is well known, Ernout dealt with the manuscript tradition independently and with good results and produced a recension that has been recognized for a long time. The translation into French is judged outstanding. In the introduction Ernout takes a clear and critical position on all of the important questions of Petronian philology. At the same time, the real and doubtful fragments are presented in a greater profusion than in Buecheler and in Heraeus. They too pose very interesting problems for the scholar. Léon Herrmann has put together a well-thought-out selection with translation (*Douze poèmes d'exil de Sénèque et vingt-quatre poèmes de Pétrone*, Brussels, 1955).

We now have another critical text with translation and extensive commentary by A. Cesareo and N. Terzaghi (Florence, 1950). The names of the editors responsible for this edition are well enough known to make any word of recommendation unnecessary. In Germany many readers will refer to the edition of Carl Hoffmann (Heimeran, Munich, 1948), which is accompanied by a translation that is both accurate and readable. E. Koestermann has reviewed this work which deserves every praise (*Gnomon* 21, 1949, 266–67). But many will perhaps give priority to Otto Weinreich's translation in his *Römische Satiren* (pp. 305–416) over Hoffmann's, in part more for emotional reasons than for anything else.

Structure: Vicenzo Ciaffi deals with the structure of the novel (*Struttura del Satyricon*, Turin, 1955).

Cena Trimalchionis: This is a much-studied piece, and it is very welcome news that now a small critical edition is once again available in Germany. This is the fourth edition of H. Schmeck's text with abundant ancillary material in Winter's collection of vulgar Latin texts (Heidelberg, 1954). Schmeck's thoughts about problems and methods of research in vulgar Latin deserve careful consideration. Enzo V. Marmorale has also published a text edition of the *Cena* with commentary (Florence, 1947 and last in 1955), while W. B. Sedgwick's text has appeared in a second edition (Oxford, 1950), once again with the *Apocolocyntosis* and a selection of wall graffiti from Pompeii. The separate edition of the *Cena* in French by Paul Perrochat has appeared in a second edition (*Le festin de Trimalcion*, Paris, 1952); it contains a critical and exegetic commentary. An article by J. Colin is devoted to a detail of this episode ("All'uscita del banchetto di Trimalchione, Petronio 79," *Rivista di filologia e d'istruzione classica* 30, 1952, 97–110) and a study of V. Ciaffi to another ("Intermezzo nella Cena Petroniana [XLI. 10–LVI. 8]," *Rivista di filologia e d'istruzione classica* 33, 1955, 113–45).

H. L. Nelson treats the *speech of the freedmen* in the *Cena* fully and effectively along with the difficult problem of what now should be considered vulgar Latin in it and what should be taken as colloquial (*Petro-nius en zijn "vulgair" Latijn*, Utrecht, 1947, diss., and in a second study as well: "Les rapports entre le latin littéraire, la langue de conversation et la langue vulgaire au temps de Pétrone," *Actes du premier congrès de la Fédération Internationale des Associationes des Études Classiques*, 1951, 220–29). W. Süss, who himself has dealt with the problem au-thoritatively for more than thirty years, reviewed both of these studies (*Gnomon* 27, 1955, 378–79). Giovanni Tarditi has produced a brief study on the diminutive in Petronius (*I diminutivi nel Satyricon di Petronio*, Genoa, 1951).

The Widow of Ephesus: Another brillant episode in our novel is this ever popular tale. J. Colin has produced an article on it also ("Il soldato della matrone d'Efeso e l'aceto dei crocefissi, Petronio 111," *Rivista di filologia e d'istruzione classica* 31, 1953, 97–128).

Details: Many particulars in Petronius need further clarification, and scholarship is fully aware of this. Here are only a few indications of this. The article of G. Bagnani is useful ("Encolpius, *Gladiator obscenus*," *Classical Philology* 51, 1956, 24–27; cf. Andreas Thierfelder, "*Obscaenus*," in *Navicula Chiloniensis, Studia philologica F. Jacoby*, Leiden, 1956, 98–106). Useful in a completely different way is the cul-ture-critical essay on Petronius, chapter 5, by H. L. W. Nelson ("Ein Unterrichtsprogramm aus Neronischer Zeit auf Grund von Petrons Satiricon, c. 5," *Nieuwe Reeks* 19, 1956, 201–28).

Translations: Finally, after mention has been made of the very good German, French, and Italian translations, the most recent one in English should not be overlooked. This is the much-praised version of Paul Dinnage (*The Satyricon of Petronius*, London and New York, 1954).

Chapter X. *Aules Persius Flaccus*

In the intervening years there have been a number of very important contributions that have added considerably to our understanding of Persius, a poet who with his capricious style has proved capable of instilling enthusiam in some of his readers to the same degree that he has tortured and repelled others.

Monograph: The extensive monograph of Enzo V. Marmorale has appeared in a second edition (*Persio*, Florence, 1956).

Text editions: The poems now also exist in several good text editions newly edited. In France the Budé edition of A. Cartault, which has been highly regarded for a very long time, has gone into a third edition (Paris,

1951). In Italy Augusto Mancini published the text with introduction, translation, and notes under the patronage of Castiglioni, Pasquali, and Terzaghi (Florence, 1950); that of Nino Scivoletto, also with commentary, followed this (Florence, 1956). In Germany, Otto Seel produced the satires in the bilingual Tusculum series of Heimeran (Munich, 1950). This valuable and capricious book offers far more than just text and translation, however, for there is also a survey of the text tradition, an *adnotatio critica* (critical note), notes which for Persius are absolutely necessary and an epilogue well worth reading and one which can perhaps serve as an introduction to Persius. Since in the meantime Seel's Persius has become a standard work in our scholarship, I can be satisfied here with briefly mentioning H. Wieland's review of it (*Gnomon* 23, 1951, 226–28).

But if I am not completely deceived by what is at present still a first impression, the best critical pocket edition of the poet there is has been in print for a few weeks now, coming from the pen of an American scholar, Wendell Clausen (*A. Persi Flacci saturarum liber*, Oxford, 1956). Clausen has undertaken to independently rework the Persius tradition which is almost limitless and which even today is not yet definitively and completely known. Through his work a reliable documentary basis has been attained which up until now has necessarily been missing. From the *mare magnum* (great sea) of manuscripts Clausen draws a small group, and the initiate can breathe a sigh of relief as he imagines what a plethora of useless texts has been pushed to one side—though the editor first had to determine their worthlessness himself in laborious detail. The apparatus is in essence meant to present only the divergency of the tradition in the case of genuine, that is to say ancient, variants, and so a sequence can be sketched. This surely deserves our thanks and our praise. It follows further that upon closer inspection we cannot any longer agree with Otto Jahn's view of a bipartite Persius tradition—an idea which was recognized as admirable and well proven for his time—for even manuscripts of secondary quality can contain the best and most valuable material from the tradition, as Clausen shows convincingly in a few pages in his preface. Furthermore, Clausen has also carried out a fresh investigation of the old Persius scholia themselves and has made them of use for the history of the tradition as well as for establishing a text; he is really the first to do this with consistency. For it has long been known that the scholia editions of Otto Jahn (1843) and of Buecheler and Leo (1910) which followed were quite incomplete and actually inadequate. Perhaps we may now also expect from Clausen the new critical edition of the scholia that is much desired, possibly along the lines of Wessner's Juvenal scholia.

Clausen's Persius text, then, is put together on a considerably more solid basis than all the editions of his predecessors. What results from the editor's sober judgment and sharp sensitivity seems to me to be a plainly excellent text. And in all the difficult passages, which are really quite numerous in Persius, the apparatus makes the editor's thoughts amply clear and substantiates them in the way Housman usually does in his master editions, though even more fully. I do, however, miss a comment on the interpolated verse at Satire 5.59a which Kugler had discovered and had explained as being genuine. To this summary recommendation of this book I can only add: "In brief, this edition provides the first critical text of Persius to be accompanied by an accurate report of the manuscript tradition on which it rests."

Persius' art: Teodoro Ciresola addresses himself to this (*La formazione del linguaggio poetico di Persio*, Rovereto, 1953). There is also the study of D. Henss ("Die Imitationstechnik des Persius," *Philologus* 99, 1955, 277–94); this article, which demonstrates how fruitful the inquiry really is, is an extract from Henss' dissertation (*Studien zur Imitationstechnik des Persius*, Marburg, 1951). Mention might also be made of an article by H. Hommel ("Die Frühwerke des Persius," *Philologus* 99, 1955, 266–76).

Details: In the case of Persius these continually demand fresh attention and explanation. Only very little that has been done may be noted here: R. E. Wycherley on Pers. 3.53f. (*Phoenix* 7, 1953, 20–35); P. Frassinetti, "Note a Persio e a Giovenale," *Rivista di filologia e d'istruzione classica* 33, 1955, 405–15; R. Verdière, "Notes critiques sur Perse," in *Hommage à M. Niedermann*, Brussels, 1956, 339–50.

Translations: Finally, besides mentioning the very recent translation of O. Seel, I want to draw attention to O. Weinreich's reproduction and completion of the translation of H. Blümner (1897) in his *Römische Satiren* (pp. 166–200). Weinreich himself speaks about the way he deals with the translation into rhymed iambics (p. 420), which in my opinion is still a little too smooth. He says himself that he only stands behind the relatively good portions of it.

Chapter XI. *Satire in the Time of Domitian*

The seventy hexameters of Sulpicia, about which I feel no differently today than I did earlier, have been subjected to a more searching investigation by Italo Lana (*La satira di Sulpicia*, Turin, 1949). Through a happy discovery by A. Campana we now also have a handwritten witness for the verses. This is the *Codex Vaticanus Latinus 2836*, a miscellaneous manuscript of the fifteenth or sixteenth century, which is a copy of a lost *Codex Bobiensis*. Like the lost original, it contains a collection of rather short and very short poems which had been collected in the fourth century after Christ. Of these No. 27 is the so-called *Satura* of Sulpicia. With this discovery the hypothesis of a possible medieval origin for this series of verses collapses once and for all; the lines are ancient. The collection has now been published, edited with the usual superior skill (*Epigrammata Bobiensia*, detexit A. Campana, ed. Franco Munari, vol. 2, Rome, 1955 [*Edizioni di Storia e Letteratura*]; H. Dahlmann's review of this is worth reading [*Gymnasium* 6, 1956, 558–64]).

Chapter XII. *Decimus Junius Juvenalis*

General studies: In the year 1949 there appeared, among others, the brief general appreciation of Juvenal by M. Puelma Piwonka (*Lucilius und Kallimachos*, pp. 104–07) and that of Otto Weinreich in the introduction to his *Römische Satiren* (pp. LVIII-LXV) that is very much to the point. Soon after this came K. Büchner's contribution in his survey of scholarship (Berne, 1951). The great monograph of Gilbert Highet now has much greater pretensions (*Juvenal the Satirist*, Oxford, 1954; rev. B. L. Ullman, *American Journal of Philology* 77, 1956, 321–23; the review [by U. Knoche] in *Gnomon* 29, 1957, 54–65 is more detailed). Highet deals with Juvenal's life, his literary work, and his survival from antiquity to the present in three main sections. Voluminous, though certainly not always systematic, notes supplement the text. The book is directed both to experts as well as to a wider circle of interested readers to whom it also has quite a lot to say. It is skillfully written and presents a goodly number of quite brilliant formulations. This is a book that surely provides no mean evidence of contemporary American humanism, a sphere in which Highet stands out probably as one of the most important personalities. Highet's purpose is to understand Juvenal's satires mainly from the personal experiences of the poet. Such an attempt in and of itself should not be faulted, for important differences between the individual satires do in fact exist. But to go on and understand these from the poet's changing fortunes seems to me a very problematic tack to take. For the externals of Juvenal's life can no longer be determined today with any certainty, and this is especially true of his inner life. And such knowledge would be a necessary prerequisite. Highet lets other possible explanations go completely by the board and yet these in particular deserve serious consideration also.

The picture that Highet sketches of Juvenal as a satiric poet is backed by a well-considered paraphrase of the individual satires which also has much to offer for questions of structure. His general opinion reads: "His poetry is memorable, original, and fundamentally true." In a certain sense this is correct, but it needs more detailed explanation. And, as far as I am concerned, it remains doubtful whether the position of an important satiric poet can be defined so simply. Highet gets great enjoyment from the material; on the other hand, his account of Juvenal's means of expression is quite meagre. For amid all the impressive rhetoric, a substantial part of Juvenal's satiric poetry, whether it is viewed as a literary genre or as personal expression, cannot be understood from the rhetorical alone.

Highet's survey of the history of the poet's influence deserves our thanks—especially what he says about his appeal since Renaissance times. Here a real expert takes his readers over broad, even remote areas of the various literatures of Europe. His observations support his presentation very well, and besides containing a great deal of material, they include many a pithy suggestion. All-in-all the monograph strikes me as being a useful Juvenal handbook. It will also certainly provoke no little disagreement and it urgently needs supplementing through critical refinement on a number of important points.

Enzo V. Marmorale seeks to deepen the understanding of Juvenal from the aesthetic point of view (*Giovenale*, Bari, 1950). This is a second edition of his work; I earlier reviewed the first edition not without several reservations (*Gnomon* 15, 1939, 368–72). An article of W. S. Anderson on matters of chronology is to be noted ("Juvenal, Evidence on the Years A. D. 117–28," *Classical Philology* 50, 1955, 255–57), while for an appreciation of the poetic form there is the dissertation of Karl Heindl (*Bilder, Vergleiche und Beschreibungen bei Juvenal*, Vienna, 1951). For understanding the subject matter there is M. A. Levi's "Aspetti sociali della poesia di Giovenale" (in *Studi in onore di G. Funaioli*, Rome, 1955, 170–80) and before him G. Highet's "The Philosophy of Juvenal" (*Transactions and Proceedings of the American Philological Association* 80, 1949, 254–70), where in my opinion, at any rate, Juvenal's inclination to Epicureanism in his later years is probably overestimated. There is another article by Highet that is very fresh and original ("Juvenal's Bookcase," *American Journal of Philology* 72, 1951, 369–94).

Critical editions: There is now the fourth edition of the Budé text with translation into French by P. de Labriolle and F. Villeneuve (Paris, 1950) which was introduced a long time ago. An Italian edition has not been accessible for me up until now (*Satire, testo e versione a cura dell'Istituto di Letteratura Latina della Facoltà di Magistero di Roma*, Naples, 1954). My own pocket edition with critical apparatus preceded this (U. Knoche, *D. Junius Juvenalis, Saturae*, Munich, 1950), and the translation volume appeared the next year (U. Knoche, *Juvenal, Satiren*, Munich, 1951, also at Max Hueber). I attempted to put together a critical recension using basic documentary material that had been worked through independently. The apparatus is meant to present the actual state of the tradition clearly and to make it verifiable at any given point. It is not just a mechanical apparatus, but its purpose is to serve as much as possible in each instance the needs of the person consulting it as he comes to his own conclusions. The edition has enjoyed a favorable reception both by H. Fuchs and by Sesto Prete (*Gnomon* 24, 1952, 328–31). I alone am best aware of the fact that several defects need to be remedied—typographical errors, mistakes, and inaccuracies. E.g., *Sat.* 6.56—*agro*; *Sat.* 11.70—*praeterea*; *Sat.* 7.45 —*constant*: without period. In the apparatus: *Sat.* 1.35—the *second quem* appears in P¹ as *que*; *Sat.* 1.161—the stroke after the word *Vallae* is to be removed; *Sat.* 4.141—*post*: italics; *Sat.* 7—superscription, line 4: STERILITATE; *Sat.* 7.154—*crambe*: G, not g; *Sat.* 7.167—*Vel* no longer stands today in the fragment from Antinoë; *Sat.* 8.7—*Fabricium* is not in Ω, but in ς; *Sat.* 15—superscription, line 2: "u" is to be removed (cf. line 3); *Sat.* 15.2—(*A*)*egyptus*, not (*A*)*epyptus*. Also, the lacuna after *Sat.* 5.64 no longer seems to me quite as likely as it did earlier. The suggestion has a better place, then, in the apparatus than in the text. Pulman had already deleted *Sat.* 5.90. Bertil Axelson proposes *tamquam* instead of *quamquam* in *Sat.* 4.79; this should at least have appeared in the apparatus.

Manuscripts: A book by Alexander Gružewski provides access to new manuscript material (*De XVI Juvenalis codicibus qui in Polonia asservantur*, Warsaw, 1956). Of these texts the *Zamoscianus* from the year 1529, which Gružewski discusses in detail (p. 59), seems to have the greatest value, relatively speaking (*Codex Bibliothecae Nationalis Varsaviensis Cim. 108*). The book provides a gratifying and valuable addition to our knowledge, even though the manuscripts which it deals with are quite late, coming as they do from the fourteenth through the sixteenth centuries.

Text-criticism: Even today there are still widely divergent opinions as to the correct way to deal with the text itself. Generally speaking, the existence of extensive interpolations in Juvenal is much more readily recognized now than it was earlier, only there is no agreement as to their extent. Franz Dornseiff has certainly remained firm (*Deutsche Literatur-Zeitung* 72, 1951, 250–51; "Überscharfe Philologie, verschwendet an Propertius und Juvenalis," *Wiss. Zeitschr. der Univ. Leipzig, Ges.- und Sprachwiss. Reihe* vol. 3, 1951/2, 48–54). On the other hand, W. C. Helmbold, for instance, attempts to identify interpolations in Juvenal to a much greater extent than Jachmann and I have recommended. He published structural analyses of several of Juvenal's satires and at the same time did not hesitate to suggest broad deletions (Satire 1: *University of California Publications in Classical Philology* 14, 1951, 47–60; Satire 12: *Classical Philology* 51, 1956, 14–23). Here Helmbold in my opinion goes much to far. An example is his deletion of the whole digression with the elephants (*Sat.* 12.102–10) which then makes a painful and by no means probable textual emendation necessary in line 101. But his objections could bring about a new and energetic examination of the stylistic characteristics of the real Juvenal—of the techniques he uses in digressions, for example.

At the same time the debate over the Oxford verses seems not to have been decided yet. Highet, for instance, once again clearly takes the passage as being genuine. Finally, the old hypothesis of author variants has found a new adherent in John G. Griffith ("Author Variants in Juvenal, a Reconsideration," in *Festschrift Bruno Snell*, Munich, 1956, 101–11). I cannot accept the results of this study, though there is not only a sharp, critical intelligence at work, but also a gallantry toward his learned opponent such as we would like to find more often.

Word index: There is now a valuable resource for criticism and observation in the *Index verborum Juvenalis* by Lucile Kelling and Albert Suskin (Chapel Hill, N.C., 1951; cf. my review of this, *Gnomon* 24, 1952, 331–37). The work represents a very welcome improvement over the old word index of Franz Atorf which concludes Friedlaender's edition (Leipzig, 1895).

Structure: Corrado Gallo, whose name has been well known in Juvenal philology for thirty years, has dealt with the structure of individual satires of the poet in a series of articles. He treats the first, second, third, fifth, and sixth satires. W. C. Helmbold and E. N. O'Neil discuss the structure of Satire 4 (*American Journal of Philology* 77, 1956, 68–73).

Individual passages: I shall have to forgo enumerating the many studies which provide help with individual passages, such as B. L. Ullman's brief article ("The Goddess Pecunia [Juvenal 1.113]," in *Studies Presented to D. M. Robinson*, St. Louis, 1951, 1092–95).

Translations: That of Otto Weinreich, I think, reads more easily than mine which has already been mentioned. But our versions are identical in many half-verses, though they were produced independently of each other. At other places they show a correlation with the translation done earlier by Ed. Casp. Jac. von Siebold (Leipzig, 1858) which is still probably unsurpassed. This is perhaps one indication that we have not gone about it all in the wrong way.

Hamburg, January 18, 1957

Ulrich Knoche

Bibliographical Supplements
for the Years 1956-1968/9

COMPILED BY W. WOLFGANG EHLERS

The titles are arranged in the following order: A = Editions, Translations, Commentaries; B= Surveys of Scholarship and Bibliographies; C = Other Literature. Histories of literature are not included; titles of periodicals are given in such a way that a list of abbreviations is unnecessary. Sum. = summary, diss. = dissertation.

Chapters I and II. *Satire, a Roman Literary Genre; Origin and Name of the* Satura

A

La poesia popolare in Roma durante la repubblica e l'impero, text, transl., comm. by E. BOLISANI, Mem. Accad. Patav., Cl. sc. mor. e lett. 77, 3, 1965, 461–82.

B

W.S. ANDERSON, Recent Work in Roman Satire (1937–1955), Class. World 50, 1956, 33–40. (1955–1962) Class. World 57, 1964, 293–301, 343–48.

C

W.S. ANDERSON, Anger in Juvenal and Seneca, Univ. of Calif. Publ. Class. Phil. 19, 3, Berkeley 1964.

J.-P. CÈBE, La satura dramatique et le divertissement fascennin, Rev. Belge Phil. 39, 1961, 26–34.

———, La caricature et la parodie dans le monde romain antique des origines a Juvénal, Bibl. des Éc. franc. d'Ath. et Rome 206, Paris 1966.

R.C. ELLIOTT, Satire und Magie, Antaios 4, 1962, 313–26.

P. GREEN, Essays in Antiquity, Ch. 7: Roman Satire and Roman Society, London 1960.

J. HEURGON, Les éléments italiques dans la satire romaine, Wiss. Zs. Univ. Rostock, Ges.- u. sprachwiss. R. 15, 1966, 431–39.

G. HIGHET, The Anatomy of Satire, Princeton 1962.

J. IRMSCHER, Römische Satire und byzantinische Satire, Wiss. Zs. Univ. Rostock, Ges.- u. sprachwiss. R. 15, 1966, 441–46.

J.W. JOLIFFE, Satyre, *satura, σάτυρος*. A Study in Confusion, Bibl. d'Human. et Renaiss. 18, 1956, 84–95 (Geneva).

U. KNOCHE, Erlebnis und dichterischer Ausdruck in der lateinischen Poesie, Gymnasium 65, 1958, 146–65.

———, review of G. Highet, The Anatomy of Satire, Anz. Alt. Wiss. 17, 1964, 18–27.

W. KRENKEL, Römische Satire und römische Gesellschaft, Wiss. Zs. Univ. Rostock, Ges.- u. sprachwiss. R. 15, 1966, 471–77.

F. KÜHNERT, *Ambitio* in der römischen Satire, Wiss. Zs. Univ. Rostock, Ges.- u. sprachwiss. R. 15, 1966, 485–88.

E. PASOLI, Satura drammatica e satura letteraria, Vichiana 1, 2, 1964, 1–41.

C.A. VAN ROOY, Studies in Classical Satire and Related Literary Theory, Leiden 1965.

E.G. SCHMIDT, Diatribe und Satire, Wiss. Zs. Univ. Rostock, Ges.- u. sprachwiss. R. 15, 1966, 507–15.

J. SCHNEIDER, Zum Nachleben der römischen Satiriker in den mittellateinischen satirischen Dichtungen des deutschen Bereiches in der Zeit der Salier und Staufer, Wiss. Zs. Univ. Rostock, Ges.- u. sprachwiss R. 15, 1966, 517–24.

H. SZELEST, Die römische Satire und der Philhellenismus, Wiss. Zs. Univ. Rostock, Ges.- u. sprachwiss. R. 15, 1966, 541–46.

J.S. WILLIAMS, Towards a Definition of Menippean Satire, Diss. Vanderbilt Univ., Nashville 1966 (Microf.), sum. Diss. Abstr. 27, 1966, 1350A–1351A.

E.C. WITKE, Latin Satire. The Classical Genre and its Medieval Development, Harvard Stud. 66, 1962, 277–79 (sum. of diss.).

Chapter III. *The Satires of Quintus Ennius*

A

Scriptorum Romanorum quae extant omnia, III: Ennius, Venice 1964.

C

D. BO, Su gli *Hedyphagetica* di Ennio, Rendic. Ist. Lombardo, Cl. Lett., sc. mor. e stor., Milan 89–90, 1956, 107–20.

N. CATONE, Grammatica Enniana, Florence 1964.

M. COFFEY, Die Saturae des Ennius, Wiss. Zs. Univ. Rostock, Ges.- u. sprachwiss. R. 15, 1966, 417f.

T. DOHRN, Der vatikanische "Ennius" und der *poeta laureatus*, Mitt. Dt. Arch. Institut, Röm. Abt. 69, 1962, 76–95.

A. GRILLI, Studi Enniani, Pubblic. Sodalic. glottol. Milanese III, Brescia 1965.

I. GUALANDRI, Problemi di stile enniano, Helikon 5, 1965, 390–410.

A. KAMBYLIS, Die Dichterweihe und ihre Symbolik. Untersuchungen zu Hesiod, Kallimachos, Properz und Ennius, Diss. Kiel 1959, Heidelberg 1965.

M.R. LEFKOWITZ, Metaphor and Simile in Ennius, Class. Journ. 55, 1959, 123–25.

A. MARASTONI, Studio critico su Ennio minore, Aevum 35, 1961, 1–27.

S. MARIOTTI, Lezioni su Ennio, Turin[2] 1963.

W. RICHTER, Staat, Gesellschaft und Dichtung in Rom im 3. und 2. Jahrhundert v. Chr., Gymnasium 69, 1962, 286–310.

O. SKUTSCH, Studia Enniana, London 1968.

W. SUERBAUM, Untersuchungen zur Selbstdarstellung älterer römischer Dichter. Livius Andronicus, Naevius, Ennius, Spudasmata 19, Hildesheim 1968.

R. VERDIÈRE, Enniana, Rhein. Mus. 110, 1967, 158–64.

J.H. WASZINK, Tradition and Personal Achievement in Early Latin Literature, Mnemosyne 13, 1960, 16–33.

Chapter IV. *Gaius Lucilius*

A

Saturarum reliquiae, in usum maxime acad. 3 dig. brevissimaque adnot. crit. instr. N. TERZAGHI, I. MARIOTTI adiuvante, Leiden 1970.

Lucilius, Satiren, Lat.-Germ. by W. KRENKEL, 2 vols., Leiden 1970.

C

R. ARGENIO, I grecismi in Lucilio, Riv. Stud. Class. 11, 1963, 5–17.

D. ARMSTRONG, Horace, Sat. 1. 1–3, see Horace: Armstrong.

A. DI BENEDETTO, La satira oraziana del seccatore, Lucilio, ed alcune reminiscenze dell'Eunuchus di Terenzio, Rendic. Accad. Arch., Lett. e Belle Arti, Naples, 35, 1960, 57–64.

J. HEURGON, Lucilius, Paris 1959.

W. KRENKEL, Luciliana, in Miscellanea Critica, aus Anl. des 150j. Bestehens der Verlagsgesellschaft . . . B.G. Teubner, Leipzig, ed. by J. Irmscher, B. Doer, U. Peters, R. Müller, vol. 2, 136–96, Leipzig 1965.

———, Irreversibles bei Lucilius, Wiss. Zs. Univ. Rostock, Ges.- u. sprachwiss. R. 15, 1966, 479–83.

I. MARIOTTI, Due note di critica testuale, Stud. It. Fil. Class. 29, 1957, 255–58.

———, Studi Luciliani, Studi e Testi Pisa 25, Florence 1961.

———, L'età di Lucilio (Interventi di I. MARIOTTI, F. DELLA CORTE, W. KRENKEL), Maia 20, 1968, 254–70.

J.R.C. MARTYN, Lucilius 1165–6 M., Am. Journ. Phil. 85, 1964, 66–70.

———, Imagery in Lucilius, Wiss. Zs. Univ. Rostock, Ges.- u. sprachwiss. R. 15, 1966, 493–505.

J. MICHELFEIT, Zum Aufbau des ersten Buches des Lucilius, Hermes 93, 1965, 113–28.

M. MOSCA, I presunti modelli del *concilium deorum* di Lucilio, Parola del Pass. 15, 1960, 373–84.

A. RONCONI, Lucilio critico letterario, Maia 15, 1963, 515–25.

J. TER VRUGT-LENTZ, Lucili ritu, Mnemosyne 19, 1966, 349–58.

J.H. WASZINK, Zur ersten Satire des Lucilius, Wiener Stud. 70, 1957, 322–28.

T. WEEPLE, Lucilius. An Introduction to the Satires, and a Commentary on the First Book, Harvard Stud. 70, 1965, 270–73 (sum. of diss.).

Chapter V. *Varro's Menippeans*

A

Scriptorum Romanorum quae extant omnia, XXXIX–XLVI: Terentius Varro, quae extant, ed. by F. SEMI, Padua 1966.

B

B. CARDAUNS, Bibliographie Varronienne (1950–1963), see Varron: Entretiens 209–12.

C

Varron: Entretiens sur l'antiquité classique 9, Geneva, Fondation Hardt 1963.

H. DAHLMANN, Bemerkungen zu Varros Menippea *Tithonus*, in Studien zur Textgeschichte und Textkritik, ed. by H. Dahlmann und R. Merkelbach (Festschrift Jachmann), Cologne 1959, 37–46.

H. GELLER, Varros Menippea *Parmeno*, Diss. Cologne 1966.

K. LATTE, Zu Varros Menipp. fr. 363 Bchl., Studi in onore di U. E. Paoli 1955, 449–52 = Kleine Schriften, Munich 1968, 848–52.

E. LAUGHTON, Observations on the Style of Varro, Class. Quart. 10, 1960, 1–28.

P. LENKEIT, Varros Menippea *Gerontodidaskalos*, Diss. Cologne 1966.

Chapter VI. *Satire at the End of the Republic*

C

E. BOLISANI, La poesia di Varrone Atacino nei testimonia e nei frammenti, Atti Ist. Veneto Sc., Lett. ed Arti, Cl. sc. mor. e lett., 123, 1964–5, 339–51.

Chapter VII. *Horace's Satires and Epistles*

A

Opera II: Sermonum libri II. Epistularum libri II. De arte Poetica liber, ed. by D. BO, Turin 1959.

———— III: De Horatii poetico eloquio, indices by D. BO, Turin 1960.

Sämtliche Werke, Lat.-Germ. ed. by F. BURGER, H. FÄRBER, W. SCHÖNE, Munich[4] 1967.

Epistles, Book I, ed. with comm. by O.A.W. DILKE, London[2] 1961.

Satiren und Briefe, Lat.-Germ., introd. and transl. by R. HELM, Zurich 1962.

Quintus Horatius Flaccus, ed. by A. KIESSLING, rev. by R. HEINZE, Nachwort und bibliogr. Nachträge by E. BURCK, vol. 2, Satiren, Berlin[8] 1961; vol. 3, Episteln, Berlin[7] 1961.

Opera, ed. by F. KLINGNER, Leipzig[3] 1959.

Épîtres livre I, ed. with introd. and comm. by J. PRÉAUX, Paris 1968.

De arte poetica liber, Lat.-Germ. ed. by H. RÜDIGER, Zurich 1961.

Satire ed Epistole, ed. by A. SERAFINI, Turin 1966.

Q. Orazio Flacco, text, transl., comm. by E. TUROLLA, Turin 1957–1962 (Satire 1958, Epistole 1962).

Episteln, Lat.-Germ., transl. and comm. by Chr. M. WIELAND, rev. by G. WIRTH, Hamburg 1963.

Lexica, Indices:

D. BO, Lexicon Horatianum, 2 vols., Hildesheim 1965–6.

E. STAEDLER, Thesaurus Horatianus, zum Druck besorgt von R. Müller, Schriften Akad. Wiss. Berlin 31, 1962.

B

R.J. GETTY, Recent Work on Horace (1945–57), Class. World 52, 1959, 167–88. 246–47.

E. THUMMER, Horaz 1958–1962, Anz. Alt. Wiss. 15, 1962, 129–50.

D. WIEGAND, Die Natur bei Vergil und Horaz, Bibl. 1920–1959, Gymnasium 67, 1960, 344–58.

C

K. ABEL, Horaz auf der Suche nach dem wahren Selbst, Antike u. Abendl. 15, 1969, 29–46.

V. D'AGOSTINO, *Solve senescentem equum* (Ep. 1.1.8), Riv. Stud. Class. 9, 1961, 293–98.

W. ALLEN, *O fortunatam natam. . . ,* Transact. Proc. Am. Phil. Ass. 87, 1956, 130–46 (Ep. 2.1. 256).

W.S. ANDERSON, Imagery in the Satires of Horace and Juvenal, Am. Journ. Phil. 81, 1960, 225–60.

J.M. ANDRÉ, L'évolution morale de la poésie d'Horace, in L'otium dans la vie morale et intellectuelle romaine des origines à l'époque augustéenne, Publ. Fac. Lettr. Paris, Sér. Recherches 30, Paris 1966, 455–99.

A. ARDIZZONI, Orazio Sat. 1.10. 27–30, Riv. Fil. Istruz. Class. 93, 1965, 170–72.

D. ARMSTRONG, Horace, Satires 1.1–3. A Structural Study, Arion 3,2, 1964, 86–96.

W.D. ASHWORTH and M. ANDREWES, Horace Sat. 1.6.104–5, Class. Rev. 7, 1957, 107f.

F. BANFI, *Roma civitas regia* (Ep. 1.7.44–5), Studi Romani 10, 1962, 510–28.

H. BARDON, L'obstacle. Métaphore et comparaison en latin, Latomus 23, 1964, 3–20.

D.S. BARRETT, Horace, Satirist and Assembler of Words, Class. Bull. 40, 1963, 5–13.

C. BECKER, Das Spätwerk des Horaz, Göttingen 1962.

A. DI BENEDETTO, La satira oraziana del seccatore, Lucilio, ed alcune reminiscenze dell'Eunuchus di Terenzio, Rendic. Accad. Arch., Lett. e Belle Arti, Naples 35, 1960, 57–64.

G. BERNARDI PERINI, *Suspendere naso*, Mem. Accad. Patavina, Cl. Sc. mor., Lett. ed Arti 79, 1966–7, 233–64.

F. BÖMER, Beiträge zum Verständnis der augusteischen Dichtersprache, Gymnasium 64, 1957, 1–21.

R. BOGAERT, *Est tibi mater. . . ?* (Horace Sat. 1.9.26ff.), Les Ét. Class. 31, 1963, 159–66.

H. BOLKESTEIN, A.F. DEKKER, J. VAN GELDER, A. D. LEEMAN, H.L.W. NELSON, J.H. WASZINK, H. C. SCHNUR: Horatius, Amsterdam 1965.

B. BOLZ, Eine unbekannte Handschrift von Horaz' Epistulae, Gnesnensis 246, Eos 54, 1964, 139–50.

B. BORECKÝ, Some Occupations in the Poetry of Horace (The Influence of the Craftsman's Manual Work on the Imagination of Horace), in J. Irmscher, K. Kumaniecki et al., Römische Literatur der augusteischen Zeit, Schriften Akad. Wiss. Berlin 22, 1960, 9–14.

C.O. BRINK, Horace and Aristotle. Second Thoughts on the A.P., sum. Proc. Class. Ass. 56, 1959, 26f.

———, Horace on Poetry. Prolegomena to the Literary Epistles, Cambridge 1963.

G. BRUGNOLI, Vita di Orazio, Testi e Studi per la scuola universitaria, Testi 2, Rome 1967.

V. BUCHHEIT, Homerparodie und Literaturkritik in Horazens Satire 1.7 und 1.9, Gymnasium 75, 1968, 519-55.

K. BÜCHNER, Horaz, Studien zur römischen Literatur 3, Wiesbaden 1962.

———, Über ein Komma in Horaz, Riv. Cult. Class. e Med. 5, 1963, 71-87.

E. BURCK, see above, Kießling-Heinze.

———, Vom Sinn des *otium* im alten Rom. Ἐπιστημονικὴ Ἐπετηρὶς τῆς φιλοσοφικῆς Σχολῆς τοῦ Πανεπιστημίου Ἀθηνῶν, 13, 1962-3, 548-57.

W. BUSCH, Horaz in Rußland, Forum Slavicum 2, Munich 1964.

G. CAMBIER, *Equi te esse feri similem dico*, Latomus 19, 1960, 59-64.

A. CAMERON, Horace Ep. 2.2.87ff., Class. Rev. 15, 1965, 11-13.

A.Y. CAMPBELL, Serm. 2.7.75-83, Rhein. Mus. 100, 1957, 385-89.

———, Two Notes on Horace, Ars Poetica, Bull. Inst. Class. Stud. London 5, 1958, 65-68.

R.W. CARRUBBA, The Technique of the Double Structure in Horace, Mnemosyne 20, 1967, 68-71.

E. CASTORINA, La poesia di Orazio, Rome 1965.

W. CLAUSEN, An Interpolated Verse in Horace, Philologus 106, 1962, 205f.

N.E. COLLINGE, The Structure of Horace's Odes, Oxford 1961.

S. COMMAGER, The Odes of Horace. A Critical Study, New Haven (Yale UP) 1962.

J.A. COULTER, An Unnoted Allusion to Aristotle's Nicomachean Ethics in Horace Serm. 2.2, Class. Phil. 62, 1967, 39-41.

F. CUPAIUOLO, Orazio e la poesia, Naples 1965.

A. DEMAN, Avec Horace sur la route de Brindes (Satires 1.5), Ludus Magistralis 1965, 2, 1-12; 1966, 3, 8-13; 1966, 4, 5-11.

R. DESMED, Une scène de magie (Hor. Sat. 1.8), Ludus Magistralis 1966, 7, 1-6; 1967, 8, 6-13; 1967, 9, 1-11; 1967, 10, 1-11.

C. DESSEN, The Poetic Unity of Horace's Serm. 1.4, Am. Journ. Phil. 88, 1967, 78-81.

———, The Sexual and Financial Mean in Horace's Serm. 1.2, Am. Journ. Phil. 89, 1968, 200-08.

C. DIANO, Orazio e l'epicureismo, Atti Ist. Veneto Sc., Lett., Arti, Cl. sc. mor. e lett., 120, 1961-2, 43-58.

D.R. DICKS, Astrology and Astronomy in Horace, Hermes 91, 1963, 60-73.

H. DIERKS, Selbstwiederholungen und Selbstzitationen bei Horaz, Diss. Hamburg 1959 (typewr.).

O.A.W. DILKE, When Was the Ars Poetica Written?, Bull. Inst. Class. Stud. London 5, 1958, 49-57.

E. DOBLHOFER, Die Augustuspanegyrik des Horaz in formalhistorischer Sicht, Heidelberg 1966.

G. DONINI, Horatius in Martiale, Am. Journ. Phil. 85, 1964, 56-60.

D.J. DOOLEY, Horace, Portrait Artist in Words, Class. Bull. 37, 1961, 58–61.

F. DORNSEIFF, Die sibyllinischen Orakel in der augusteischen Dichtung, in J. Irmscher, K. Kumaniecki et al., Römische Literatur in augusteischer Zeit, Schriften Akad. Wiss. Berlin 22, 1960, 43–51.

H. DREXLER, Zwei Horaz-Interpretationen (Sat. 1.6; 1.4. 105ff.), Romanitas 4, 1962, 132–54.

————, Zur Komposition von Horaz Sat. 1.1, Romanitas 6–7, 1965, 267–75.

————, Nochmals zu Horaz Ep. 1.7, Romanitas 9, 1967, 53–67.

G.E. DUCKWORTH, *Animae dimidium meae*. Two Poets of Rome, Transact. Proc. Am. Phil. Ass. 87, 1956, 281–316.

————, Horace's Hexameters and the Date of the Ars Poetica, Transact. Proc. Am. Phil. Ass. 96, 1965, 73–95.

K. ECKERT, *O et praesidium et dulce decus meum*. Horazens Freundschaft mit Maecenas als eine Seite seiner Religiosität, Wiener Stud. 74, 1961, 61–95.

R. EINBERGER, Behandlung gleicher Motive bei Horaz und Ovid, Diss. Heidelberg 1961 (typewr.).

V. ESTEVEZ, Problem of Unity. Horace to Bullatius (Epist. 1.11), Class. Bull. 37, 1961, 36f.

B.H.P. FARRER, An Interpretation of Horace, Sat. 1.3.117–24, Acta Class. 9, 1966, 149f.

J. FERGUSON, Catullus and Horace, Am. Journ. Phil. 77, 1956, 1–18.

D. FLACH, Das literarische Verhältnis von Horaz und Properz, Gießen 1967.

A. FONTÁN, *Tenuis . . . Musa?* La teoría de los χαρακτῆρες en la poesía augústea (sum. in English), Emerita 32, 1964, 193–208.

E. FRAENKEL, Horace, Oxford 1957.

H. FUCHS, Zum Wettgesang der Hirten in Vergils siebenter Ekloge, Mus. Helv. 23, 1966, 218–23.

K. GANTAR, Die Anfangsverse und die Komposition der horazischen Epistel über die Dichtkunst, Symb. Oslo. 39, 1964, 89–98.

————, Horazens *amicus sibi*, Acta Ant. Acad. Sc. Hungariae 12, 1964, 129–35.

R.J. GETTY, Horace Satires 1.6.126 and the Blandinius vetustissimus, in Class., Med. and Renaiss. Stud. in Honor of B.L. Ullman, ed. by Ch. Henderson Jr., Rome 1964, I, 119–31.

G. GIANGRANDE, Lateinische Beiträge (Serm. 1.6), Mnemosyne 20, 1967, 414–21.

————, Emendation einer horazischen Korruptel (Ep. 1.7.29ff.), Rhein. Mus. 111, 1968, 55–58.

G.C. GIARDINA, Orazio e Properzio. A proposito di Hor. Epist. 2.2.91ff., Riv. Fil. Istruz. Class. 93, 1965, 24–44.

M. GIGANTE, Margini ascripta (Sat. 1.9.59f.), Parola del Pass. 18, 1963, 54–56.

F. GILLEN, Symbolic Dimensions in Horace's Poetry, Class. Bull. 37, 1961, 65–67.

C. GRASSI, Sull' interpretazione di Hor. Ep. 1.6.67–68, Maia 21, 1969, 159f.

N.A. GREENBERG, The Use of *poiema* and *poiesis*, Harv. Stud. Class. Phil. 65, 1961, 263–89.

J.G. GRIFFITH, Horace, Ars Poet. 372–3, Class. Rev. 10, 1960, 104.

P. GRIMAL, Horace, Paris 1958.

————, Horace, Art poétique. Commentaire et étude, Cours prof. à la Fac. Lettr. 1963–4, Paris 1964.

————, Horace. De l'art de vivre à l'Art poétique, Bull. Ass. Budé, 1964, 436–47.

P. HÄNDEL, Zur Ars poetica des Horaz, Rhein. Mus. 106, 1963, 164–86.

————, Zur Augustusepistel des Horaz, Wiener Stud. 79, 1966, 383–96.

E.L. HARRISON, Horace's Tribute to his Father (Sat. 1.6), Class Phil. 60, 1965, 111–14.

J.L. HELLER, Horace Epistles 1.1.47–54, Am. Journ. Phil. 85, 1964, 297–303.

L. HERRMANN, Canidia, Latomus 17, 1958, 665–68.

————, Les deux parties de l'Art poétique d'Horace, Latomus 23, 1964, 506–10.

O. HILTBRUNNER, Der Gutsverwalter des Horaz (Ep.1.14), Gymnasium 74, 1967, 297–314.

H.H. HOLFELDER, Zu Horaz, Ep. 1.7.29–33 und Cyrill, *Speculum Sapientiae* 3.11, Hermes 96, 1968, 638–40.

A.O. HULTON, The Death Theme in Horace, Orpheus 11, 1964, 19–23.

W. HUPPERTH, Horaz über die *scaenicae origines* der Römer, Diss. Cologne 1961.

S. JANNACCONE, Il segreto di Orazio, Giorn. It. Fil. 13, 1960, 289–97.

————, *Vicina Trivici villa*, Giorn. It. Fil. 19, 1966, 97–106.

D. JONES, Horace's Idea of Poetry and the Poet, Diss. Bryn Mawr Coll. 1963 (Microf.).

S. JOSIFOVIĆ, Horaz in der serbokroat. Lit. des 15. und 16. Jhs., Ziva Antika, Skopje, 15, 1965–6, 429–56.

H. JUHNKE, Das dichterische Selbstverständnis des Horaz und Properz, Diss. Kiel 1963 (typewr.).

R.S. KILPATRICK, Horace to Albinovanus Celsus: Ep. 1.8, Mnemosyne 21, 1968, 408–14.

U. KNOCHE, Über Horazens satirische Dichtung: Witz und Weisheit, Gymnasium 67, 1960, 56–72.

————, review of W. Wimmel, Zur Form der horazischen Diatribensatire, Gnomon 35, 1963, 470–75.

D. KUIJPER, *Minorem ad lunam*, Mnemosyne 19, 1966, 38–41.

B. KYTZLER, Das früheste Aeneiszitat, in Gedenkschrift Rohde = Aparchai, 4 ed. by G. Radke, Tübingen 1961, 151–67.

W. LUDWIG, Die Komposition der beiden Satirenbücher des Horaz, Poetica 2, 1968, 304–25.

O. LUSCHNAT, Horaz Epistel 1.2, Theologia Viatorum 9, 1963, 142–55.

J. MARMIER, Horace en France au XVIIe siècle, Paris 1962.

————, La survie d'Horace à l'époque romantique, Paris 1965.

J. MARTIN, Zwei Interpretationsversuche zu Horaz, in Studi in onore di L. Castiglioni, Florence 1960, 595–611.

G. MAURACH, Der Grundriß von Horazens erstem Epistelbuch, Acta Class. 11, 1968, 73–124.

M.J. McGANN, The Sixteenth Epistle of Horace, Class. Quart. 10, 1960, 205–12.

————, Horace, Ep. 2.2.87ff. Another View, Class. Rev. 16, 1966, 266f.

H.J. METTE, *Genus tenue* und *mensa tenuis* bei Horaz, Mus. Helv. 18, 1961, 136–39.

A. MICHEL, A propos de la théorie du *decorum*. L'Art poétique d'Horace et la philosophie de son temps, in Antiquitas Graeco-Romana ac tempora nostra. Acta Congr. Intern. habiti Brunae diebus 12–16 mensis Aprilis 1966, ed. by J. Burian and L. Vidman, Prague 1968, 345–52.

W. MONECKE, Wieland und Horaz, Cologne 1964.

A.L. MOTTO, Stoic Elements in the Satires of Horace, in Class., Med. and Renaiss. Stud. in Honor of B.L. Ullman, ed. by Ch. Henderson Jr., Rome 1964, I, 133–41.

R. MULLIN, The Use of the Terms *rus* and *urbs* in the Poetry of Horace, Diss. Univ. Washington, Seattle 1967, sum. Diss. Abstr. 28, 1967, 650A–651A.

G. NENCI, Reminiscenze oraziane nell'epistolario augusteo, Parola del Pass. 16, 1961, 119–23.

R.G.M. NISBET, Notes on Horace Ep. I, Class. Quart. 9, 1959, 73–76.

H. OPPERMANN, Das Göttliche im Spiegel der Dichtkunst des Horaz, Altspr. Unterricht 9, 1956, 54–67.

E. PASOLI, Le Epistole Letterarie di Orazio, Corso tenuto nella Fac. di Magistero, Univ. di Bologna, 1963–4, Bologna 1964.

――――, Spunti di critica letteraria nella satira oraziana, Convivium (Bologna) 32, 1964, 449–78.

――――, Sueton, Vit. Hor. 38–43 Rostagni, Latinitas 13, 1965, 278–81.

――――, Per una lettura dell'Epistola di Orazio a Giulio Floro (2.2), Il Verri, Riv. di Lett., Milan 19, 1965, 129–41.

G. PASQUALI, Orazio lirico, Studi, ed. by A. LA PENNA, Florence 1964.

Z. PAVLOVSKIS, Aristotle, Horace and the Ironic Man, Class. Phil. 63, 1968, 22–41.

A. LA PENNA, Due note sulla cultura filosofica delle Epistole oraziane, Stud. It. Fil. Class. 27–8, 1956, 192–201.

――――, Orazio e l'ideologia del principato, Saggi 332, Turin 1963.

――――, A proposito del classicismo latino, Maia 18, 1966, 170f.

――――, Due questioni oraziane (Sat. 1.5.51ff. Ep. 2.2.92–96), Maia 19, 1967, 154–61.

J. PERRET, Horace, Coll. Conn. des lettres 53, Paris 1959.

V. POESCHL, Horaz und die Politik, Sitzb. Ak. Wiss. Heidelberg, Phil.-hist. Kl., 1956, 4.

A. RONCONI, *Quaeque notando* (Sat. 10.1.6a(!)), Stud. It. Fil. Class. 29, 1957, 124f.

――――, Interpretatiunculae II (Sat. 1.1.70), Atene e Roma 6, 1961, 167f.

M. RUCH, Horace et les fondements de la *iunctura* dans l'ordre de la création poétique (A.P. 46–72), Rev. Ét. Lat. 41, 1963, 246–69.

N. RUDD, The Satires of Horace, Cambridge 1966.

V. SACK, Ironie bei Horaz, Diss. Würzburg 1965.

E. DE SAINT-DENIS, La fantasie et le coq-à-l'âne dans l'Art poétique d'Horace, Latomus 22, 1963, 664–84.

――――, L'humour dans les satires d'Horace, Rev. Phil. 38, 1964, 24–35.

J.J.H. SAVAGE, The Cyclops, the Sibyl and the Poet, Transact. Proc. Am. Phil. Assoc. 93, 1962, 410–42.

————, Variations on a Theme by Augustus, Transact. Proc. Am. Phil. Assoc. 97, 1966, 431–57.

R. SCHRÖTER, Horazens Sat. 1.7 und die antike Eposparodie, Poetica 1, 1967, 8–23.

G. SCHWIND, Zeit, Tod und Endlichkeit bei Horaz, Diss. Freiburg/Brsg. 1964.

E.R. SCHWINGE, Zur Kunsttheorie des Horaz, Philologus 107, 1963, 75–96.

E.T. SILK, The God and the Searchers for Happiness. Notes on Horace's Repetition and Variation of a Favorite Topos, Yale Class. Stud. 19, 1966, 233–50.

E. SKARD, Zu Horaz, Ep. 1.11, Symb. Oslo. 40, 1965, 81f.

O. SKUTSCH, Horaz, Ep. 1.6.66–67, Hermes 88, 1960, 504f.

W. STEFFEN, Kritische Bemerkungen zu Suetons Vita Horati, in J. Irmscher, K. Kumaniecki et al., Römische Literatur der augusteischen Zeit, Schriften Akad. Wiss. Berlin 22, 1960, 18–25.

G. STÉGEN, L'unité et la clarté des Épîtres d'Horace. Études sur sept pièces du premier livre (1.4, 6, 7, 9, 13, 14, 16), Namur 1963.

————, La douzième Épître d'Horace, à Iccius, Les Ét. Class. 31, 1963, 375–91.

H. SZELEST, Martials satirische Epigramme und Horaz, Altertum 9, 1963, 27–37.

M.E. TAYLOR, Horace, *laudator temporis acti*, Am. Journ. Phil. 83, 1962, 23–43.

N. TERZAGHI, Il padre di Orazio, Atene e Roma 10, 1965, 66–71.

I. TRENCSENYI-WALDAPFEL, Horatius, Budapest 1964.

I. TROXLER-KELLER, Die Dichterlandschaft des Horaz, Diss. Zurich, Heidelberg 1964.

R. VERDIÈRE, Notes critiques sur les Sermones d'Horace, Eos 52, 1, 1962, 111–24.

J.H. WASZINK, Bemerkungen zu den Literaturbriefen des Horaz, Mnemosyne 21, 1968, 394–407.

D. WEST, Reading Horace, Edinburgh 1967.

W. WILI, Horaz und die augusteische Kultur, Basel² 1965.

L.P. WILKINSON, The Language of Vergil and Horace, Class. Quart. 9, 1959, 181–92.

G. WILLIAMS, Poetry in the Moral Climate of Augustan Rome, Journ. Rom. Stud. 52, 1962, 28–46.

W. WILLIGE, Horaz und Tibull, Gymnasium 64, 1957, 98–100.

W. WIMMEL, Kallimachos in Rom. Die Nachfolge seines apologetischen Dichtens in der Augusteerzeit, Hermes Einzelschr. 16, Wiesbaden 1960.

————, Zur Form der horazischen Diatribensatire, Frankfurt 1962.

————, Zur Satzerwartung bei Horaz, Sat. 1.3.70, Wiener Stud. 77, 1964, 128–37.

————, *Quid oportet nos facere a volgo longe longeque remotos?* Zur Frage von Horaz S. 1.6.17f. und zum Eingang dieser Satire, Wiener Stud. 79, 1966, 351–64.

E. WISTRAND, Politik och litteratur i antikens Rom, Stockholm 1962.

K. ZARZYCKA, Literarische Problematik in den Satiren von Horaz, Wiss. Zs. Univ. Rostock, Ges.- u. sprachwiss. R. 15, 1966, 547–49.

E. ZINN, Elemente des Humors in augusteischer Dichtung, Gymnasium 67, 1960, 41-56; 152-55.

Chapter VIII. *Seneca's Apocolocyntosis*

A

'Αποκολοκύντωσις, introd., text, transl., comm., indic. by C.F. RUSSO, Bibl. Stud. Sup. 3, Florence[5] 1965.

Apocolocyntosis. Die Verkürbissung des Kaisers Claudius, Lat.-Germ. by W. SCHOENE, Munich 1957.

The Deification of Claudius the Clod, transl. by J.P. SULLIVAN, Arion 5, 1966, 378–99.

B

M. COFFEY, Seneca, Apocolocyntosis 1922–1958, Lustrum 6, 1961, 239–71.

A.L. MOTTO, Recent Scholarship on Seneca's Prose Works, 1940–57, Class. World 54, 1960, 13–18; 37–48; 70f.

————, Addenda 1957–58, Class. World 55, 1961, 111f.

P.G. VAN DER NAT, Seneca Philosophus I, Lampadion 5, 1965, 49–67.

C

H. MACL. CURRIE, The Purpose of the Apocolocyntosis, L'Antiqu. Class. 31, 1962, 91–97.

———— and R. SEALEY, Apocolocyntosis 6, Rhein. Mus. 105, 1962, 95.

————, Apocolocyntosis. A Suggestion, Rhein. Mus. 105, 1962, 187f.

————, The Younger Seneca's Style. Some Observations, Bull. Inst. Class. Stud. London 13, 1966, 76–87.

H. HAFFTER, Senecas Apocolocyntosis, in Römische Politik und römische Politiker, Heidelberg 1967.

N.I. HERESCU, La constellation des Trois Boeufs (Sén. Apoc. 11.2), Rhein. Mus. 105, 1962, 263–69.

W. JUST, Senecas Satire auf die Apotheose des Kaisers Claudius in ihrer politischen Bedeutung, Wiss. Zs. Univ. Rostock, Ges.- u. sprachwiss. R. 15, 1966, 447–51.

U. KNOCHE, Das Bild des Kaisers Augustus in Senecas Apocolocyntosis, Wiss. Zs. Univ. Rostock, Ges.- u. sprachwiss. R. 15, 1966, 463–70.

K. KRAFT, Der politische Hintergrund von Senecas Apocolocyntosis, Historia 15, 1966, 96–122.

R.M.W. KRILL, Character of Claudius from the Apocolocyntosis, Class. Bull. 41, 1965, 85–87.

I. LANA, L. Anneo Seneca e la posizione degli intelettuali Romani di fronte al principato, Turin 1964.

C. PRATO, Sen. Apoc. 3.1, Stud. It. Fil. Class. 30, 1958, 124f.

G. RAMBELLI, Il finale dell'Apocolocyntosis e la catabasi dell'Hercules furens, in Studi di Fil. Class., Pavia 1957, 9–28.

A. RONCONI, *Quaeque notando* (Apoc. 8.2), Stud. It. Fil. Class 29, 1957, 129f.

N. SCIVOLETTO, Quando nacque Seneca? Giorn. It. Fil. 19, 1966, 21–31.

O. SPECCHIA, Tracce dei mimi di Eroda nell'Apokolokyntosis di Seneca, Liceo-Ginn. Stat. Palmieri, Lecce, 1958–9, 45–50.

J.G. SZILAGYI, 'Αποκολοκύντωσις, Acta Ant. Acad. Sc. Hungariae 11, 1963 235–44.

V. TANDOI, Il trionfo di Claudio sulla Britannia e il suo cantore (Anth. lat. 419–26 R.), Stud. It. Fil. Class. 34, 1962, 83–129; 137–68.

H. WAGENVOORT, Quid significet Apocolocyntosis, Mnemosyne 11, 1958, 340–42.

Chapter IX. *Petronius' Novel*

A

Satyricon, text, transl. by V. CIAFFI, Turin 1967.

Satyricon, ed. by A. ERNOUT, Paris⁵ 1962.

Cena Trimalchionis, text and comm. by E.V. MARMORALE, Florence² 1961.

Satyricon, ed. by K. MÜLLER, Munich 1961.

Satyrica, ed. by K. MÜLLER, transl. by Wilh. EHLERS, Munich 1965.

Le festin de Trimalcion, ed. by P. PERROCHAT, Paris³ 1962.

Satyricon. Ein römischer Schelmenroman, transl. and comm. by H.C. SCHNUR, Stuttgart 1968.

The Satyricon and the Fragments, transl. by J.P. SULLIVAN, Baltimore 1965.

B

G. SCHMELING, Petronian Scholarship Since 1957, Class. World 62, 1969, 157–64; 352f.

C

L. ALFONSI, Topica erotico-elegiaca in Petronio, Aevum 34, 1960, 254f.

P.J.M. VAN ALPHEN, Petronius' Cena Trimalchionis en de Pompejaanse muurschilderingen, Hermeneus 36, 1964–5, 94–106; 117–29.

W. ARROWSMITH, Luxury and Death in the Satyricon, Arion 5, 1966, 304–31.

E.E. BESTMAN, Attitudes Toward Literacy Reflected in Petronius, Class. Journ. 61, 1965, 72–76.

P. BICKNELL, Opimian Bitters or "Opimian" Wine? Am. Journ. Phil. 89, 1968, 347–49.

M. BROŻEK, De Petronii Satyricon librorum numero ac natura, Acta Class. Univ. Sc. Debreceniensis 4, 1968, 65–67.

————, De Petronii Satyricon excerptorum pleniorum origine, in Hommages à M. Renard, ed. by J. Bibauw, Coll. Latomus 101, Brussels 1969, 176–79.

J.A. CABANISS, The Satiricon and the Christian Oral Tradition, Greek, Rom. and Byz. Stud. 3, 1960, 36–39.

E. CAMPANILE, Osservazioni sulla lingua di Petronio, Annali Scuola Norm. Sup. Pisa 26, 1957, 54–69.

————, Un glossario medioevale attribuito a Petronio, Stud. Urb. 35, 1961, 118–34.

J.-P. CÈBE and P. VEYNE, Proverbes chez Pétrone, Annal. Fac. Lettr. et Sc. hum. Aix, Sér. Class. 39, 1965, 173–80.

V. CIAFFI, Petronio in Apuleio, Univ. Torino, Fac. Lett. Fil., Fond. Parini-Chirio 1960.

E. CIZEK, Autour de la date du Satyricon de Pétrone, Studii Clas. 7, 1965, 197–207.

E. COURTNEY, Parody and Literary Allusion in Menippean Satire, Philologus 106, 1962, 86–100.

A. DELL'ERA, L'uso delle congiunzioni copulative in Petronio, Riv. Cult. Class. e Med. 8, 1966, 58–61.

——, L'uso del diminutivo in Petronio, Quaderni Urbin. Cult. Class. 1967, 3, 95–123.

H. FUCHS, Verderbnisse im Petrontext, in Stud. z. Textgesch. u. Textkritik, ed. by H. Dahlmann and R. Merkelbach (Festschrift Jachmann), Cologne 1959, 57–82.

P. GEORGE, Style and Character in the Satyricon, Arion 5, 1966, 336–58.

E.V. MARMORALE, Il Petronio della biblioteca di des Esseintes, Giorn. It. Fil. 12, 1959, 1–3.

A. MARZULLO, Elementi satirici e popolareschi nella Cena Trimalchionis, Atti e Mem. Acc. Sc. Lett. Arti Modena Ser. 4a, 1, 1959, 175–227.

W.C. McDERMOTT, Isidore and Petronius, Class. et Mediaev. 23, 1962, 143–47.

P. MORENO, Aspetti di vita economica nel Satyricon, Ann. Ist. Ital. di Numism. 9–11, 1962–4, 53–73.

J. NOVÁKOVÁ, Nochmals zum Petrontext 119–124, Eunomia 4, 1960, 9–15.

R. PACK, The Criminal Dossier of Encolpius, Class. Phil. 55, 1960, 31f.

C. PELLEGRINO, Su alcuni problemi della tradizione manoscritta del Satyricon, Riv. Cult. Class. e Med. 10, 1968, 72–85.

L. PEPE, Studi Petroniani, Bibl. G.I.F. 6, Naples 1957.

——, Sul monumento sepolcrale di Trimalchione, Giorn. It. Fil. 10, 1957, 293–300.

——, Appunti sulla lingua di Petronio, Giorn. It. Fil. 12, 1959, 314–21.

P. PERROCHAT, Mentalité et expression populaires dans la Cena Trimalchionis, L'Inform. Litt. 13, 1961, 62–69.

B.E. PERRY, The Ancient Romances, Berkeley 1967.

O. RAITH, Petronius, ein Epikureer. Seine literarische, philosophische und weltanschauliche Nachfolge von Lukrez und Epikur. Ein Zeit- und Persönlichkeitsbild, Erlanger Beitr. zur Sprach- und Kunstwiss., Nuremberg 1963.

H.D. RANKIN, On Tacitus' Biography of Petronius, Class. et Mediaev. 26, 1965, 233–45.

——, Petronius, Priapus and Priapeum 68, Class. et Mediaev. 27, 1966, 225–42.

H. RÖMER, Ausdrucks- und Darstellungstendenzen in den urbanen Erzählungspartien von Petrons Satyricon, Diss. Göttingen 1961 (typewr.).

C. RONCAIOLI, Il diminutivo e l'età di Petronio, Giorn. It. Fil. 14, 1961, 1–27.

K.F.C. ROSE, Time and Place in the Satyricon, Transact. Proc. Am. Phil. Ass. 93, 1962, 402–09.

——, The Petronian Inquisition. An auto-da-fe, Arion 5, 1966, 275–301.

——, Petroniana, Latomus 26, 1967, 130–38.

——, Petroniana, Rhein. Mus. 111, 1968, 253–60.

H.C. SCHNUR, The Age of Petronius Arbiter, Diss. New York Univ. 1957 (Microf.), sum. Diss. Abstr. 17, 1957, 2263.

——, The Economic Background of the Satyricon, Latomus 18, 1959, 790–99.

T. SINKO, De reconstructione fabulae menippeae Petronii (Polish with Lat. sum.), Meander 12, 1957, 79–96; 119; 121–41.

A.F. SOCHATOFF, The Purpose of Petronius' Bellum Civile. A Reexamination, Transact. Proc. Am. Phil. Ass. 93, 1962, 449–58.

A. STEFFENELLI, Die Volkssprache im Werk des Petron (im Hinblick auf die romanischen Sprachen), Wiener Roman. Arb. 1, Vienna 1962.

J.H. STUCKEY, The Reputation and Influence of C. Petronius Arbiter among English Men of Letters from 1660 to 1700, Diss. Yale Univ. New Haven 1966 (Microf.), sum. Diss. Abstr. 27, 1966, 188A–189A.

J.P. SULLIVAN, The Satyricon of Petronius. A Literary Study, Bloomington, Ind. 1968.

D.C. SWANSON, A Formal Analysis of Petronius' Vocabulary, Minneapolis 1963.

P. VEYNE, Le "je" dans le Satiricon, Rev. Et. Lat. 42, 1964, 301–24.

P.G. WALSH, Eumolpus, the *Halosis Troiae*, and *De Bello Civili*, Class. Phil. 63, 1968, 208–12.

F. WEHRLI, Einheit und Vorgeschichte der griechisch-römischen Romanliteratur, Mus. Helv. 22, 1965, 133–54.

Chapter X. *Aules Persius Flaccus*

A

H. BEIKIRCHER, Kommentar zur 6. Satire des A. Persius Flaccus, Wiener Stud. Bh. 1, Vienna-Cologne-Graz 1969.

A. Persi Flacci et D. Iuni Iuvenalis Saturae, ed. by W.V. CLAUSEN, Oxford 1959.

Persio e Giovenale. Le satire, ed. by P. FRASSINETTI, Turin 1956.

Saturarum liber, ed. by A. MARSILI, Studi e Testi 19, Pisa 1960.

I. REIGL, Persius' 5. Satire. Kommentar, Diss. Vienna 1956 (typewr.).

Lexica, Indices:

L. BERKOWITZ and T.F. BRUNNER, Index verborum quae in saturis Auli Persi Flacci reperiuntur, Hildesheim 1967.

D. BO, Persii Lexicon, Hildesheim 1967.

B

V. D'AGOSTINO, Nuova bibliografia su Persio (1946–1957), Riv. Stud. Class. 6, 1958, 63–72.

————, Gli studi sul Persio dal 1957 al 1962. Nota bibliografica, Riv. Stud. Class. 11, 1963, 54–64.

C

W.S. ANDERSON, Part Versus Whole in Persius' Fifth Satire, Philol. Quart. 39, 1960, 66–81.

————, Persius and the Rejection of Society, Wiss. Zs. Univ. Rostock, Ges.- u. sprachwiss. R. 15, 1966, 409–16.

D. BO, Note a Persio, Rendic. Ist. Lombardo, Cl. Lett. Sc. mor. e stor. 101, 1967, 133–60.

P. COURCELLE, *Habitare secum* selon Perse et selon Grégoire le Grand, Rev. Ét. Anc. 69, 1967, 266–79.

C.S. DESSEN, The Satires of Persius. A Poetic Study, Diss. Johns Hopkins Univ. Baltimore 1964 (Microf.), sum. Diss. Abstr. 27, 1967, 3026A.

H. ERDLE, Augusteische Vorlage und neronische Überformung, Diss. Munich 1968.

J. HEURGON, Les éléments étrusques dans les satires de Perse, sum. Rev. Ét. Lat. 44, 1966, 30–32.

————, Les éléments italiques dans la satire romaine, see Satire: Heurgon.

S. JANNACCONE, Rapporti di codici nella tradizione degli scolii a Persio, Giorn. It. Fil. 12, 1959, 198–213.

E. PARATORE, Biografia e poetica di Persio, Florence 1968.

K.J. RECKFORD, Studies in Persius, Hermes 90, 1962, 476–504.

W. RICHTER, Varia Persiana, Beobachtungen zu den Satiren 4 und 6, Wiener Stud. 78, 1965, 139–75.

U.W. SCHOLZ, Rem populi tractas? Zu Persius' 4. Satire, Wiss. Zs. Univ. Rostock, Ges.- u. sprachwiss. R. 15, 1966, 525–31.

N. SCIVOLETTO, Ancora sul testo di Persio, Giorn. It. Fil. 13, 1960, 298–309.

————, Retractatio Persiana, in Studi di letteratura latina imperiale, Bibl. del G.I.F. 14, Naples 1963, 85–105.

O. SEEL, Zum Persius-Titel des Codex Pithoeanus, Hermes 88, 1960, 82–98.

W.H. SEMPLE, The Poet Persius, Literary and Social Critic, Bull. J. Rylands Libr. 44, 1961–2, 157–74.

V. TANDOI, Morituri verba Catonis (3.45f.), Maia 17, 1965, 315–39.

J. TER VRUGT-LENTZ, Die Choliamben des Persius, Philologus 111, 1967, 80–85.

J.H. WASZINK, Das Einleitungsgedicht des Persius, Wiener Stud. 76, 1963, 79–91.

Chapter XI. *Satire in the Time of Domitian*

A

Das Klagelied der Sulpicia über die Gewaltherrschaft des Kaisers Domitian, text, transl., comm. by H. FUCHS in Discordia concors, Festschrift für E. Bonjour, Basel-Stuttgart 1968, 32–47.

Epigrammata Bobiensia, ed. by W. SPEYER, Leipzig 1963.

B

S. MARIOTTI, Epigrammata Bobiensia, RE Suppl. 9, 1962, 37–63.

C

W. SPEYER, Naucellius und sein Kreis. Studien zu den Epigrammata Bobiensia, Zetemata 21, Munich 1959.

Chapter XII. *Decimus Junius Juvenalis*

A

Satires, see Persius, ed. by Clausen.

Extraits des Satires, introd., text, transl., comm. by J. HELLEGOUARC'H, Catania 1967.

Martial, Juvenal. Römisches Alltagsleben, transl. with introd. by R. HELM, Zurich 1963.

Saturae 3, 4, 5, ed. with introd., comm. by R. MARACHE, Coll. Érasme 15, Paris 1965.

Satires, transl. by J. MAZZARO, introd. and notes by R.E. BRAUN, Ann Arbor 1965.
Satira prima, text, transl., comm. by E. ZORZI, Milan 1966.

B

M. COFFEY, Juvenal Report for the Years 1941–1961, Lustrum 8, 1963, 161–215.

C

V. ALFANO, Elementi storici nelle Satire di Giovenale, Naples 1963.
W.S. ANDERSON, Studies in Book I of Juvenal, Yale Class. Stud. 15, 1957, 31–90.
––––––, *Venusina lucerna*. The Horatian Model for Juvenal, Transact. Proc. Am. Phil. Ass. 92, 1961, 1–12.
––––––, The Programs of Juvenal's Later Books, Class. Phil. 57, 1962, 145–60.
––––––, Anger in Juvenal, see Satire: Anderson.
––––––, Imagery, see Horace: Anderson.
M. BALASCH, Contribución al estudio de la lengua de Juvenal, Madrid 1966.
B. BALDWIN, Cover-names and Dead Victims in Juvenal, Athenaeum 45, 1967, 304–12.
J.J. BODOH, An Analysis of the Ideas of Juvenal, Diss. Univ. Wisconsin 1966 (Microf.), sum. Diss. Abstr. 27, 1966, 1042A.
E. BOLISANI, Persio imitato da Giovenale, Atti Ist. Veneto di Sc., Lett. ed. Arti, Cl. sc. mor. e lett., 121, 1962–3, 367–89.
S. BORSZÁK, *Nona aetas?* Meander 22, 1967, 305–17.
G. BRUGNOLI, Vita Juvenalis, Stud. Urb. 37, 1963, 5–14.
A.D.E. CAMERON, Literary Allusions in the Historia Augusta, Hermes 92, 1964, 363–77.
R.E. COLTON, Juvenal and Martial, Diss. Columbia Univ. 1959 (Microf.), sum. Diss. Abstr. 20, 1959, 664–665.
––––––, Dinner Invitation. Juvenal 11.56–208, Class. Bull. 41, 1965, 39–45.
––––––, Echoes of Martial in Juvenal's Third Satire, Traditio 22, 1966, 403–19.
––––––, Juvenal and Propertius, Traditio 23, 1967, 442–61.
E. COURTNEY, The Transmission of Juvenal's Text, Bull. Inst. Class. Stud. London 14, 1967, 38–50.
M. DUBROCARD, Recherches par ordinateur sur la langue et le vocabulaire de Juvénal, sum. Rev. Ét. Lat. 45, 1967, 37–39.
D.E. EICHHOLZ, The Art of Juvenal and His Tenth Satire, Greece and Rome 3, 1956, 61–69.
E. FLORES, Origini e ceto di Giovenale e loro riflessi nella problematica sociale delle Satire, Annali Fac. Lett. e Fil. Univ. Napoli 10, 1962–3, 3–32.
J. GÉRARD, Présence de l'histoire dans les satires de Juvenal, L'Inform. Litt. 16, 1964, 103–09. 154–59.
C. GNILKA, "Scholiastenweisheit" und moderne Exegese. Zu Juv. Sat. 6.231ff. und 247ff., Wiener Stud. N.F. 2, 1968, 193–205.
––––––, Eine typische Fehlerquelle der Juvenalinterpretation, Symb. Oslo. 44, 1969, 90–108.
J.G. GRIFFITH, The Survival of the Longer of the So-called Oxford Fragments of Juvenal's Sixth Satire, Hermes 91, 1963, 104–14.

————, A Taxonomic Study of the Manuscript Tradition of Juvenal, Mus. Helv. 25, 1968, 101–38.

W. HEILMANN, Zur Komposition der vierten Satire und des ersten Satiren-buches Juvenals, Rhein. Mus. 110, 1967, 358–70.

W.C. HELMBOLD and E.N. O'NEIL, The Structure of Juvenal 4, Am. Journ. Phil. 77, 1956, 68–73.

———— and E.N. O'NEIL, The Form and Purpose of Juvenal's Seventh Satire, Class. Phil. 54, 1959, 100–08.

J. IRMSCHER, Römische Satire und byzantinische Satire, see Satire: Irmscher.

F. JACOBY, Zwei Doppelfassungen im Juvenaltext, Hermes 87, 1959, 449–62.

E.J. KENNEY, The First Satire of Juvenal, Proc. Cambr. Phil. Soc. 8, 1962, 29–40.

————, Juvenal, Satirist or Rhetorician? Latomus 22, 1963, 704–20.

U. KNOCHE, review of G. Highet, Juvenal the Satirist, Gnomon 29, 1957, 54–65.

————, Juvenals Maßstäbe der Gesellschaftskritik, Wiss. Zs. Univ. Rostock, Ges.-u. sprachwiss. R. 15, 1966, 453–62.

F. KÜHNERT, *Ambitio*, see Satire: Kühnert.

R. MARACHE, La revendication sociale chez Martial et Juvénal, Riv. Cult. Class. e Med. 3, 1961, 30–67.

————, Crime et épouvante dans les satires de Juvénal, in Hommages à M. Renard, ed. by J. Bibauw, Coll. Latomus 101, Brussels 1969, 587–94.

C. MARXSEN, Das Kompositionsprinzip Juvenals. Eine Strukturanalyse der Satiren, Diss. Humboldt Univ. Berlin 1958 (typewr.).

H.A. MASON, Is Juvenal a Classic? An Introductory Essay, Arion 1, 1, 1962, 8–44; 1, 2, 1962, 39–79.

M.J. McGANN, Juvenal's Ninth Age (13. 28ff.), Hermes 96, 1968, 509–14.

A.L. MOTTO and J.R. CLARK, *Per iter tenebricosum*. The Mythos of Juvenal 3, Transact. Proc. Am. Phil. Ass. 96, 1965, 267–76.

L. RICHARD, Juvénal et les galles de Cybèle, Rev. de l'Hist. des Rélig. 169, 1966, 51–67.

N. SCIVOLETTO, Plinio il Giovane e Giovenale, Giorn. It. Fil. 10, 1957, 133–46.

————, Presenza di Persio in Giovenale, Giorn. It. Fil. 16, 1963, 60–72.

A. SERAFINI, Studio sulle Satire di Giovenale, Florence 1957.

E. THOMAS, Some Aspects of Ovidian Influence on Juvenal, Orpheus 7, 1960, 35–44.

G.B. TOWNEND, Juvenal's *Automedon*, in Hommages à M. Renard, ed. by J. Bibauw, Coll. Latomus 101, Brussels 1969, 725–27.

B.L. ULLMAN, *Epiredia* (Juv. 8.66), in Hommages à L. Herrmann, Coll. Latomus 44, Brussels 1960, 745–49.

————, Miscellaneous Comments on Juvenal, in The Classical Tradition. Literary and Historical Studies in Honor of H. Caplan, Ithaca 1966, 274–84.

D. UNGER, Das Bild bei Juvenal, Diss. Kiel 1965.

L. VARCL, Verfassersverantwortlichkeit bei Juvenal und Lukian in: Γέρας. Studies Presented to G. Thomson, ed. by L. Varcl and R.F. Willetts, Acta Univ. Carolinae 1963, Phil. et Hist. 1, Graecolatina Pragensia 2, Prague 1963, 225–34.

D. WIESEN, Juvenal's Moral Character, an Introduction. Latomus 22, 1963, 440–71.

Horaz. Werke in einem Band, transl. by M. SIMON and W. RITSCHL, Berlin 1972.

Horacio, Epístolas libro I (selección), ed. by J. VACCARO, Buenos Aires 1970.

Horace. Satires, odes et épodes, épîtres, ed. and transl. by F. VILLENEUVE, Paris 1969.

B

K. BÜCHNER, Horaz. Bericht über das Schrifttum der Jahre 1929–1936, Darmstadt 1969.

F. CUPAIUOLO, Gli studi oraziani negli ultimi anni, Boll. Stud. Lat. 2, 1972, 51–79.

C

M. VON ALBRECHT, Horazens Brief an Albius, Rhein. Mus. 114, 1971, 193–209.

W. ALLEN, et al., The Addressees in Horace's First Book of Epistles, Studies in Philology 67, 1970, 255–66.

W.S. ANDERSON, The Roman Socrates, Horace and His Satires, in Critical Essays on Roman Literature. Satire, ed. by J.P. Sullivan, London 1963, 1–37.

———, The Form, Purpose, and Position of Horace's Satire 1.8, Am. Journ. Phil. 93, 1972, 4–13.

V. D'ANTÒ, Studi oraziani, Naples 1968.

A. ARDIZZONI, Satira e poesia in Orazio, in In memoriam E.V. Marmorale, Naples 1967, 1, 189ff.

———, Orazio. La satira e il linguaggio poetico, in Umanità e storia. Scritti in onore di Adelchi Attisani, Naples 1971, 2, 49–63.

———, Anticonformismo o aberrazione? (Ancora su Orazio, la satira e il linguaggio poetico), Giorn. It. Fil. 24, 1972, 489–512.

F. ARNALDI, Il viaggio di Orazio, in Studi filologici e storici in onore di V. de Falco, Naples 1971, 377–92.

L. ASCHER, A Satire Misnamed (Horace, Sat. 1.9), Class. Journ. 59, 1966, 306.

B. BALDWIN, Horace on Sex, Am. Journ. Phil. 91, 1970, 460–65.

W. BARR, Horace, Serm. 1.10.64–67, Rhein. Mus. 113, 1970, 204–11.

J.M. BAUMGARTEN, The Counting of the Sabbath in Ancient Sources (Hor. Sat. 1.9.69), Vetus Testamentum 16, 1966, 277–86.

A. DI BENEDETTO, I giambi di Callimaco e il loro influsso sugli epodi e le satire di Orazio, Rendic. Acad. Arch., Lett. e Belle Arti, Napoli 41, 1966, 23–69.

———, Quatenus et qua ratione Horatius in Brundisino itinere Lucilii iter Siculum sibi imitandum proposuerit, Helikon 9, 1969, 3–23.

J.J. BODOH, Unity in Horace Sermo I.1, L'Antiqu. Class. 39, 1970, 164–67.

L. BÖSING, Multa renascentur (Hor. Ars 70–72), Rhein. Mus. 113, 1970, 246–61.

———, Griechen und Römer im Augustusbrief des Horaz, Constance 1972.

S.F. BONNER, The Street-Teacher. An Educational Scene in Horace (Epist. 1.20.17ff.), Am. Journ. Phil. 93, 1972, 509–28.

S. BORZSÁK, Bemerkungen zu Horazens Briefen, Philologus 113, 1969, 225–34.

———, Spinas evellere (Hor., Epist. 1.14.4f.), Acta Class. 7, 1971, 55–62.

———, Zur Überlieferungsgeschichte des Horaz, Acta Ant. 20, 1973, 77–93.

P. BRIND'AMOUR, *Paulum silvae super his foret* (Horace, Satires 2.6.3), Rev. Ét. Anc. 74, 1972, 86–93.

C.O. BRINK, On Reading a Horatian Satire. An Interpretation of Sermones II.6, Todd Mem. Lect. 6, Sidney 1965.

——, Horace and Empedocles' Temperature. A Rejected Fragment of Empedocles, Phoenix 23, 1969, 138–42.

——, Horace on Poetry, II. The Ars poetica, Cambridge 1971.

C. BRUGNOLI, *Candidus* e *scholasticus* (Epist. 1.4), Giorn. It. Fil. 20, 1967, 71–79.

E.W. BUSHALA, A Note on the togata in Horace, Latomus 28, 1969, 1069f.

——, The Motif of Sexual Choice in Horace Satire 1.2, Class. Journ. 66, 1971, 312–15.

G. CASTELLI, A Orazio sat. II.8.42–78. Note critico-esegetiche, Riv. Stud. Class. 16, 1968, 212–18.

M.L. CLARKE, Horace, Epistles 1.13, Class. Rev. 22, 1972, 157–59.

C.J. CLASSEN, Orazio critico, Boll. Stud. Lat. 1, 1971, 402–18.

——, Eine unsatirische Satire des Horaz? Zu Hor. Sat. 1.5, Gymnasium 80, 1973, 235–50.

P. COLMANT, Horace. *Ibam forte via sacra* (1.9), Les Ét. Class. 37, 1969, 60–64.

C.D.N. COSTA ed., Greek and Latin Studies. Classical Literature and its Influence. Horace, London 1973 (see below DILKE, McGANN, RUSSELL).

L.C. CURRAN, Nature, Convention, and Obscenity in Horace, Satires 1.2, Arion 9, 1970, 220–45.

J. DELZ, Glossen im Horaztext? Mus. Helv. 30, 1973, 51–54.

O.A.W. DILKE, Horace and the Verse Letter, in Greek and Latin Studies. Classical Literature and its Influence. Horace, ed. by C.D.N. Costa, London 1973, 94–112.

H. DREXLER, Zur Epistel 1.7 des Horaz, in Studi in onore di Gennaro Perrotta, Bologna 1964, 24–35.

A. ERNOUT, *Ira* = gr. ὀργή (Sat. 1.2.68ff.), in Omagiu lui A. Rosetti, Bucharest 1965, 205–07.

B.H.P. FARRER, The Different Moods of Horace, Acta Class. 10, 1967, 1–10.

J.M. FERNÁNDEZ, Vida, pensamiento y psicología de Horacio en sus textos, Humanidades 13, 1961, 7–31.

E. FLINTOFF, Lines 116–136 of Horace, Satire II, 2, Latomus 32, 1973, 814–17.

J. FOSTER, Horace, Epistles 1.16.35ff., Class. Quart. 21, 1971, 214.

——, Horace, Epistles 1.3.25ff., Mnemosyne 25, 1972, 303–06.

E. FRAENKEL, Kallimachos bei Horaz (Epist. 2.2.70ff.), Mus. Helv. 26, 1969, 113f.

H. FUCHS, Zu Horaz, Epistulae 1.18, Rhein. Mus. 117, 1974, 186–89.

D. GAGLIARDI, Orazio, Epist. 1.15.19–21, Vichiana 6, 1969, 347f.

——, Orazio e la tradizione neoterica, Collana di Studi Classici 10, Naples 1971.

——, Una reminiscenza di Catullo in un'epistola oraziana, Boll. Stud. Lat. 1, 1971, 15f.

*C.D. GILBERT, Horace, *Ep.* 1.19.37–40, Class. Quart. 25(?), 1975(?).

J. GLAZEWSKI, *Plenus vitae conviva*. A Lucretian Concept in Horace's Satires, Class. Bull. 47, 1971, 85–88.

R. GODEL, *Rudis et Graecis intacti carminis auctor* (Horace, Serm. 1.10.66), Mus. Helv. 30, 1973, 117-21.

N.A. GREENBERG, Metrical Expectations in the Ars poetica, Revue de l'Organisation Internationale pour l'Étude des Langues Anciennes par Ordinateur 3, 1970, 111-29.

P. GRIMAL, Horace et la question du théâtre à Rome, Dioniso 41, 1967, 291-98.

L. HERRMANN, L'ordre du livre I des Épîtres d'Horace, Latomus 28, 1969, 372-77.

R.S. KILPATRICK, Fact and Fable in Horace Epistle 1.7, Class. Phil. 68, 1973, 47-53.

K.Q. KRAFT, Q. Aelius L. f. Lamia. Münzmeister und Freund des Horaz (Epist. 1.14), Jahrbuch für Numismatik und Geldgeschichte 16, 1966, 23-31.

W. KRENKEL, Horace's Approach to Satire, Arethusa 5, 1972, 7-16.

E.W. LEACH, Horace's *Pater optimus* and Terence's Demea. Autobiographical Fiction and Comedy in Sermo 1.4, Am. Journ. Phil. 92, 1971, 616-32.

G. LIEBERG, Individualismo ed impegno politico nell'opera di Orazio, Parola del Pass. 18, 1963, 337-54.

M.P. LOICQ-BERGER, Horace, Plaute et Épicharme. Autour de Épîtres II.1.58, in Hommages à M. Renard, ed. by J. Bibauw, Coll. Latomus 101, Brussels 1969, 1, 561-72.

A. MANZO, Dottrina e problematica del faceto in Orazio, Rendic. Ist. Lomb. 102, 1968, 445-71.

M. McGANN, Studies in Horace's First Book of Epistles, Coll. Latomus 100, Brussels 1969.

————, The Three Worlds of Horace's Satires, in Greek and Latin Studies. Classical Literature and its Influence. Horace, ed. by C.D.N. Costa, London 1973, 59-93.

H.A. MUSURILLO, Horace and the Bore. The Character Dramaticus of Sat. 1.9, Class. Bull. 40, 1964, 65-68.

————, A Formula for Happiness. Horace Epist. 1.6 to Numicius, Class. World 67, 1974, 193-204.

E. NICOLAY, L'emploi stylistique de la diérèse bucolique dans Horace, Satire 1.9, Ludus Magistralis 29/30, 1971, 12-15.

H. OPPERMANN, Wege zu Horaz, Darmstadt 1972 (see below, ZINN).

M. ORBAN, *Sapere et ringi*. Horace, Ep. 2.2, in Mélanges offerts à René Fohalle, Gembloux 1969, 239-48.

W. OTT, Metrische Analysen zur Ars poetica des Horaz, Göppinger Akademische Beiträge 6, Göppingen 1970.

E. PARATORE, Satira e poesia in Orazio, Giorn. It. Filol. 20, 1967, 189-233.

————, De Persio Horati interprete, Latinitas 17, 1969, 245-50.

————, Il bimillenario delle Satire di Orazio, Ann. Lib. Univ. Tuscia 1969-70, 3f.

————, Di alcuni questioni vivamente discusse. Il Orazio, Persio e la satira, Riv. Cult. Class. e Med. 14, 1972, 44-56.

E. PASOLI, Il contributo del Rostagni e dell'esegesi posteriore all'interpretazione di Orazio, Ars poet. 128-30, Atti Accad. Sc. Torino 106, 1971-72, 39-54.

A. LA PENNA, Orazio e la morale mondana europea, Florence 1969.

J. PERRET, transl. by B. Humez, Horace, New York 1969.

R.G. PETERSON, The Unity of Horace, Epistle 1.7, Class. Journ. 63, 1968, 309–14.

J. PREAUX, *Scholastici domini* (Epist. 1.4; Epist. 1.1.16–19), in Mélanges offerts à René Fohalle, Gembloux 1969, 249–57.

C. RAMBAUX, La composition d'ensemble du livre 1 des satires d'Horace, Rev. Ét. Lat. 49, 1971, 179–204.

K. RECKFORD, Horace, New York 1969.

H. ROHDICH, Die 18. Epistel des Horaz, Rhein. Mus. 115, 1972, 261–88.

C.A. VAN ROOY, Arrangement and Structure of Satires in Horace Sermones, Book 1, Acta Class. 11, 1968, 38–72.

————, Arrangement and Structure of Satires in Horace Sermones Book 1. Satires 1.4 and 1.10, Acta Class. 13, 1970, 7–27; Satires 5 and 6, Acta Class. 13, 1970, 45–59.

————, Arrangement and Structure of Satires in Horace Sermones Book 1. Satire 7 as related to Satires 10 and 8, Acta Class. 14, 1971, 67–90.

————, Arrangement and Structure of Satires in Horace Sermones Book 1. Satires 9 and 10, Acta Class. 15, 1972, 37–52.

————, Horace, Sat. 1.1 and 1.6, and the Topos of Cardinal Vices, in Antidosis. Festschrift für Walther Kraus, ed. by R. Hanslik, A. Lesky, H. Schwabl, Vienna 1972, 297–305.

M. RUCH, Horace, Satires 1.3, Les Ét. Class. 38, 1970, 517–27.

N. RUDD, Horace on the Origins of Satura, Phoenix 14, 1960, 36–44.

D.A. RUSSELL, Ars poetica, in Greek and Latin Studies. Classical Literature and Its Influence. Horace, ed. by C.D.N. Costa, London 1973, 113–34.

K. SALLMANN, Satirische Technik in Horaz' Erbschleichersatire (II.5), Hermes 98, 1970, 178–203.

————, Die seltsame Reise nach Brundisium. Aufbau und Deutung der Horazsatire 1.5, in Musa iocosa, Arbeiten über Humor und Witz, Komik und Komödie der Antike, for Andreas Thierfelder, Hildesheim 1974, pp. 179–206.

W. SCHETTER, Zum Aufbau der Horazsatire 1.8, Antike u. Abendl. 17, 1971, 144–61.

N. SCIVOLETTO, Orazio negli studi italiani più recenti, Cultura e Scuola 36, 1970, 56–65.

O. SEEL, Horazens sabinisches Glück (Sat. 2.6), in Verschlüsselte Gegenwart. Drei Interpretationen antiker Texte, Stuttgart 1972, 13–93.

R. SKALITZKY, Good Wine in a New Vase (Horace, Epistles 1.2), Transact. Proc. Am. Phil. Ass. 99, 1968, 443–52.

H-P. STAHL, Peinliche Erfahrungen eines kleinen Gottes: Horaz in seinen Satiren, Antike und Abendl. 20, 1974, 25–53.

A. TERRANOVA, A proposito dell'epistola I. 4 di Orazio, Siculorum Gymnasium 22, 1969, 190–201.

K.M. THOMAS, Evolution of the Horatian Hexameter, Class. Bull. 45, 1969, 81f; 96.

S. TREGGIARI, Cicero, Horace, and Mutual Friends, Lamiae and Varrones Murenae, Phoenix 27, 1973, 245–61.

G. VANELLA, Il mondo di Orazio satiro. Fonti, Pensiero, Originalità, Naples 1968.

A. WALTZ, Des variations de la langue et de la métrique d'Horace dans ses différents ouvrages, Rome 1968 (anastat. repr. of 1881 ed.).

W. WIMMEL, *Vir bonus et sapiens dignis ait esse paratus.* Zur horazischen Epistel 1.7, Wiener Stud. 82, 1969, 60–74.

L. WINNICZUK, Horatian *Humanitas* (In the Margin of the Satires), transl. by B.Z. Kielar, Studia Filozoficzne 5, 1971, 49–58.

E. WISTRAND, Archilochus and Horace (Epist. 2.2.41–54; 1.9.50ff.), in Archiloque, Fondation Hardt, Entretiens sur l'antiquité classique 10, Geneva 1963, 257–79.

E. WOLTER, Théâtre et satire chez Horace, Caesarodunum 5, 1970, 203–21.

E. ZINN, Ironie und Pathos bei Horaz, in Ironie und Dichtung. Sechs Essays, Munich 1970, 39–58.

————, Erlebnis und Dichtung bei Horaz, in Wege zu Horaz, ed. by H. Oppermann, Darmstadt 1972, 369–89.

N.K. ZUMWALT, Horace's Evasion of Grand Poetry, Diss. Berkeley 1970 (Microf.), sum. Diss. Abstr. 31, 1970, 6576A–6577A.

Chapter VIII. *Seneca's Apocolocyntosis*

A

The Pumpkinification of Claudius. A Satire in Prose and Verse by Lucius Annaeus Seneca, in Claudius the God by R. GRAVES, New York 1935, 566–82.

Apokolokyntosis, ed. with introd. and transl. by A. RONCONI, Milan² 1968.

L. Annaei Senecae Divi Claudii apotheosis per saturam quae Apocolocyntosis vulgo dicitur, ed. by O. ROSSBACH, Berlin² 1967.

B

A.L. MOTTO, Seneca's Prose Writings. A Decade of Scholarship, 1958–68, Class. World 64, 1971, 141–58; 177–91.

C

D. ALTMURA, Apocolocyntosis et Satyricon, Latinitas 7, 1959, 43–54.

A. ATHANASSAKIS, Some Thoughts on Double Entendres in Seneca, Apocolocyntosis 3 and 4, Class. Phil. 68, 1973, 292–94.

————, Some Evidence in Defense of the Title *Apocolocyntosis* for Seneca's Satire, Transact. Proc. Am. Phil. Ass. 104, 1974, 11–22.

R.H. AUBRETON, Una sátira maliciosa de Sêneca, Alfa 9, 1966, 77–92.

B. BALDWIN, Executions under Claudius. Seneca's *Ludus de morte Claudii*, Phoenix 18, 1964, 39–48.

G. BELLARDI, L'Apocolocyntosis senecana e la prima bucolica di Calpurnio, Atene e Roma 8, 1963, 44–52.

K. BRINGMANN, Senecas Apocolocyntosis und die politische Satire in Rom, Antike u. Abendl. 17, 1971, 56–69.

E. CIZEK, L'Apocoloquintose. Pamphlet de l'aristocratie latine, Acta Antiqua Philippopolitana, Sofia, 1963, 295–303.

J.L. HELLER, Some Points of Natural History in Seneca's Apocolocyntosis, in Homenaje a A. Tovar, Madrid 1972, 181–92.

L. HERRMANN, Hercule selon Sénèque et selon Phèdre, in Hommages à Marcel
Renard, ed. by J. Bibauw, Coll. Latomus 101, Brussels 1969, 431–42.
D. NONY, Claude et les Espagnols. Sur un passage de l'Apocoloquintose, Mélanges
de la Casa de Velázquez 4, 1968, 51–72.
R. RONCALI, Tradizione medioevale della satira di Anneo Seneca, in Omaggio
a Eduard Fraenkel, Roma 1968, 225–28.
———, Citazioni nell'Apocolocyntosis di Seneca, Annali Fac. Lett. Fil. Univ.
Bari 14, 1969, 401–14.
———, Seneca satirico nel nono-dodicesimo secolo, Belfagor 25, 1970, 694f.
———, Divisione in capitoli dell'Apocolocyntosis di Seneca, Bari 1972.
———, *Marci municipem*, Annali Fac. Let. Fil. Univ. Bari 16, 1973, 537–40.
———, Partizione scenica della satira di Seneca, Belfagor 28, 1973, 425–29.
R. SCARCIA, Per l'interpretazione del titolo del ludus senecano, in Latina Siren.
Note di critica semantica, Rome 1964, 49–168.
R. VERDIÈRE, Notes critiques sur l'Apocolocyntosis, Riv. Stud. Class. 11, 1963,
249–63.
V. ZAPPACOSTA, Senecae 'Ἀποκολοκύντωσις, Latinitas 17, 1969, 86–95.

Chapter IX. *Petronius' Novel*

A

Petronius, The Satyricon, transl. by W. ARROWSMITH, Ann Arbor 1959.
Satyricon, ed. with transl. (Polish) by M. BROŻEK, Wrocław 1968.
Dal Satyricon. Cena Trimalchionis. Troiae halosis. Bellum civile, ed. with introd.
and transl. by E. CASTORINA, Bologna 1970.
Cena Trimalchionis, ed. by T. CUTT, rev. by J.E. NYENHUIS, Detroit 1970.
C. Petronius Arbiter. Cena Trimalchionis, ed. by R. DEMAN, Anvers 1968.
Satiricón (chaps. 1–60), ed. with transl. by M.C. DIAZ Y DIAZ, Barcelona 1968.
Petronius, with an English Translation, transl. by M. HESELTINE, rev. by
E.H. WARMINGTON, Loeb Class. Library, London[2] 1969.
Cena Trimalchionis, transl. (Finnish) with introd. by E. LINKOMIES, Helsinki[4]
1968.
Petronio. Cena Trimalchionis, ed. with introd., transl., and comment. by G.
PUCCIONI, Genoa 1970.
Petronius. The Satyricon, ed. by E.T. SAGE, rev. by B. GILLELAND, New
York[2] 1969.

B

G.N. SANDY, Recent Scholarship on the Prose Fiction of Antiquity, Class.
World 67, 1974, 321–59 (Petronius, 355–57).
H.C. SCHNUR, Recent Petronian Scholarship, Class. World 50, 1957, 133–36;
141–43.

C

G. ALESSIO, Hapax legomena ed altre cruces in Petronio, Istit. Glottologia Univ.
Napoli, Quaderni linguistici 6/7, 1960–61, Naples 1967.
D. ALTMURA, Apocolocyntosis et Satyricon, Latinitas 7, 1959, 43–54.
B. BALDWIN, A Note on Trimalchio's Zodiac Dish, Class. Quart. 20, 1970, 364.
———, Trimalchio's Poetry, Class. Journ. 66, 1971, 254f.

————, Trimalchio's Corinthian Plate, Class. Phil. 68, 1973, 46f.

————, *Ira Priapi*, Class. Phil. 68, 1973, 294–96.

J. BALKENSTEIN, Trimalchio, een naam met een betekenis? Hermeneus 43, 1971, 12–17.

E.J. BARNES, The Poems of Petronius, Diss. Toronto 1971 (Microf. from National Library of Canada, Ottawa).

————, Petronius, Philo and Stoic Rhetoric, Latomus 32, 1973, 787–98.

S. BASTOMSKY, Petronius, Satyricon 35, 4. Some Possible Emendations, Emerita 37, 1969, 367–70.

R. BECK, Some Observations on the Narrative Technique of Petronius, Phoenix 27, 1973, 42–61.

F. BORNMANN, Petronio c. 96.1, in Studi in onore di Gennaro Perrotta, Bologna 1964, 1–3.

T. BRANDIS and W. EHLERS, Zu den Petronexzerpten des Florilegium Gallicum, Philologus 118, 1974, 85–112.

M. BROŻEK, Petronii Satyricon capita 27.1–37.5, Acta conventus XI Eirene, 21–25 Oct. 1968, Warsaw 1971, 539–53.

————, Szeneriebeschreibungen bei Petronius, Eos 60, 1972, 285–91.

A. CAMERON, Petronius and Plato, Class. Quart. 19, 1969, 367–70.

————, Myth and Meaning in Petronius. Some Modern Comparisons, Latomus 29, 1970, 397–425.

H.D. CAMERON, The Sibyl in the Satyricon, Class. Journ. 65, 1970, 337–39.

E. CASTORINA, Petronio, Lucano e Vergilio, in Vergiliana, Leiden 1971, 97–112.

————, La lingua di Petronio e la figura di Trimalchione, Siculorum Gymnasium 26, 1973, 18–40.

E. CIZEK, L'ironie détachée, procédé de composition dans le Satyricon de Pétrone, Studii Clas. 9, 1966, 171–81.

*————, A propos des premiers chapitres du Satyricon, Latomus.

M. COCCIA, Le interpolazioni in Petronio, Rome 1973.

P.B. CORBETT, Petronius, New York 1970.

J.C. DAVIES, Petronius Satyricon 39.12, Rhein. Mus. 114, 1971, 288.

B.C. DIETRICH, Petronius Satyr of Satirist, Orpheus 17, 1970, 17–43.

E. DOBROIU, Contributions à l'explication de la loterie de Trimalcion, Analele Univ. Bucureşti, Şt. soc. filol. 14, 1965, 101–11.

————, *Muraena et littera* (Sat. 56.9), Analele Univ. Bucureşti, Şt. soc. filol. 16, 1967, 285–98.

————, Pour une édition du Satiricon, Studii Clas. 10, 1968, 159–70; 11, 1969, 115–28; 12, 1970, 79–93.

————, Allusions à l'empereur Tibère dans le Satiricon, Analele Univ. Bucureşti, Şt. soc. filol. 18, 1969, 17–45.

————, Două studii petroniene, Studii Clas. 14, 1972, 239–44.

————, Quid Petronius de Latino vulgari sermone cogitaverit, Act. Convent. Bucureşti 1970, Bucharest 1972, 257–59.

R.P. DUNCAN-JONES, Scaurus at the House of Trimalchio, Latomus 32, 1973, 364–67.

V. EBERSBACH, Petrons Stellung zu den sozialen Kräften der frühen Kaiserzeit, Altertum 19, 1973, 96–104.

A. DELL'ERA, La geminazione in Petronio, Giorn. It. Fil. 22, 3, 1970, 22-31.
———, Problemi di lingua e stile in Petronio, Roma 1970.
J.R. EVENHUIS, Petronius, Hermeneus 41, 1969, 16-23.
I. GAROFALO, Un nuovo saggio su Petronio, Maia 25, 1973, 77-80.
P.A. GEORGE, Petronius and Lucan De bello civili, Class. Quart. 24, 1974, 119-33.
G.C. GIARDINA, *Augusto patri patriae feliciter*. Petronio 60.7, Maia 24, 1972, 67f.
———, Note a Petronio, Mus. Crit. 5/7, 1970-72, 178-87.
C.H. GILL, The Sexual Episodes in the Satyricon, Class. Phil. 68, 1973, 172-85.
M. GONZÁLEZ-HABA, Petron. 38.9 *est tamen subalapa*, Glotta 47, 1969, 253-64.
H.B. GOTTSCHALK, *Hircus in ervilia* (Petronius 57.11), Class. Phil. 66, 1971, 187f.
P. GRIMAL, Une intention possible de Pétrone dans le Satiricon, Bull. Ass. Budé 31, 1972, 297-310.
R. GUERRINI, Petronio e Céline (ovvero la "denigrazione" del reale), Rendic. Ist. Lomb. 107, 1973, 380-92.
R.B. HARLOW, *Pharmace*: Petronius 107.15, Hermes 102, 1974, 377.
H.H. HUXLEY, "Marked Literary Inferiority" in the Poems of the Satyricon, Class. Journ. 77, 1970, 69f.
C. IANDOLO, *Tangomenas faciāmus* (Sat. 34.7, 73.6), Vichiana 5, 1968, 134-42.
———, *Dispare pallavit* del Satyricon (nuova congettura testuale-semantica), Vichiana 6, 1969, 155-61.
H. JACOBSON, A Note on Petronius Sat. 31.2, Class. Phil. 66, 1971, 183-86.
J.F. KILLEEN, Petronius 28.15, Hermes 96, 1968, 127.
———, Petronius 43.6, Orpheus 15, 1968, 179-81.
———, Petronius 9.8, Hermes 97, 1969, 127f.
A.D. LEEMAN, Morte e scambio nel romanzo picaresco di Petronio, Giorn. It. Fil. 20, 1967, 147-57.
———, Petronius als Dichter, Hermeneus 40, 1968, 65-69.
G. LUCK, On Petronius' Bellum civile, Am. Journ. Phil. 93, 1972, 133-41.
S. LUNDSTRÖM, Reminiszenzen an Properz bei Petron, Hum. Vetensk.-Samfundets i Uppsala Årsbok 1967-68, 68-97.
F. MAGI, L'adventus di Trimalchione e il fregio a della Cancelleria, Archaeol. Class. 23, 1971, 88-92.
P. MANTOVANELLI, *Curiosa felicitas*, in Quaderni del'Istituto di Filologia latina, Univ. di Padua, Bologna 1972, 59-71.
*W.O. MOELLER, Once More *matavitatu*, Class. Phil. 70, 1975.
D.D. MULROY, Petronius 81.3, Class. Phil. 65, 1970, 254-56.
H.L.W. NELSON, Bemerkungen zu einem neuen Petrontext, Mnemosyne 24, 1971, 60-87.
W.R. NETHERCUTT, Petronius. Epicurean and Moralist, Class. Bull. 43, 1967, 53-55.
R.A. PACK, Trimalchio's Game (Petronius 33), Class. Phil. 69, 1974, 214f.
E. PARATORE, Petronio, Studi Romani 14, 1966, 385-405.
C. PELLEGRINO, Nuove ricerche sulla tradizione manoscritta del Satiricon, Riv. Cult. Class. e Med. 11, 1969, 203-13.

————, Il "Bellum civile" nel "Satyricon." Possibilità di una nuova riscostruzione del testo, Riv. Cult. Class. e Med. 14, 1972, 155–64.

G. PUCCIONI, *Libera cena* in Petronio, Giorn. It. Fil. 24, 1972, 323–26.

————, *L'Ilioupersis* di Petronio, in Argentea Aetas, for V. Marmorale, Genoa 1973, 107–38.

H. PUZIS, Zagadnienia romansu rzymskiego pt. Satyrikon, Meander 22, 1967, 29–43. (Lat. sum. p. 63).

O. RAITH, Unschuldsbeteuerung und Sündenbekenntnis im Gebet des Enkolp an Priap (Petr. 133.3), Studii Clas. 13, 1971, 109–25.

H.D. RANKIN, Did Tacitus Quote Petronius? L'Antiqu. Class. 37, 1968, 641–43.

————, Petronius 44.3–5. Who Receives the Beating? Hermes 96, 1968, 254–56.

————, Eating People Is Right. Petronius 141 and a τόπος, Hermes 97, 1969, 381–84.

————, Some Themes of Concealment and Pretence in Petronius' Satyricon, Latomus 28, 1969, 99–119.

————, Petronius. A Portrait of the Artist, Symb. Oslo. 45, 1970, 118–28.

————, Some Comments on Petronius' Portrayal of Character, Eranos 68, 1970, 123–47.

————, Petronius the Artist, Essays on the Satyricon and its Author, The Hague 1971.

F. RASTIER, La morale de l'histoire. Notes sur la Matrone d'Éphèse (Satiricon 111–112), Latomus 30, 1971, 1025–56.

T.W. RICHARDSON, A Further Note on Trimalchio's Zodiac Dish, Class. Quart. 22, 1972, 149.

K.F.C. ROSE, Petroniana, Class. et. Mediaev. 26, 1965, 222–32.

————, Petronius' Accountant, Class. Phil. 62, 1967, 258–59.

———— and J.P. SULLIVAN, Trimalchio's Zodiac Dish (Petronius 35.1–5), Class. Quart. 60, 1968, 180–84.

————, The Date and Author of the Satyricon, Mnemosyne Sup. 16, Leiden 1971.

L.E. ROSSI, *Qui te primus "deurode" fecit* (Petron. 58.7), Stud. It. Fil. Class. 45, 1973, 28–45.

G.N. SANDY, Satire in the Satiricon, Am. Journ. Phil. 90, 1969, 293–303.

————, Petronius and the Tradition of the Interpolated Narrative, Transact. Proc. Am. Phil. Ass. 101, 1970, 463–76.

————, Scaenica Petroniana, Transact. Proc. Am. Phil. Assoc. 104, 1974, 329–46.

E. SANGUINETTI, Il giuoco del Satyricon, un'imitazione da Petronio, Turin 1970.

G. SCHMELING, Studies in Petronius, Diss. Univ. of Wisconsin 1968 (Microf.), sum. Diss. Abstr. 29, 1969, 3116A.

————, The Literary Use of Names in Petronius' Satyricon, Riv. Stud. Class. 17, 1969, 5–10.

————, Petronius. Satirist, Moralist, Epicurean, Artist, Class. Bull. 45, 1969, 49f; 64.

————, A Note on Petronius 62.9, Riv. Cult. Class. e Med. 12, 1970, 38f.

————, Trimalchio's Menu and Wine List, Class. Phil. 65, 1970, 248–51.

————, The Exclusus Amator Motif in Petronius, in Fons perennis. Saggi critici in onore di Vittorio d'Agostino, Turin 1971, 333–57.

————, The Satyricon. Forms in Search of a Genre, Class. Bull. 47, 1971, 49–52.

H.C. SCHNUR, Petronius, Sense and Nonsense, Class. World 66, 1972, 13–20.

A. SCOBIE, Aspects of the Ancient Romance and Its Heritage. Essays on Apuleius, Petronius and the Greek Romances, Meisenheim 1969.

H.J. SHEY, Petronius and Plato's Gorgias, Class. Bull. 47, 1971, 81–84.

D. SLUŞANSCHI, Le vocabulaire de la critique littéraire et le langage des personnages illetrés de la Cena Trimalchionis, Studii Clas. 12, 1970, 95–104 (Romanian, sum. in French).

A.F. SOCHATOFF, Imagery in the Poems of the Satyricon, Class. Journ. 65, 1970, 340–44 (cf. CJ 66, 1971, 254–57).

G. STÉGEN, Trois notes de lecture (Pétrone fragment 50), Giorn. It. Fil. 21, 1969, 357–59.

C. STOECKER, Humor bei Petron, Diss. Erlangen-Nuremberg 1969.

J.P. SULLIVAN, Petronius. Artist or Moralist? Arion 6, 1967, 71–88.

————, Petronius, Seneca and Lucan. A Neronian Literary Feud? Transact. Proc. Am. Phil. Ass. 99, 1968, 453–67.

————, Petronius and His Modern Critics, Bucknell Review 19, 1971, 107–24.

————, On Translating Petronius, in Neronians and Flavians, ed. by D.R. Dudley, London, 1972, 155–83.

A. SZANTYR, Zu Petron. 108.1, Hermes 102, 1974, 358–63.

V. TANDOI, Una proposta di matrimonio per Trimalchione (Petr., Satyr. 74.15), in Studia Florentina A. Ronconi oblata, Rome 1970, 431–53.

R.G. TANNER, Petronius 44, Hermes 100, 1972, 496–98.

H. VAN THIEL, Sulla tradizione di Petronio, Maia 22, 1970, 238–60; Maia 23, 1971, 57–64.

————, Petron. Überlieferung und Rekonstruktion, Mnemosyne Sup. 20, Leiden 1971.

A. TRELOAR, Animae ebullitio, Glotta 47, 1969, 264f.

R. VERDIÈRE, Jeux de mots chez Pétrone, Giorn. It. Fil. 20, 1967, 309–12.

P.G. WALSH, The Roman Novel. The Satyricon of Petronius and the Metamorphoses of Apuleius, Cambridge 1970.

————, Was Petronius a Moralist?, Greece and Rome 21, 1974, 181–90.

N.J. WOODALL, Trimalchio's Limping Pentameters, Class. Journ. 66, 1971, 256f.

F.I. ZEITLIN, Petronius as Paradox. Anarchy and Artistic Integrity, Transact. Proc. Am. Phil. Ass. 102, 1971, 631–84.

————, Romanus Petronius. A Study of the Troiae halosis and the Bellum civile, Latomus 30, 1971, 56–82.

M. ZICÀRI, Note a Petronio e a Marziale, in Lanx satura N. Terzaghi oblata, Genoa 1963, 343–54.

Chapter X. *Aules Persius Flaccus*

A

Saturarum liber, ed. with comm. by D. BO, Turin 1969.

The Satires of Persius, transl. by W.S. MERWIN, Bloomington, Ind. 1961.

Le Satire, ed. with life, introd., transl., and comm. by M. PAGLIANO, Bologna 1967.

The Satires of Horace and Persius, transl. by N. RUDD, Baltimore 1973.

Persius, Die Satiren, ed. and transl. by O. SEIL, Munich² 1974.

Aulo Persio Flacco, Le Satire, ed. by S. VOLLARO, transl. and notes by V. MONTI, Turin 1971.

C

G. D'ANNA, Persio *semipaganus*, Riv. Cult. Class. e Med. 6, 1964, 181–85.

F. BALLOTTO, Cronologia ed evoluzione spirituale nelle satire di Persio, Messina 1964.

F. BELLANDI, Persio e la poetica del *semipaganus*, Maia 24, 1972, 317–41.

E. BOLISANI, Quaenam Persius e Lucilio sumpserit, Atti Accad. Patavina 75, 1962–63, 139–59.

L. and P. BRIND'AMOUR, La deuxième satire de Perse et le *dies lustricus*, Latomus 30, 1971, 999–1024.

J.H. BROUWERS, Allitération, anaphore et chiasme chez Perse, Mnemosyne 26, 1973, 249–64.

G. BRUGNOLI, *Verba togae*, Riv. Cult. Class. e Med. 10, 1968, 190–92.

————, Persio e Properzio, Riv. Cult. Class. e Med. 11, 1969, 190–202.

T.F. BRUNNER, A Note on Persius 5.179ff., Univ. of Calif. Stud. Class. Ant. 1, 1968, 63f.

A.L. CASTELLI, La tecnica imitativa di Persio vista nelle sue caratteristiche e in riferimento alla II satira, Atti Accad. Sc. Ist. Bologna 60, 1971–72, 42–60.

W.V. CLAUSEN, Sabinus Ms. of Persius, Philologus 91, 1963, 252–56.

N.E. COLLINGE, A Conversation in Persius (Sat. 1.1–3), Class. Rev. 17, 1967, 132.

C. DESSEN, *Iunctura callidus acri*. A Study of Persius' Satires, Illinois Studies in Language and Literature 59, Urbana 1968.

V. FERRARO, *Semipaganus—semivillanus—semipoeta*, Maia 22, 1970, 139–46.

————, Accione Labeone. Una creatura degli scolastici di Persio, Stud. It. Fil. Class. 43, 1971, 79–100.

G.C. GIARDINA, Persio 4.49, Philologus 116, 1972, 152–55.

S. GRIMES, Structure of the Satires of Persius, in Neronians and Flavians, ed. by D. R. Dudley, London, 1972, 113–54.

L. HERRMANN, Néron et la mort de Perse, Latomus 22, 1963, 236–39.

R. JENKINSON, Interpretations of Persius' Satires III and IV, Latomus 32, 1973, 521–49.

R.R. JOHNSON, *Bicolor membrana*, Class. Quart. 67, 1973, 249–64.

D. KORZENIEWSKI, Die erste Satire des Persius, in Die römische Satire, Darmstadt 1970, 384–438.

————, Die zweite Satire des Persius, Gymnasium 77, 1970, 199–210.

————, Die dritte Satire des Persius, Helikon 11/12, 1971–72, 289–308.

S. MARIOTTI, Congetture alla Vita Persi, Riv. Fil. Istruz. Class. 93, 1965, 185–87.

E.V. MARMORALE, Commemorando Persio, Giorn. It. Fil. 15, 1962, 289–302.

G. MAZZOLI, Sui Choliambi di Persio, Athenaeum 50, 1972, 407–14.

E. MERONE, Aspetti prosodico-metrici della flessione nominale in Persio, Naples 1971.

M. MOGGI, *Trossulus* (Pers. 1.82), Maia 25, 1973, 31–49.

S. MONTI, Contenuto e strutura del fascicolo che comprese il foglio di Bobbio

(Vat. 5750) di Giovenale e Persio, Annali Fac. Lett. e Fil. Univ. Napoli 11, 1964-68, 57-68.

R.G.M. NISBET, Persius, in Essays on Roman Literature. Satire, ed. J.P. Sullivan, London 1963, 39-71.

E. PARATORE, Persio e Lucano, Riv. Cult. Class. e Med. 5, 1963, 88-130.

————, De Persio Horati interprete, Latinitas 17, 1969, 245-50.

————, Di alcuni questioni vivamente discusse. II Orazio, Persio e la satira, Riv. Cult. Class. e Med. 14, 1972, 44-56.

E. PASOLI, Pers. 1.121 e i principi della critica testuale, Maia 22, 1970, 38-40.

————, Persio 4.14-16, Philologus 116, 1972, 148-52.

O. PECERE, In margine a un nuovo commento della 6 satira di Persio, Riv. Fil. Istruz. Class. 99, 1971, 217-42.

A. PENNACINI, I procedimenti stilistici nella I satira di Persio, Atti Accad. Sc. Torino, Cl. Sc. mor. stor. e fil., 104, 1970, 417-87.

R. REGGIANI, Una probabile eco Enniana in Pers. Chol. 5-6, Maia 26, 1974, 29-32.

R. DE RISI, I choliambi. Prologo delle Satire di Persio, Annali Fac. Lett. e Filos. Univ. Napoli 11, 1964-68, 29-48.

N. RUDD, Persiana, Class. Rev. 20, 1970, 282-88.

R.E. RUSSELL, Dryden's Juvenal and Persius, Diss. Univ. Calif., Davis 1966 (Microf.), sum. in Diss. Abstr. 28, 1967, 209A.

R. SCARCIA, A proposito della Vita di Persio, Riv. Cult. Class. e Med. 6, 1964, 298-302.

R. SCHOTTLÄNDER, Persius und Seneca über die Problematik der Freilassungen, Wiss. Zs. Univ. Rostock, Ges.- u. sprachwiss. R. 15, 1966, 533-39.

D. DE SIMONE, Il nome di Persio, Riv. Fil. Istruz. Class. 96, 1968, 419-35.

D. SLUŞANSCHI, Ansambluri de termeni figurati in critica literara a lui Persius, Studii Clas. 10, 1968, 171-76.

W.S. SMITH, Speakers in the Third Satire of Persius, Class. Journ. 64, 1969, 305-08.

J.P. SULLIVAN, In Defense of Persius, Ramus 1, 1972, 48-62.

M. TARTARI, Brisaei venosus liber Acci (Pers. 1.76), Maia 23, 1971, 349-55.

L.J. VIGNOLI, Studies in Persius, Diss. Stanford Univ. 1968 (Microf.), sum. Diss. Abstr. 29, 1969, 2237A.

J. TER VRUGT-LENTZ, Satire und Gesellschaft bei Horaz und Persius, Gymnasium 77, 1970, 480-84.

E.C. WITKE, The Function of Persius' Choliambics, Mnemosyne 15, 1962, 153-58.

*J.E.G. ZETZEL, Lucilius, Lucretius, and Persius 1.1, Class. Phil. 71, 1976.

Chapter XI. *Satire in the Time of Domitian*

C

C.J. HEMER, Sulpicia, Satire 58-61, Class. Rev. 23, 1973, 12f.

Chapter XII. *Decimus Junius Juvenalis*

A

Saturae XIV. Fourteen Satires of Juvenal, ed. by J.D. DUFF, introd. by M. COFFEY, Cambridge 1970.

Juvenal. The Sixteen Satires, transl. by P. GREEN, Harmondsworth 1967.

The Satires of Juvenal, transl. by R. HUMPHRIES, Bloomington, Ind., 1958.

Satiren, introd. and transl. by H.C. SCHNUR, Stuttgart 1969.

Iuvenalis saturae XVI fragmentum nuperrime repertum, ed. by H.C. SCHNUR, in Silvae. Festschrift für E. Zinn, ed. by M. Von Albrecht and E. Heck, Tübingen 1970, 211–15.

Scholia in Juvenalem vetustiora, ed. by P. WESSNER, Stuttgart 1967.

C

J. ADAMIETZ, Untersuchungen zu Juvenal, Hermes Einzelschr. 26, Wiesbaden 1973.

W.S. ANDERSON, Juvenal 6. A Problem in Structure, Class. Phil. 51, 1956, 73–94.

———, Juvenal and Quintilian, Yale Class. Stud. 17, 1961, 3–93.

———, Valla, Juvenal, and Probus, Traditio 21, 1965, 383–424.

———, *Lascivia* vs. *Ira*. Martial and Juvenal, Univ. of Calif. Stud. Class. Ant. 3, 1970, 1–34.

F. ARNALDI, Giovenale, Studi Romani 10, 1962, 121–35.

*R. ASTBURY, Juvenal 10. 148–50, Mnemosyne 28, 1975.

B. BALDWIN, Three Characters in Juvenal, Class. World 66, 1972, 101–04.

N.I. BARBU, Les esclaves chez Martial et Juvénal, Acta Antiqua Philippopolitana, Sofia 1963, 67–74.

W. BARR, Juvenal's Other Elephants, Latomus 32, 1973, 856–58.

A. BARTALUCCI, Il "Probus" di Giorgio Valla e il "Commentum vetustum" a Giovenale, Stud. It. Fil. Class. 45, 1973, 233–57.

J. BEAUJEU, La religion de Juvénal, in Mélanges offerts à Jérôme Carcopino, Paris 1966, 71–81.

F. BELLANDI, Poetica dell'*indignatio* e "sublime" satirico in Giovenale, Annali Scuola Norm. Sup. Pisa 1973, 53–94.

S.S. BERTMAN, Fire Symbolism in Juvenal's First Satire, Class. Journ. 63, 1968, 265f.

J.J. BODOH, Artistic Control in the Satires of Juvenal, Aevum 44, 1970, 475–82.

E.W. BOWER, Notes on Juvenal and Statius, Class. Rev. 8, 1958, 9–11.

G. BRUGNOLI, Il dialogus e Giovenale, Riv. Cult. Class. e Med. 10, 1968, 252–59.

L. CANALI, Giovenale, Rome 1967.

M.L. CLARKE, Juvenal VII. 150–53, Class. Phil. 63, 1968, 295f.

———, Juvenal 7.242–3, Class. Rev. 23, 1973, 12.

R.E. COLTON, Juvenal and Martial on Literary and Professional Men, Class. Bull. 39, 1963, 49–52.

———, Cabinet Meeting. Juvenal's Fourth Satire, Class. Bull. 40, 1963, 1–4.

———, Juvenal's Second Satire and Martial, Class. Journ. 61, 1965, 68–71.

———, Echoes of Martial in Juvenal's Twelfth Satire, Latomus 31, 1972, 164–73.

———, Ausonius and Juvenal, Class. Journ. 69, 1973, 41–51.

———, Cruelty and Vanity. Juvenal 6.490; 6.502–06 and Martial, Class. Bull. 50, 1973, 5f.

———, Juvenal and Martial on Women Who Ape Greek Ways, Class. Bull. 50, 1973, 42–44.

*————, Juvenal's Thirteenth Satire and Martial, Class. Bull. 51, 1975.

G.H. COSOI, Interpretari din Juvenal. Pe Marginea versiunilor romanesti (1.1–6), Analee Stiintifice ale Univ. Al I Cuza din Jasi 15, 1969, 131–36.

F. DAVEY, Juvenal 7.242ff., Class. Rev. 21, 1971, 11.

B.F. DICK, Seneca and Juvenal 10, Harv. Stud. Class. Phil. 73, 1969, 237–46.

M. DUBROCARD, Quelques remarques sur la distribution et la signification des hapax dans les satires de Juvénal, Annales Fac. Lettr. et Sc. hum. Nice 11, 1970, 131–40.

M. DURRY, Cosmetae (Juvénal VI. 477), in Hommages à M. Renard, ed. by J. Bibauw, Coll. Latomus 101, Brussels 1969, 1, 329–44.

————, Juvénal et les pretoriens, Rev. Ét. Lat. 47 bis, 1969, 153–64.

D. EBENER, Juvenal. Mensch, Dichter, Gesellschaftskritiker, Altertum 10, 1964, 55–60.

L. EDMUNDS, Juvenal's Thirteenth Satire, Rhein. Mus. 115, 1972, 59–73.

C.E. FINCH, Juvenal in Codex Vat. Lat. 5204, Class. Phil. 65, 1970, 47f.

*FLETCHER, Juvenalia, Latomus.

R.A. LAFLEUR, A Note on Juvenal 10.201f., Am. Journ. Phil. 93, 1972, 598–600.

————, Artorius and Catulus in Juvenal 3, Riv. Stud. Class. 22, 1974, 5–9.

*————, Amicus and Amicitia in Juvenal, Class. Bull. 51, 1975.

S.C. FREDERICKS, Mos Maiorum in Juvenal and Tacitus, Diss. Univ. of Pennsylvania 1969 (Microf.), sum. Diss. Abstr. 30, 1969, 2505A–2506A.

————, Calvinus in Juvenal's Thirteenth Satire, Arethusa 4, 1971, 219–31.

————, Rhetoric and Morality in Juvenal's 8th Satire, Transact. Proc. Am. Phil. Ass. 102, 1971, 111–32.

————, Daedalus in Juvenal's Third Satire, Class. Bull. 49, 1972, 11–13.

————, The Function of the Prologue (1–20) in the Organization of Juvenal's Third Satire, Phoenix 27, 1973, 62–67.

A. FROLÍKOVÁ, Quid Iuvenalis in saturis de plebe Romana censuerit, Zprávy Jednoty Kl. Fil. 3, 1961, 63–69.

J.V. GARRIDO, El asalariado griego y el mecenas romano vistos por Luciano y Juvenal, in ΔΩΡΩΙ ΣΤΝ ΟΛΙΓΩΙ, Homenaje a José Alsina, Barcelona 1969, 165–74.

J. GÉRARD, Juvénal et les associations d'artistes grecs à Rome, Rev. Ét. Lat. 48, 1970, 309–31.

C. GNILKA, Maura Maurae collactea. Zu Juv. Sat. 6, 306–308, Riv. Filol. Istruz. Class. 96, 1968, 47–54.

————, Juvenalinterpretation, Symb. Oslo. 49, 1973, 141–46.

J.G. GRIFFITH, Juvenal, Statius and the Flavian Establishment, Greece and Rome 16, 1969, 134–50.

————, The Ending of Juvenal's First Satire and Lucilius, Book XXX, Hermes 98, 1970, 56–72.

————, On Synecdoche of the Verb ponere in Juvenal, Symb. Oslo. 46, 1971, 135–41.

————, Caper exstat in Ansa, Greece and Rome 20, 1973, 79f.

J. HELLEGOUARC'H, Les idées politiques et l'appartenance sociale de Juvénal, Studi in onore di E. Volterra, Milan 1969, 2, 233–45.

————, La ponctuation bucolique dans les Satires de Juvénal, in Mélanges offerts à M. René Fohalle, Gembloux 1969, 173–89.

G. HIGHET, Masks and Faces in Satire, Hermes 102, 1974, 321-37.

H. HOEGG, Interpolationen bei Juvenal?, Diss. Freiburg 1971.

D. JOLY, Juvénal et les Géorgiques, in Hommages à Jean Bayet, Coll. Latomus 70, Brussels 1964, 290-308.

K. KELTON and K.H. LEE, The Theme of Juvenal's Eleventh Satire, Latomus 31, 1972, 1041-46.

D.A. KIDD, Juvenal 10.175-6, Class. Quart. 19, 1969, 196f.

J.F. KILLEEN, Juvenal 7.126ff., Glotta 47, 1969, 265f.

R.S. KILPATRICK, Juvenal's "Patchwork" Satires 4 and 7, Yale Class. Stud. 23, 1973, 229-41.

F.J. LELIEVRE, Virgil and Juvenal's Third Satire, Euphrosyne 5, 1972, 457-62.

L. I. LINDO, The Evolution of Juvenal's Later Satires, Class. Phil. 69, 1974, 17-27.

G. LUCK, The Textual History of Juvenal and the Oxford Lines, Harv. Stud. Class. Phil. 76, 1972, 217-31.

R. MARACHE, La poésie romaine et le problème social à la fin du 1er siècle. Martial et Juvénal, L'Inform. Litt. 13, 1961, 12-19.

————, Rhétorique et humour chez Juvénal, in Hommages à Jean Bayet, Coll. Latomus 70, Brussels 1964, 474-78.

————, Un usage particulier de *ergo* chez Juvénal? Giorn. It. Fil. 21, 1969, 241-43.

J.R.C. MARTYN transl., L. Friedlaender's Essays on Juvenal, Amsterdam 1969.

————, Juvenal 2.78-81 and Virgil's Plague, Class. Phil. 65, 1970, 49f.

————, A New Approach to Juvenal's First Satire, Antichthon 4, 1970, 53-61.

————, Juvenal and *ne quid nimis*, Hermes 102, 1974, 338-45.

A.S. McDEVITT, The Structure of Juvenal's Eleventh Satire, Greece and Rome 15, 1968, 173-79.

A. MICHEL, La date des Satires. Juvénal, Héliodore e le tribun d'Arménie, Rev. Ét. Lat. 41, 1963, 315-27.

W.O. MOELLER, Juvenal III.29-40 and 152-159, Mnemosyne 22, 1969, 383-88.

S. MONTI, Contenuto e strutura del fascicolo che comprese il foglio di Bobbio (Vat. 5750) di Giovenale e Persio, Annali Fac. Lett. e Fil. Univ. Napoli 11, 1964-68, 57-68.

M. MORFORD, A Note on Juvenal 6.627-61, Class. Phil. 67, 1972, 198.

————, Juvenal's Thirteenth Satire, Am. Journ. Phil. 94, 1973, 26-36.

D. NARDO, La sesta satira di Giovenale e la tradizione erotico-elegiaca latina, Padua 1973.

E.N. O'NEIL, The Structure of Juvenal's Fourteenth Satire, Class. Phil. 55, 1960, 251-53.

L. PERELLI, Per una nuova interpretazione di Giovenale 7.228-43, Maia 25, 1973, 107-12.

————, Considerazioni sulla poetica di Giovenale, Boll. Stud. Lat. 4, 1974, 34-48.

P. PERNAVIEJA, *Ludia*, un terme sportif latin chez Juvénal et Martial, Latomus 31, 1972, 1037-40.

A.D. PRYOR, Juvenal's False Consolation, Journ. Austral. Univ. Lang. Lit. Ass. 18, 1962, 167-80.

T. REEKMANS, Juvenal's Views on Social Change, Ancient Society 2, 1971, 117-61.

M.D. REEVE, Gladiators in Juvenal's Sixth Satire, Class. Rev. 23, 1973, 124f.

G.R. ROCHEFORT, Laughter as a Satirical Device in Juvenal, Diss. Tufts Univ. 1972.

R.E. RUSSELL, Dryden's Juvenal and Persius, Diss. Univ. Calif., Davis 1966 (Microf.), sum. in Diss. Abstr. 28, 1967, 209A.

R. SCARCIA, Osservazioni critiche sulla vita di Persio, Riv. Cult. Class. e Med. 6, 1964, 287–302.

F. SCHREIBER, Juvenal 14.265–269, Hermes 99, 1971, 383f.

S. SETTIS, *Qui multas facies pingit cito* (Juven. 9.146), Atene e Roma 15, 1970, 117–21.

D. SINGLETON, Juvenal 6.1–2, and Some Ancient Attitudes to the Golden Age, Greece and Rome 19, 1972, 151–65.

J.P. STEIN, The Unity and Scope of Juvenal's Fourteenth Satire, Class. Phil. 65, 1970, 34–36.

V. TANDOI, Giovenale e il mecenatismo a Roma fra I e II secolo, Atene e Roma 13, 1968, 125–45.

————, Il ricordo di Stazio dolce poeta nella Sat. VII di Giovenale, in Omaggio a Eduard Fraenkel, Roma 1968, 248–70; also in Maia 21, 1969, 103–22.

E. THOMAS, Ovidian Echoes in Juvenal, in Ovidiana, ed. by N. Herescu, Paris 1958, 505–25.

G.B. TOWNEND, The Earliest Scholiast on Juvenal, Class. Quart. 22, 1972, 376–87.

————, The Literary Substrata to Juvenal's Satires, Journ. Rom. Stud. 63, 1973, 148–60.

G. VIONI, Considerazioni sulla settima satira di Giovenale, Atti Acad. Sc. Ist. Bologna, Cl. sc. mor. 61, 1972–73, 240–71.

K.H. WATERS, The Character of Domitian, Phoenix 18, 1964, 49–77.

————, Juvenal and the Reign of Trajan, Antichthon 4, 1970, 62–77.

W.J. WATTS, A Literary Reminiscence in Juvenal (9.96), Latomus 31, 1972, 519f.

K. WEISINGER, Irony and Moderation in Juvenal XI, Univ. Calif. Stud. Class. Ant. 5, 1972, 227–40.

D. WIESEN, Juvenal 10.358, Class. Phil. 64, 1969, 73–80.

————, *Classis Numerosa.* Juvenal Satire 7.151, Class. Quart. 21, 1971, 506–08.

————, Juvenal and the Intellectuals, Hermes 101, 1973, 464–83.

L. WINNICZUK, Osservazioni sui valori della satira di Giovenale, Eos 53, 1963, 191–203.

E.C. WITKE, Juvenal 3. An Eclogue for the Urban Poor, Hermes 90, 1962, 244–46.

Index of Passages Cited

Aesop *Fab.* 379, *161n21*
Anthologia Latina 950.8.3, *170n18*
Appian *Bell. civ.* 5.549, *165n7*
Apuleius *Met.* 1.15, *168n4*
Athenaeus *Deipn.* 15.669E, *161n34*
Augustine *Civ. Dei* 6.5, *165n49*
Ausonius *Caes.* 5, *168n10*
Epist. 11, *173n23*; 15.9, *162n8*; 23, *168n11*
Avianus *Fab.* 21, *161n21*
Babrius *Fab.* 88, *161n21*
Callimachus (ed. Pf.) frag. 192, *161n31*; frag. 194, *161n30*. *Ox. Pap.* 7, 1910, 31, *165n16*
Cassius Dio *Hist.* 48.54, *165n5(ch.7)*; 60.35.2, *101*; 60.35.3, 99, *182*; 61.10, *168n6, 168n7*
Catullus *Carm.* 10, 79; 38, 45
Cicero *Acad.* 1.8, *159n6(ch.1)*, *164n5*, *164n10*, *164n30*; 2.102, *162n15*. *Att.* 13.6.4, *161n2*. *Brut.* 160, *163n45*. *Cat. Mai.* 10, *160n8*; 14, *160n13(ch.3)*. *De or.* 1.72, *162n16*; 2.276, *160n10(ch.3)*, *160n12(ch.3)*; 2.284, *162n12*. *Fam.* 12.16, *165n5(ch.6)*. *Lucull.* 51, *161n33*. *Nat. Deor.* 1.97, 30
Claudian *Cons. Stil.* 3. *praef.*, *160n7*
Corpus Inscript. Latin. 5, *sup. It.* 898, *161n4*; 9, 6415a, *159n10(ch.2)*; 10, 5382, *171n6(ch.12)*
Diogenes Laertius *Vit. Phil.* 4.46–57, *166n19*; 6.8, *164n8*
Diomedes *Gramm. Lat.* ed. Keil 1.485, *159n3(ch.2)*, *160n18*, *161n1*, *161n5*
Donatus (on Terence) *Phorm.* 339, *161n18*
Ennius (ed. Vahlen³) *Ann.* 60–65, *163n40*; 213–17, *160n15(ch.3)*; 376, *160n2*; 377, *160n9*. *Sat.* 2, *161n36*; 3–4, 26, 27; 5, 26; 6, 25; 6–7, *161n35*; 8–9, *161n36*; 10–11, 26; 12–13, *161n35*; 14–19, 25, 26, *161n35*; 17, 26; 19, 26; 57–58, 23, *161n36*; 59–62, 26; 63, 25; 65, 23; 66, 27; 69, 30; 70, *161n36*
Festus (ed. Lindsay) 306, *160n26*; 416, *160n23*

Gellius, Aulus *Noct. Att.* 2.18, *159n6(ch. 1)*; 2.18.7, *164n3*; 2.24.4, *162n26*; 2.29.1, *161n20*; 4.73, *161n37*; 6.3.28, *162n14*; 6.9, *161n38*; 6.16, *165n50*; 12.4.5, *160n11*; 13.11, *165n47*; 17.17.1, *160n4*; 18.8, *163n43*
Helenius Acron (on Persius) *Sat.* 2.56, *170n16*
Herodotus *Hist.* 1.141, *161n24*
Horace *Ars poet.* 101, *166n42*; 178, *181*; 197, *166n42*; 421, *181*. *Epist.* 1.1.1, *165n12*; 1.1.14–18, 90; 1.1.19, 90; 1.1.30, *166n50*; 1.1.56, *181*; 1.1.61, *181*; 1.1.73, *161n28*; 1.1.104, *181*; 1.2, 90; 1.3, *167n1*; 1.4.1, *165n10*; 1.4.15–16, 90; 1.6, 90; 1.7, 90; 1.7.29–33, *161n28*; 1.7.69, *166n50*; 1.7.98, *166n21*; 1.11, *166n29*; 1.13, 88, 90; 1.14, 90; 1.16, 90, *165n9*, *166n29*; 1.16.43, *166n41*; 1.16.52, *166n38*, *181*; 1.17.7, *181*; 1.17.31, *166n42*; 1.18.37, *166n42*; 1.18.91, *181*; 1.19, *166n31*; 1.19.23–25, 74; 1.19.48–49, *181*; 1.20, 88; 1.20.17–18, 94; 2.1, *91*; 2.1.4, 78, *166n27*; 2.1.101, *181*; 2.1.139–70, *159n5(ch.2)*; 2.1.250–59, *165n16*, *166n27*; 2.2, *91*; 167n1; 2.2.43–45, 73; 2.2.51–52, 74; 2.2.58–60, *159n4(ch.1)*; 2.2.60, 82, *165n10*; 2.2.114, *181*. *Epod.* 4, 75; 7, 75; 16, 75. *Odes* 1.34, 86, 90; 2.2, 86; 4.8, *161n39*. *Satires* 1.1, 76, *182*; 1.1.1, *165n12*; 1.1.114–16, 77; 1.2, 46, 49, 76, 86; 1.2.25, 76; 1.2.27, *165n3*; 1.3, 76; 1.3.131–32, *166n38*; 1.4, *51*, 76, 85, 86, *159n4*, *166n17*; 1.4.1–7, *161n5*; 1.4.6–8, *163n52*; 1.4.9–13, *162n23*; 1.4.11, *165n4(ch.7)*; 1.4.13, *181*; 1.4.35, *166n39*; 1.4.42, 78; 1.4.45–48, *165n16*; 1.4.50, *181*; 1.4.52, *181*; 1.4.56–62, *165n16*; 1.4.63–143, *163n36*; 1.4.71–74, *165n2(ch.7)*; 1.4.87, *166n42*; 1.4.90, *165n4(ch.7)*; 1.4.92, *165n3(ch.7)*; 1.5, 76, *182*, *163n41*; 1.5.30, *181*; 1.5.92, *181*; 1.5.104, 75; 1.6, 74, 75, 76, *163n38*; 1.6.12–44, 79; 1.6.28, *181*; 1.6.102, *166n42*; 1.6.126, *166n38*; 1.7, 45, 76; 1.7.35, *181*; 1.8, 76, 86; 1.8.11, *165n1(ch.7)*;

GENERAL INDEX

76
77
79
83
85

8 **The Peopling of Newfoundland: Essays in Historical Geography**—John J. Mannion (ed.)

7 **The White Arctic: Anthropological Essays on Tutelage and Ethnicity**—Robert Paine (ed.)

6 **Consequences of Offshore Oil and Gas—Norway, Scotland and Newfoundland**—M.J. Scarlett (ed.)

5 **North Atlantic Fishermen: Anthropological Essays on Modern Fishing**—Raoul Andersen and Cato Wadel (eds.)

4 **Intermediate Adaptation in Newfoundland and the Arctic: A Strategy of Social and Economic Development**—M.M.R. Freeman (ed.)

3 **The Compact: Selected Dimensions of Friendship**—Elliott Leyton (ed.)

2 **Patrons and Brokers in the East Arctic**—Robert Paine (ed.)

1 **Viewpoints on Communities in Crisis**—Michael L. Skolnik (ed.)

Mailing Address:

ISER Books (Institute of Social and Economic Research)
Memorial University of Newfoundland
St. John's, Newfoundland, Canada, A1C 5S7